Looking f
working with you!

Eric

Creative
Execution

Creative Execution

WHAT GREAT LEADERS DO TO UNLEASH BOLD THINKING AND INNOVATION

ERIC BEAUDAN

John Wiley & Sons Canada, Ltd.

Library and Archives Canada Cataloguing in Publication Data
Phillips-Beaudan, Eric
    Creative execution : what great leaders do to unleash bold thinking and innovation /
Eric Beaudan.

Includes index.
Issued also in electronic formats.
ISBN 978-1-118-35109-3

    1. Creative ability in business—Management.   2. Organizational change—
Management.   3. Leadership.   4. Creative ability in business—Management—Case
studies.   5. Organizational change—Management—Case studies.   6. Leadership—Case
studies.   I. Title.

HD53.P55 2012   658.4'063   C2012-901354-4

ISBN 978-1-11835650-0 (ebk); 978-1-11835651-7 (ebk); 978-1-11835652-4 (ebk)

Production Credits
Cover design: Adrian So
Interior text design: Laserwords
Maps: Crowle Art Group
Typesetter: Laserwords
Cover printer: Friesens
Printer: Friesens

John Wiley & Sons Canada, Ltd.
6045 Freemont Blvd.
Mississauga, Ontario
L5R 4J3

Printed in Canada

1 2 3 4 5 FP 16 15 14 13 12

For Troy and Ashley

CONTENTS

FOREWORD   ix

ACKNOWLEDGEMENTS   xiii

INTRODUCTION   1

CHAPTER 1: ALEXANDER AT GAUGAMELA   17

CHAPTER 2: NELSON AT TRAFALGAR   39

CHAPTER 3: YAMAMOTO AT PEARL HARBOR   57

CHAPTER 4: FROM DESERT STORM TO IRAQI FREEDOM   81

CHAPTER 5: CREATIVE EXECUTION MARCHES EAST   111

CHAPTER 6: TOYOTA'S ROAD TO SUPREMACY   127

CHAPTER 7: THE FOUR SEASONS PUTS ON THE RITZ   149

CHAPTER 8: GOOGLE OGLES MICROSOFT   173

CHAPTER 9: CREATIVE EXECUTION IN ACTION   197

CHAPTER 10: BECOMING A CREATIVE EXECUTION LEADER   217

ENDNOTES   231

INDEX   243

ABOUT THE AUTHOR   253

FOREWORD

Every organization knows that its future—its success or failure—depends above all on its leaders. So it is not surprising that millions of words are written about leadership. But despite these words and the research behind them, leadership remains an elusive concept. There is no template for leadership. Even if we can list the world's most famous leaders, recognising leadership potential is an art, not a science. In different circumstances, in different cultures and at different times, leadership qualities will be adapted in different ways.

One of the reasons why it is so difficult to define leadership—or to isolate the qualities that make for a good leader—is that leaders are like artists: they come in a bewildering array of shapes and sizes. Artists may be musicians, painters, or architects—they might dance or sing or write. Leaders may be consistent or mercurial, charismatic or low-key, kind or harsh. And leadership is practiced in such a bewildering range of organizations from businesses and governments to charities and sports teams.

With so many variations and contradictions, it is easy to resort to defining leadership in a circular way. We can say that a leader is someone who can take people with him or her, who can inspire action, who can get results. But saying this simply begs the question: Which qualities does a leader really need to achieve those things?

Eric Beaudan's insight is to identify just five core characteristics and to illustrate them not by developing a theory or list of "competencies" but with examples of leaders in war and business. With the difficulty of defining leadership, these examples are more helpful than abstract definition. Eric's stimulating account of very different military, business, and political leaders brings to life the importance of the five characteristics that he proposes as the qualities for effective leadership in the twenty-first century.

The leaders in this book are willing—even eager—to break rules. Battles are not won by generals who fight "by the book" and success in business or war usually depends on identifying new strategies. That, in its turn, requires the leader to persuade people to do unfamiliar things and gain the trust of large numbers of people. Warfare demands a mix of thought leadership and action leadership. Great leaders, whether they lead armies into battle or turn around a struggling business, develop novel strategies and then turn strategy into action.

That we live in a rapidly changing world is a cliché because there is no period in modern history when the world has not been changing in a way that seemed bewildering at the time. The great leaders of the twentieth century lived in turbulent times and succeeded mightily because they developed new ways of doing business and turned their ideas into reality. Now as the East comes to dominate our thinking, and as economic dominance seems to be slipping from the West, it is as true as ever that the winners in business will be those who develop bold strategies and are willing to be visible leaders who take judicious risks and defy the odds.

Although war—especially wars as long ago as those of Alexander the Great—seems far removed from business, the leaders in this book help to demonstrate the essence of the qualities that Eric identifies as core to any leader's success. A leader in business—as in war—must develop a unique strategy, communicate it, determine who should do what, implement boldly, and be visible to those whom he or she has to take on this dangerous journey. The stories from Four Seasons, Toyota, and Google aptly mirror these requirements.

At Odgers Berndtson, our partners and consultants around the world have a special responsibility: to find and recognize leadership potential and matching them to organizations with different styles and challenges. We constantly advise boards, CEOs, and leaders of some of the world's most fascinating private and public organizations on how to find and assess people to lead them into new directions. From our vantage point, I can tell you that leadership isn't a lofty topic that only briefly emerges on organizations' agendas. It is by far the single most important subject that consumes boards, executive teams, and decision makers as they respond to the massive economic and political shifts that have erupted around us.

Just as organizations know that their future depends on how well they select their leaders, so ambitious individuals know that they must develop leadership skills. They know that to rise to the top of their organizations, and to be successful when they get there, they must constantly challenge their own thinking and develop their leadership.

And so whether you're the newly appointed CEO of a company wondering how to chart a course for the future, or steering a public-sector agency in an era of austerity and high anxiety, this book will help you set in motion the critical leadership decisions that will make you successful. There is a Creative Execution leader inside all of us, and there is an unbounded supply of opportunities and challenges around the world that require all of us to apply these leadership qualities.

Richard Boggis-Rolfe
Chairman, Odgers Berndtson

London, United Kingdom
February 2012

ACKNOWLEDGEMENTS

Many friends, mentors, colleagues and clients have inspired the writing of this book. For simplicity's sake, I will acknowledge them in chronological order—to parallel the writing of Creative Execution.

The genesis of the book was an assignment I conducted for Gary McDonald when he was the CEO of Thomas Cook North America and implemented his SPF25 formula. I was introduced to Gary and his team by David MacCoy, our OD Practice Leader at Watson Wyatt Worldwide (now Towers Watson). David ended up moving to the UK for several years to pursue his executive coaching work with Thomas Cook and complete his Ph.D. Both David and Gary were generous with their time and feedback as I slowly fleshed out the book, and I thank them both for their support and insights.

While working at Watson Wyatt, I first met Bob Rosen, founder of a consulting firm based in Arlington, Virginia, called Healthy Companies International. Bob became a mentor and good friend, along with his partners Leigh Shields, Eric Sass and Jim Mathews. I partnered with Bob to start interviewing CEOs such as Issy Sharp of the Four Seasons, which lifted my understanding of what CEOs do to build great companies. Bob and I have written about dozens of CEOs around the world, including the former president of Toyota and Major-General Patrick Cordingley, who can be found in the book. Our interviews have been a great source of knowledge and inspiration, and are now co-published by Odgers Berndtson and HCI under the title CEO Spotlight.

Odgers Berndtson has provided the support to make this book possible, and I can't thank our UK Chairman Richard Boggis-Rolfe and Canadian Chair Carl Lovas enough for their belief in this project. A special thanks to the partners in Toronto who have given me new wings since joining Odgers Berndtson, and have fueled the growth of our leadership practice: my mentor Paul Stanley, Sal Badali, Michael Mundy, Gillian Landsdowne, Sheila Ross, Carrie Mandel, Deborah

Lucas, Ken Rutherford, Jane Matthews, Sue Banting, Rob Quinn, Penny Mirams, Margaret Campbell, Malcolm Bernstein, Tanya Todorovic and Roberta Chow. Jacqueline Foley in Canada and Robin Balfour in the UK were outstanding in their marketing support. Our other partners and consultants in Canada—from our offices in Montreal, Ottawa, Calgary, Vancouver and Halifax—are too numerous to acknowledge, but their support has been equally invaluable. My assistant Kristen, always patient and cheerful, managed my calendar around some pretty tight deadlines.

From the many sources who contributed to my research, I would like to single out Katie Taylor and Nick Mutton of the Four Seasons who graciously put up with my requests for interviews and information. The Four Seasons is a beacon for Canadian businesses which so often find it difficult to sustain their global success.

The wonderful staff at Wiley Canada, including my editor Don Loney, production editor Elizabeth McCurdy and copy editor Jacqueline Lee worked overtime to get the book in final form. Deborah Crowle did a terrific job rendering the battle maps. Special thanks to Paula Sloss who put me in touch with the team at Wiley to get the project started.

My parents, Jacques and Colette, nurtured my love of history and writing early on, and let me accumulate insane amounts of military books and model ships despite any evidence that this would do any good. I hope that the lessons in this book will inspire my children, Troy and Ashley, to better appreciate history, which they always muse about. I'm not sure how many times I uttered the sentence "Not now, Dad is writing"—but probably far too many!

My newfound life partner Theresa shared my excitement for this book, reading early drafts and sitting through my first presentation to executives in Portugal. Ana Loya and her team in our Lisbon office did a wonderful job organizing this event, and the executives who attended gave us unexpected encouragement. I'm looking forward to many more opportunities where we can share the power of Creative Execution with our clients and friends around the world.

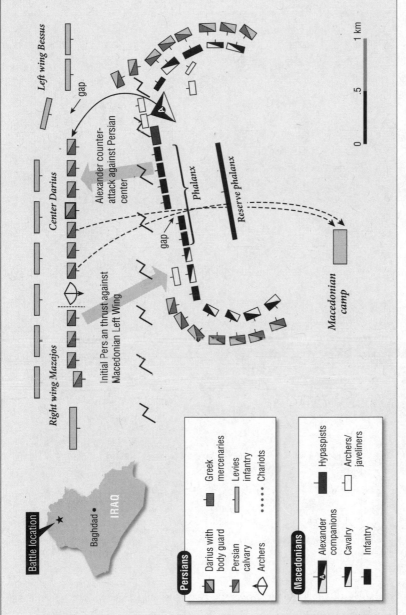

Persians

- Darius with body guard
- Persian calvary
- Archers
- Greek mercenaries
- Levies infantry
- Chariots

Macedonians

- Alexander companions
- Cavalry
- Infantry
- Hypaspists
- Archers/ javeliners

Battle location

Baghdad

IRAQ

Right wing Mazajos

Center Darius

Left wing Bessus

gap

Alexander counter-attack against Persian center

Initial Pers an thrust against Macedonian Left Wing

gap

Phalanx

Reserve phalanx

Macedonian camp

0   .5   1 km

Creative Execution in action: this map of the battle of Gaugamela shows the early action with the Persian attack on the Macedonian left wing, which Alexander ordered to hold. The Persian cavalry broke through the Macedonian lines and ransacked the Macedonian baggage camp in the rear. Meanwhile Alexander took his Companion Cavalry straight into Darius's center and caused the Persian king to flee.

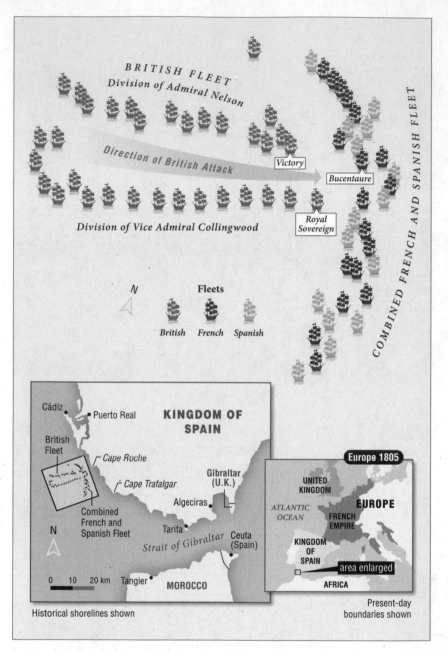

This map of the Battle of Trafalgar shows the two English lines converging on the French and Spanish Combined Fleet. Nelson's bold approach became known as the Nelson Touch.

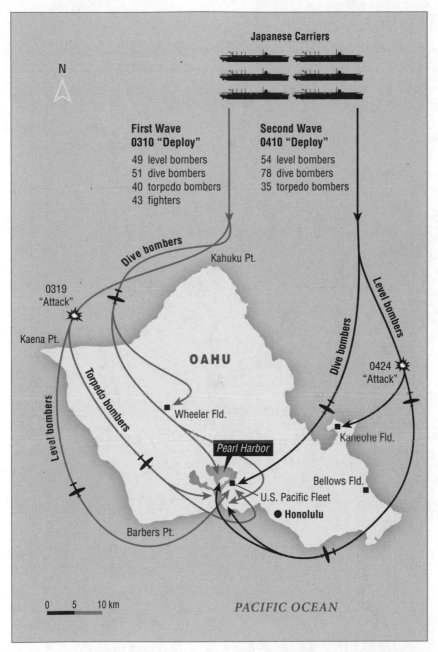

Japanese Carriers

First Wave
0310 "Deploy"

49 level bombers
51 dive bombers
40 torpedo bombers
43 fighters

Second Wave
0410 "Deploy"

54 level bombers
78 dive bombers
35 torpedo bombers

N

Dive bombers

Kahuku Pt.

0319
"Attack"

Kaena Pt.

Level bombers

Level bombers

Torpedo bombers

OAHU

Wheeler Fld.

Pearl Harbor

Dive bombers

0424
"Attack"

Kaneohe Fld.

Bellows Fld.

U.S. Pacific Fleet

● **Honolulu**

Barbers Pt.

0   5   10 km

PACIFIC OCEAN

Despite the imminent threat of war, no one in the US Navy or War Department thought the Japanese would have the audacity to mass their fleet carriers within a two hour striking distance of Pearl Harbor, and execute a well-coordinated attack against the Pacific Fleet.

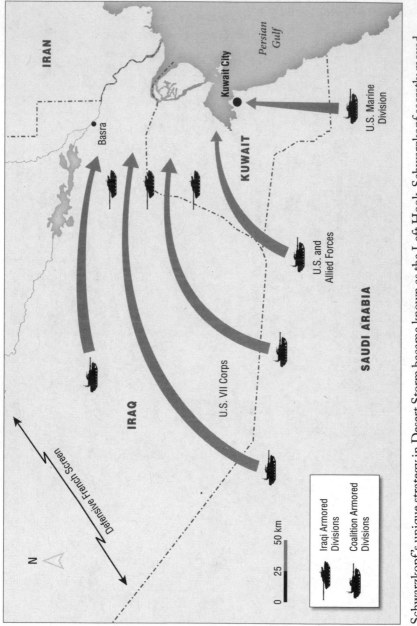

Schwarzkopf's unique strategy in Desert Storm became known as the Left Hook. Schwarzkopf secretly moved US armored divisions to the west in order to hit the Iraqi Republican Guards on their flank. This move ended the "Mother of All Battles" in 72 hours.

Who Needs Creative Execution?

- We must be bold. [1]

—John F. Kennedy

KATRINA WIPES OUT FEMA

When Katrina made landfall near New Orleans on August 29, 2005, no one believed that the Category 5 hurricane was about to become one of the worst natural disasters in U.S. history. The city's levees and flood walls failed, leading to the deaths of 1,200 people. The federal organization charged with the rescue and response effort, the Federal Emergency Management Agency (FEMA), soon became overwhelmed with the task at hand. Despite assurances by FEMA director Michael Brown that the federal government was ready to respond to the crisis, there were no emergency response teams from FEMA in New Orleans, or buses and ships ready to evacuate wounded or sick people from the area. Michael Chertoff, head of Homeland Security, was attending a conference at the Centers for Disease Control and Prevention, while President Bush was vacationing at his ranch in Crawford, Texas. While the 9/11 attacks had sensitized the Bush administration to the need for high vigilance in preventing another act of terrorism on American soil, the thought of a hurricane devastating New Orleans was nowhere near the top of the secretary of homeland security's priority list. As the devastating break in the 17th Street Canal levee widened to 500 feet and water from Lake Pontchartrain spewed into New Orleans, residents were left scrambling to deal with dead bodies and the 22 million tons of debris strewn around the Louisiana coast, including 350,000 automobiles and 35,000 boats destroyed by the storm.

FEMA's inability to respond to the worsening situation in New Orleans, evidenced by its leaders' panicked reactions, was a total failure of an agency created at the height of the Cold War—believe it or not—to coordinate national relief efforts in the event of a Soviet nuclear attack on American cities. FEMA's local deputy, Marty Bahamonde, admitted in congressional testimony that "there was a systematic failure at all levels of government to understand the magnitude of the situation. The leadership from top down in our agency was unprepared and out of touch."[2] Arkansas senator Mark Pryor was less kind: "When FEMA finally did show up, everybody was angry because all they had was a Web site and a flyer," he testified in front of a bipartisan congressional committee.[3] FEMA's disgraced director, Michael Brown, resigned in September 2005. It didn't help Brown that, before his appointment by the Bush administration, his most prestigious pedigree had been commissioner of the Arabian Horse Association.

While FEMA was fumbling for resources in Washington, DC, and trying to decide whether it was safe to send supplies into New Orleans, its sister agency inside the Department of Homeland Security, the United States Coast Guard, was exerting itself doing what everyone hoped FEMA would accomplish: saving lives and restoring order. How the Coast Guard got there isn't as straightforward as it may seem. By 2005, the 40,000-person-strong Coast Guard organization was stretched and partly orphaned. After the post-9/11 shakedown of the federal government, the Coast Guard was pulled out from the United States Navy and told to refocus its mission on port security and maritime interdiction, operating anywhere from California to the Persian Gulf. The great fear of the Department of Homeland Security at the time was that terrorists would smuggle a dirty bomb into a U.S. harbor (think Los Angeles or New York), and from 2002 onward, the Coast Guard was busy patrolling U.S. harbors and providing in-shore protection for U.S. warships deployed to the Middle East in support of Operation Iraqi Freedom.

When Katrina struck, the Coast Guard rose to the occasion and immediately deployed 5,600 personnel from every Coast Guard district, from Alaska to Maine, to New Orleans. Working nonstop in gruesome conditions, Coast Guard rescue workers saved over 24,000 lives and evacuated 9,400 people to out-of-area medical facilities. The Coast Guard rescued more people in that one week than it had the entire previous year! As Douglas Brinkley wrote in *The Great Deluge*, the Coast Guard "continued to gallantly rise to the occasion. While the section headquartered in Alexandria rescued people in boats and baskets, they welcomed the help from Coast Guard outfits all over America."[4] By contrast, FEMA refused outside offers of help, stubbornly insisting that the situation was under control until two days after Katrina hit, when Michael Brown finally called the White House to alert the president that "this is bigger than what we can handle." By that time the only assets FEMA had inserted into New Orleans were eight medical emergency response teams.

How did the Coast Guard succeed where FEMA fumbled? Did one of the two organizations have better early warning of Katrina's likely impact on New Orleans? Did the Coast Guard have a plan to redeploy the bulk of its human and technical assets to assist hurricane victims in the event of a Katrina-like disaster? In either case, the answer is no. Both organizations were relying on the same information from the U.S. National Weather Service and had contingency plans for natural and man-made disasters that could strike the U.S. mainland, Alaska, or Hawaii. What the Coast Guard did have, however, was a strong conviction that it should go out and save lives with whatever means it could string together. The core belief of the service is that "Coast Guard men and women be given latitude to act quickly and decisively . . . without waiting for direction from higher levels in the chain of command."[5] While Michael Brown and Michael Chertoff were consulting with their staff to decide how best to respond to the unfolding drama, the Coast Guard swooped down into the stricken city to rescue people from rooftops, attics, and makeshift shelters. Within two weeks, President Bush appointed Coast Guard Vice Admiral Thad Allen as the man in charge of the rescue and rebuilding effort, and sent Michael Brown and his staff packing. Allen tackled the most pressing issue decisively, sending teams to recover the hundreds of corpses that were still floating among the post-flood debris. He then explained how the Coast Guard and other agencies would help rebuild New Orleans. "If you are drowning, the first thing you want is dry land," the vice admiral explained. "If you are on dry land, the next thing you want is something to eat and drink. Having eaten, you want a place to sleep, and then you want a better place to sleep. Then you want aid to start rebuilding and getting your life back in order." At the bottom of a pyramid, Allen drew a picture of the Superdome, representing the worst part of the crisis. On top of the pyramid he scripted "New Orleans 2.0" as a symbol of the future city he wanted to rebuild.

Where FEMA and Brown fumbled, Allen took charge. He brought together a clear plan of action to deal with the crisis, identified clear priorities for search-and-rescue teams, took bold action to cut through red tape and organizational boundaries, and was a visible on-scene leader after he set up his headquarters in Baton Rouge, Louisiana.

In short, Allen and the Coast Guard demonstrated a burning desire to achieve what I call *Creative Execution*: the ability to adapt to difficult or unpredictable circumstances, and mobilize an organization to win against the odds. The Coast Guard showed New Orleans that it was possible to clean up and rebuild, supplying both the material and the emotional fuel required for the city to have the confidence to move forward. It achieved a decisive victory against a backdrop of total destruction and loss of hope.

* * *

Most organizations experience Katrina moments when they launch a new product or technology, merge with another company, or try to respond to unexpected crises. Yet from all accounts, most perform more like FEMA than they do like the United States Coast Guard. The same slow, confused reaction took place at the Fukushima Dai-ichi nuclear plant when it was hit by the tsunami that struck Japan in March 2011. Unable to make a quick decision about venting the building pressure inside the reactors, the plant's operator, Tokyo Electric Power Co. (TEPCO), quickly lost control of events. Three of the plant's six reactors experienced a partial meltdown, and a hydrogen gas explosion damaged the containment core. We now know that it will take 30 years to decommission the plant, which will be entombed in a sarcophagus similar to the one built over the Chernobyl plant. More importantly, we also know from a Norwegian Institute for Air Research study and from the French Institute for Radiological Protection and Nuclear Safety that the accident released twice as much radioactive cesium 137 into the atmosphere than TEPCO admitted, and that up to 30 times that amount leaked into the Pacific Ocean. There is nothing that TEPCO could have done to prevent the earthquake that triggered the 45-foot tsunami waves. But the company's attempts to downplay the impact of the emergency and refuse the advice that the Japanese government and global experts were providing was a catastrophic human failure on a scale that hadn't been seen since Katrina. With 43 of Japan's 54 nuclear reactors now shut down and prevented from restarting due to public outcry, TEPCO effectively crippled an industry that was supposed to provide 50 percent of Japan's energy by 2030.

The same behaviors that TEPCO and FEMA displayed in their attempts to respond to their respective crises are repeated inside organizations every day. According to the Boston Consulting Group (BCG), 61 percent of mergers and acquisitions (M&A) sealed between 1995 and 2001 reduced shareholder value. If you consider the fact that an average of 21,000 M&A transactions take place every year, and that the average value of deals has doubled since 2002 to over $110 million, a 60 percent failure rate adds up to $1.4 trillion worth of deals that fail to meet expectations each year. The figures only start to improve in

2010. BCG estimates that this is the first year since 1988 that acquirers are, on average, generating positive returns from their acquisitions. Another startling study published in *Fast Company* showed that 90 percent of people who undergo coronary artery bypass graft surgery return to their pre-surgery lifestyle within two years, rather than keeping to a healthy diet. Quoting Harvard Business School professor John Kotter, who studied dozens of organizations "in the midst of upheaval," *Fast Company* explained that "the central issue is never strategy, structure, culture, or systems. The core of the matter is always about changing the behavior of people."[6]

Why does this pattern of large-scale organization failure repeat itself so often? I believe the former CEO of Citigroup, John S. Reed, said it best: "The willingness of people to change is limited, and what you pay them seems to be inversely correlated with their willingness to change."[7] Most executives learn this lesson the hard way, over-emphasizing strategy and (many times inadvertently) undervaluing the importance of fostering creativity and execution. Inevitably, an organization's success hinges not on the strength of its strategy, but on its leaders' ability to craft a realistic view of *how* the strategy will be implemented, and to empower their people to get engaged in its execution in a meaningful way. Without this ability, the fog of change quickly turns execution into a value-destroying lip service that actually *reduces* the organization's ability to turn strategy into action.

What CEOs and executives get paid to do is not to lay out a vision and objectives, and then watch their troops perform from the top of the hill. The command-and-control approach to strategy execution—simply following a plan from a top-down, do-your-piece-and-keep-quiet perspective—is a recipe for failure in the twenty-first century. The Gen X and Millennial generation creeping down the corporate chimney isn't going to put up with this any more than you would put up with verbal or sexual abuse. It's not the way forward. What leaders in both public and private organizations need to do is unleash the creative surge and passion that is dormant in all of us, and provide the lift needed to get over strategic stall, the point at which traditional change efforts start to flutter and collapse. Without a plan to address this inevitable stall and anticipate the challenges of internal resistance and organization inertia that typically derail execution, you will end up alongside the bulk of companies and leaders who fail to lead change properly.

What are the derailers that so often turn a good strategy into refined dust? In my work on strategy implementation with hundreds of executives and organizations around the world, I have identified five culprits, which by themselves or in unison can derail the best laid plans. My bet is that you've encountered at least one in each organization you might have toiled for:

1. **Blind Belief in Strategy (BSS).** The COO of a large bank once told me that his job was done since the strategy had been developed, and all that was left to do was execute it. Right.
2. **Blue on Blue.** Parts of the organization fail to collaborate effectively to get things done, and in some cases wage guerrilla warfare on each other. This is often the number one problem in matrix organizations.
3. **Improvised Explosive Devices (IEDs).** The execution agenda becomes hijacked by emergencies, new projects, or other unexpected priorities. Think about what every candidate for political office promises during their campaign, and then fails to deliver.
4. **Russian Roulette.** Strategy, compensation, and values are so misaligned that people just choose to do their own thing, and no one knows what really matters and who is accountable for getting things done. That's what we are currently seeing in Greece.
5. **Power Surge.** So much decision making is hoarded by central functions or senior leaders that the organization becomes paralyzed. This is often the case in entrepreneurial or founder-led organizations.

DEFEATING STRATEGIC STALL

In studying and working with public and private-sector companies struggling with the challenge of executing their strategy, I have come to discover not only the importance of leaders paying more attention to the pitfalls of execution, but also that there is a universal individual need for creative achievement. People and companies aren't automatons. We don't join an organization so that our work lives can become preordained and monotonous—even though the Organization Man of the 1950s seemed to be that way. We want to contribute our creative thinking and energy to the tasks in front of us, otherwise we become disengaged. The best customer service experiences we find in life don't come from people who consult a book of rules and procedures before they decide whether or not they will help us solve our problem. They come from people who spontaneously and enthusiastically grab hold of our problem, make it their own, and come up with a creative way to solve it *on the spot*. I experienced that recently when I returned a water-damaged iPhone to an Apple Store. My customer service rep, Kevin, took the phone to open it and confirm the extent of the water damage. He then explained that he needed to answer the following question on his service iPad: "Do you want to help this customer out?" Because I had been upfront about the cause of the water damage, he answered yes. And I walked out two minutes later with a brand-new iPhone.

The key message of this book is that if you want your organization to function more like Apple—or your shareholders to be as content as Apple's investors—you need to unleash Creative Execution in your organization, and overcome the forces that trip and stall even the best strategies.

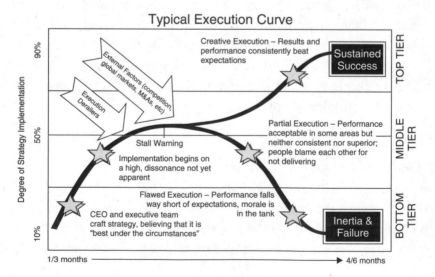

Typical Execution Curve

What exactly is Creative Execution? It isn't a form of government, religious beliefs, or didactic principles. Rather, it is the perfect storm that's generated when the organization's direction is fully embraced by its employees, stakeholders, and customers, and the total intellectual, emotional, and creative energy that resides inside all of us is unleashed in unison. This rare form of human performance inspired seemingly impossible ventures such as Alexander the Great's conquest of Asia, Google's ascent to the pinnacle of Internet companies, and the rise of the Four Seasons from a single motel to global pace setter in luxury hotels and residences.

To be successfully deployed inside any organization, Creative Execution requires five essential ingredients:

1. **A Unique Strategy**. The first step toward Creative Execution—indeed, the first step of any execution—is the creation of a simple, unambiguous strategy. There are plenty of smart people in consulting firms and corporations who insist on developing competitive strategies that fit inside volumes of three-ring binders, replete with data since the founding of the Roman Empire. For the most part, these strategies contain some good information and analyses but are not sufficiently tangible or crunchy to inspire people to action. In contrast, a crystal-clear strategy that can be explained on a single page is an indispensable starting point for seamless execution. Without a compelling, visionary, and unique strategy that you can explain to your board members, customers, or employees inside of two minutes, execution is a doomed enterprise.

2. **Candid Dialogue** about the strategy and its implementation. In his book *Winning*, Jack Welch calls lack of candor "the biggest dirty little secret in business."[8] As CEO of General Electric (GE), he made a point of letting people know exactly how he felt about them and their performance. Welch was blunt and direct with his staff and colleagues to such an extent that he told one of his GMs at a company dinner that if he underperformed the following year, he would have to fire him. Welch's insistence on candor in performance evaluations and the forced ranking of each employee using the "vitality curve"

remains controversial to this day, yet it created a culture of candor at GE that became part of the company's high-performance DNA.

Another unique leader, Mikhail Gorbachev, used Candid Dialogue to transform not just a company but an entire country. When he took over the reins of the Soviet Union in March 1985, one of Gorbachev's first acts was to request more candor and objectivity in the political reports that were presented to him and his Politburo colleagues. After decades of Soviet rule, the Russian economy was in tatters, and the country's support of Third World regimes had become a costly albatross that Gorbachev courageously decided to curtail. The KGB (now the Russian FSB) issued rather telling instructions at the end of 1985 to underscore "the impermissibility of distortions of the factual state of affairs in messages and informational reports sent to the Central Committee . . . and other ruling bodies."[9] Most of us live in organizations where the level of candor is somewhere between GE and the Soviet model, and I think it's pretty clear which model outperforms the other.

3. **Clear Roles and Accountabilities** that drive individual and team performance. In the first steps of Creative Execution, creating a Unique Strategy and Candid Dialogue, it's all talk. With Clear Roles and Accountabilities, you're matching your talk with specific expectations that align people, strategy, and execution. It's the first critical turn in translating strategy into action.

For Creative Execution to sustain itself, leaders, managers, and employees need to match the Candid Dialogue, which led to the ownership of the strategy, with roles and responsibilities that link individual and team goals to that strategy. Clear accountabilities are critical because they drive the metrics and rewards that people will use to measure their individual success. People who achieve Creative Execution rely on scorecards that allow individuals and business-unit leaders to track their progress against specific operational goals.

One leader you will meet later in the book, Gary McDonald, thrives on creating Clear Roles and Accountabilities. As the CEO of Thomas Cook for North America, Gary, one of my former consulting clients, turned around an entire business by focusing people on the execution of what he called SPF25—the alignment of Strategy, People, and Finance to achieve $25 million in net profits. Gary made each one of his direct reports accountable for the execution of a particular aspect of SPF25, and the result was staggering. In less than three years, Gary achieved his transformation of Thomas Cook Financial Services, which was then sold to Travelex for $650 million.

4. **Bold Action** that puts the strategy into play. Bold Action could entail a wholesale reorganization, the divestiture of unprofitable or misaligned operating units, a switch to a new supplier, the purchase of a new plant, a decision to stop manufacturing certain products, or outsourcing one of your business processes—all of which are clear and unequivocal signals that you're moving your pieces on the chessboard. We'll explore many examples of Bold Action, from Barack Obama's decision to forego public funds for his 2008 presidential election campaign, to Google founders Larry Page and Sergey Brin's decision to download the entire directory of the Internet onto their dorm room computers.

    Bold Action generates momentum. It firmly propels the organization toward its new direction, and provides a tangible taste of how the strategy will be deployed. It transforms doubters into believers, and passive bystanders into active participants. In the case of Barack Obama, his decision to forego federal funds in 2008 opened the door for his hyper-motivated team to reach out to millions of onlookers who contributed five or ten dollars to his first presidential election campaign.

5. **Visible Leadership** cements individual commitment to change. Without senior management's visible commitment, the wheels of Creative Execution will spin out of control or take their own, separate directions. Visible Leadership is required to maintain a common focus, set the pace, keep track of execution successes or failures, and create a positive culture centered on learning and outcomes. Visible Leadership is also accountable for making sure the organization becomes aware of the various requirements for Creative Execution— and disentangles itself from the shackles of blunt, top-down execution.

BLUNT VS. CREATIVE EXECUTION

BLUNT EXECUTION
Organization vision strategy are only debated at the top
Change & learning seen as superfluous
People follow "their version" of the plan
Failure is not addressed in a meaningful way
Leaders micro-manage, slowly eroding trust and collaboration

CREATIVE EXECUTION
Deep vision and strategy conversations at all levels
Change & learning are managed strategically
There is only "one" very explicit plan
Failure (and success) become valuable learning experiences
Leaders trust and challenge each other constructively, which stimulates collaboration

At the Battle of Trafalgar, Lord Horatio Nelson refused to remove his decorations or cover his Admiral's uniform while pacing the *Victory's* upper deck. He was convinced that his presence on deck would encourage his sailors to fight harder. He was shot and died while leading the greatest naval triumph and feat of Creative Execution of the nineteenth century. In an earlier skirmish in the Canary Islands, Nelson had been in the first boat to attack a Spanish stronghold and was struck in his right arm by grapeshot. Without the aid of anesthetics, the ship's surgeon removed the arm—and within the hour Nelson was giving orders again. That's visible leadership!

VIOLENT ROOTS

I mention Admiral Nelson for a good reason. For roughly three thousand years of our tumultuous history, the only institution organized in a way that would resonate with our concept of modern business organizations was the military. From Ramses and Alexander the Great to Julius Caesar, Kublai Khan, William the Conqueror, and Napoleon, the chief preoccupation of organized society was to field superior armies and navies that could hold at bay potential invaders, or be used as a blunt instrument of conquest. This preoccupation drew some of the best minds from East and West and resulted in a primitive—and highly destructive—form of Creative Execution: the ability to achieve total victory against larger opponents using a combination of unique tactics, weapons, and superior leadership. As Steve Forbes and John Prevas write in their book *Power Ambition Glory: The Stunning Parallels between Great Leaders of the Ancient World and Today*, "Great leaders articulate their mission in a way that the people who follow them understand what they are being asked to do, why it needs to be done, and how they are going to do it. That is what effective leadership is all about. It was that way over two thousand years ago, and it remains that way today."[10]

With the emotional armor provided by these deadly advantages, Alexander marched into Asia at the head of an army of no more than 150,000 Macedonian and Greek soldiers to defeat a Persian army that numbered a million warriors. Admiral Nelson cut down the French fleet twice, first at the Battle of the Nile and then at Trafalgar, without losing a single ship. Largely due to their successful use of Creative Execution, several great empires repeatedly resisted invasion by foreign powers, and ultimately fell as a result of internal problems. Alexander's army marched all the way to India, and turned back not because it lost a battle, but because the Macedonian soldiers under Alexander's increasingly tyrannical command grew tired of conquest and refused to go further. Rome's empire eventually crumbled under its own weight after nearly 500 years of *imperium*.

During the nineteenth century, Napoleon applied the same principles of Creative Execution to win more land battles than Alexander and Caesar combined. The fact that, at Waterloo, the French emperor broke his army's back through a senseless charge of the British center is a powerful reminder that your past victories are no guarantee of future success.

It was only in the twentieth century that a power outside of Europe, Japan, finally adopted the Creative Execution formula that had been fine-tuned during centuries of European warfare. Japan was an astute student of British naval strategy. Its Pacific squadron, led by the intrepid Admiral Togo, annihilated a Russian fleet at Tsushima in 1906. In an epic journey, the 45-ship-strong Russian Baltic fleet sailed from its European waters, around Africa and India to meet the Japanese fleet. When the two fleets faced off, Togo formed a line of battle that rained accurate and concentrated firepower over the Russian armada. One of the first victims of Togo's fire was the Russian flagship, which sank with all hands. In the end, only two Russian destroyers and one cruiser escaped the carnage. Over 6,000 Russian sailors died, versus 600 Japanese—the exact ratio Nelson had achieved at Trafalgar.

Four decades later, Admiral Yamamoto applied similar principles to sink most of the U.S. Pacific Fleet at Pearl Harbor (minus the valuable aircraft carriers, as we all know)—although his reversal at Midway was, like Napoleon's at Waterloo, swift and final. Yamamoto's successful attack at Pearl Harbor was a historical wake-up call for the naval establishments in the United States and Europe. Despite its *perceived* inferior doctrine and equipment, the Imperial Japanese Navy had been able to inflict an embarrassing defeat on the United States. Why? Yamamoto had secretly developed his own Creative Execution formula, which he unleashed on a hapless Admiral Kimmel on December 7, 1941. The United States eventually turned the tables on Yamamoto and the Imperial Japanese Navy, and demonstrated complete mastery of Creative Execution when it sent the majority of the Japanese fleet to the bottom of the Pacific in 1944.

By the beginning of the twenty-first century, Creative Execution had been orphaned by Europe and swiftly adopted by Asia and North America. It was also ready to morph from the military domain to more practical business applications.

The axiom of this book, therefore, is that Creative Execution is no longer a secret recipe. It may have been the salve that European nations used to seal their economic and military expansion since Alexander, but it's not patented or safe from duplication. Ever since the Industrial Revolution, we have moved gradually closer to a world where leaders who embrace Creative Execution, like Togo in 1905 and Yamamoto in 1941, are able to take on and win against much larger competitors. Manufacturing capabilities, technology, and human talent are now broadly shared and accessible worldwide—from the technology labs of Bangalore to Brazilian soy farms. What was once only feasible for wealthy countries or large organizations to achieve is now open to ambitious rivals around the world. And so whether you're seeking to build a company from scratch, as Toyota did in the 1950s, breathe new life into an organization, or recover from the global recession faster than your competitors, Creative Execution is for you.

GET READY FOR THE RIDE

In the first section of this book, we'll study four military masters of Creative Execution and their accomplishments: Alexander during his conquest of Asia, Nelson and his total victories at the Battle of the Nile and Trafalgar, Yamamoto at Pearl Harbor, and General Schwarzkopf in Desert Storm. Each of these unique leaders deployed a Creative Execution formula that wiped out their opposition with stunning results, and in doing so changed the rules of global warfare in a significant way. Their legacy lives with us every day. In the second section of this book, we'll look at several companies that have successfully applied Creative Execution to advance their destiny far beyond their own founders' expectations. Toyota leads the pack. Despite the "Great Recall" of 2010, Toyota's rise to the position of the world's number one carmaker remains a thought-provoking lesson in Creative Execution. Next, we'll discuss the Four Seasons, which, from its humble beginnings as a motor hotel in Toronto, grew into the most successful luxury hotel chain in the world. We'll look at Google, which started as a research project at Stanford University and now stands as the most potent threat to Microsoft's domination of the Internet. Finally we'll explore the turnaround of Thomas Cook Financial Services, a smaller organization that wielded the principles of Creative Execution just as confidently as Toyota, Four Seasons, or Google.

But before we examine these unique leaders and organizations, I need to take you back to the hallowed ground of Gaugamela, where Alexander met Darius and gave the world its first taste of total victory.

Alexander at Gaugamela

Remember, upon the conduct of each depends the fate of all.

—Alexander the Great

The date is October 1, 331 BC. On the plains of Gaugamela, roughly 60 miles east of the modern-day northern Iraqi city of Mosul, Alexander the Great faces, for the third and final time, the mighty army of King Darius III of Persia. On this balmy autumn day, a force of 150,000 Macedonian, Greek, and mercenary warriors under Alexander's command, 1,500 miles from their home and with no means of escape, defeats a Persian army at least five times its size. King Darius flees the battle, and is killed six months later by one of his advisers. Alexander, at the age of 30, finds himself the ruler of an Asian empire of 70 million people. He has become history's first master of Creative Execution.

ALEXANDER COMES OF AGE

The clash at Gaugamela was the denouement of nearly 200 years of war and rivalry between the Greek city-states and the Persian Empire. The outnumbered but highly disciplined Greeks put up remarkable fights at landmark battles such as Marathon and Salamis, and Thermopylae—the "Gates of Fire"—where King Leonidas held off the

Persians with 300 of Sparta's best warriors, giving the Greek armies enough time to regroup and halt the invaders. Just as impressive, but not yet acclaimed in a 3-D Hollywood movie, is the feat of the Ten Thousand, a Greek army of 10,700 hoplite soldiers that found itself surrounded by Persian foes in 401 BC. Rather than surrender, the Ten Thousand voted to walk back from Babylon, located in the heart of the Persian Empire, to the shores of the Black Sea. That's a journey of roughly 700 miles through what is now northern Iraq and eastern Turkey, which was—and remains—an inhospitable land settled by fierce warrior tribes. Amazingly, five out of six Greek soldiers from those Ten Thousand made it back to shore, and in the process defeated every foe that opposed their march. Stories of the Ten Thousand's retreat through Persia permeated Greek history and its rulers' belief in their superior *ethos* (moral character) and battle tactics. As Victor Davis Hanson explains in *Carnage and Culture*, "The soldiers in the ranks sought face-to-face shock battle with their enemies. All accepted the need for strict discipline and fought shoulder to shoulder whenever practicable . . . To envision the equivalent of a Persian Ten Thousand is impossible." [1]

Growing up in this warlike Macedonian society, Alexander the Great not only learned the history of Greece's ongoing cold war with Persia but also received the best classical education available at the time. His tutor, Greek philosopher Aristotle, ensured that his royal pupil understood ethics, politics, and the arcane sciences of mathematics and philosophy. The relationship between master and student persevered throughout Alexander's career. Alexander once wrote to Aristotle that he would rather "excel the rest of mankind in my knowledge of what is best than in the extent of my power."[2] Paradoxically, this sensitivity to world culture and philosophy would play a significant role in Alexander's downfall following his conquest of Persia. Instead of subjugating the Persians and imposing Greek and Macedonian customs throughout his new empire—which by classical standards would have been the norm (and was the preferred technique of the Romans, whose empire would outlast Alexander's by 500 years)—Alexander pardoned most of Darius's entourage, embraced Eastern beliefs, and dressed in the Persian style, drawing the ire of his fellow Macedonians.

By the time Alexander was in his teens, the enmity between the Greek city-states and Persia remained at an all-time high. But before they could face the Persians, the Macedonians had to tame Greece itself, which felt no compulsion to join any Macedonian adventure across the Aegean. The leading Greek city-states such as Athens, Sparta, and Thebes viewed Macedonia as an unworthy start-up, and weren't willing to commit their troops and funds to a foreign adventure as bold as the conquest of Persia. A contemporary equivalent would be a U.S.-led proposal to invade the entire Middle East in the wake of the wars in Iraq and Afghanistan. None of America's allies in Europe or elsewhere would sign up for what they would perceive as an act of folly. Yet that is precisely the task that Alexander and his father, King Philip II, set out for themselves.

Philip's contribution to this grandiose dream was to build a crack Macedonian army that defeated the Greek forces of Athens and Thebes at Chaeronea in 338 BC. Only 18 at the time, Alexander led the cavalry charge that broke through the Greek center. This decisive, powerful, and bold move would become a trademark of Alexander's strategy for fighting the Persians. Thanks to this dramatic victory, Philip secured the allegiance of the Panhellenic states and was appointed *strategos* (general) in charge of the upcoming campaign against the Persians. For the first time, the Greek city-states and their new Macedonian overlord were united in a single front to take on the Persian juggernaut.

As Philip began preparations for his ambitious campaign, Alexander wasted no time in convincing his peers and the king himself that he had grown into a mature warrior who could achieve great deeds against the odds. After watching his father's trainers approach a wild horse, Alexander asked if he could tame the creature himself. Philip consented, and announced that he would give the horse to Alexander if he succeeded. Alexander approached the animal and gently moved him away from the sun, having noticed that he became nervous at seeing his own shadow. Then he rode his new mount—which was to become the indefatigable Bucephalus—into a controlled gallop to the amazed shouts of king and courtiers.

Soon thereafter, Alexander welcomed a Persian emissary while his father was away and peppered him with questions about his journey, the geography and obstacles he had encountered on his way to Macedonia, and the conditions of the Persian army and empire. The gracious emissary did not know that Alexander would use this information to invade Persia, nor would he have believed it. The Persian Empire stretched from the Indus River in the east to Egypt in the west—what encompasses today the whole of Central Asia, the Middle East, and Turkey.

Compared to this vast empire, Macedonia was just a speck on the map. Persians had every reason to believe that their empire was vastly superior to both Greece and Macedonia, not just in military might but in sheer manpower and economic resources. In the first Greco-Persian wars, the Persians had razed Athens, whereas the Greeks had never come near the Persian capital. Persia's legendary army, including King Darius's personal guard known as the Immortals, was thought to number up to a million men—although the real number of frontline warriors was probably less than half that. To some extent the Persians had a more advanced society than the Greeks, having introduced the world's first attempt to abolish slavery and embed principles of human rights and equality in government.

THE PERSIAN ADVENTURE

Two years after Chaeronea, Philip was assassinated by one of his seven bodyguards (several theories persist about Alexander's potential role in this regicide, although his involvement was never seriously considered at the time). Alexander immediately assumed the title of *strategos*. He crossed into Asia in 334 BC, with an army consisting of 8,000 horsemen and 43,000 infantrymen. The heart of Alexander's army was the Companion Cavalry, which Alexander himself led into battle, followed by the Macedonian phalanx, a tight formation of infantry carrying 18-foot-long lances called *sarissai*. The first four or five rows of the phalanx would thrust their *sarissai* together, creating a packed wall of iron that could cleft its way through enemy infantry. Even though the Macedonians fielded far fewer men and cavalry mounts than the Persians, they were considered a crack force—much like Special Forces in today's armies. Alongside the Macedonians stood the newly allied Greeks from Athens, Thebes, and the other city-states vanquished at Chaeronea. Several thousand Greek mercenaries had also joined Darius's army, either in the belief that the untested young Alexander would crumble once he faced the entire Persian army, or simply out of spite after the humiliating defeat at the hands of Philip and Alexander.

Alexander's first test against the Persians took place at the Granicus River (modern-day Turkey) in May 334 BC. Facing the Persian army late in the day, Alexander ignored the advice of his more seasoned commanders, who wanted to wait for the following day to carry out a proper reconnaissance of the battlefield. Leaving little time for the Persians to assess the situation, Alexander deployed his troops on a wide front, with the heavy phalanx in the center and his Companion Cavalry on the right flank. Seeing Alexander to the far right, the Persians moved troops from the center to face his cavalry. Alexander's most senior general, Parmenion, launched a light charge on the left flank, thus forcing the Persians to withdraw even more troops from their center. Once this was accomplished and Alexander could see that the enemy center was depleted, he charged into the center gap with his Companions. As he reached the front line of Persian nobles, he challenged one of the enemy commanders, Rhoesaces, to fight him man to man. Alexander suffered a blow to his helmet, but recovered and struck down the Persian with his sword.

Alexander's personal triumph, after his bold crossing of the Granicus, energized his troops. The Persian center soon buckled under the double weight of the Macedonian cavalry and advancing phalanx, and the battle turned into a rout. Darius's army lost between 10,000 and 20,000 infantry and 2,500 cavalry, compared to 25 of Alexander's

Companions and 300 infantrymen, most of whom fell to Persian arrows and spears during the river crossing. This lopsided victory was a stunning achievement by the Macedonians, who not only had to ford a river while under enemy attack but also managed to conceal their intentions and strike the heart of the Persian army. So assured had Darius been of victory at the Granicus that he did not attend the battle, trusting instead several of his satraps to lead the Persian defense. Alexander showed no mercy for the Greek mercenaries who were captured, ordering the execution of more than 18,000, and condemning 2,000 to slavery. This ruthlessness would stand in stark contrast to Alexander's treatment of Persian prisoners, whom he later integrated into his army.

The Macedonian army remained in Anatolia for a year, establishing its influence and eradicating Persian strongholds. It took a year for Darius to replace the army he had lost at the Granicus. This time the king himself took charge of the army, reinforced by a staggering array of allies and mercenaries. In total, Darius had under his command 100,000 Persian infantry and cavalry, 40,000 Armenians, 30,000 Greek mercenaries, and thousands of horsemen from the Persian Empire's eastern steppes. In short, Darius had three times more soldiers and cavalry than Alexander. The Persian army's strength would be seriously tested by Alexander, who had rotated a few of his troops from Greece and Macedonia after his initial victory, but still held on to the crack Macedonian phalanx and Companion Cavalry.

Buoyed by his vastly superior numbers, Darius deployed his army near the Issus river in southern Anatolia (modern-day Turkey) in November 333 BC. He did not heed the warning of his Greek adviser Charidemus, who had led the Athenian resistance against Alexander's father and had joined Darius's ranks after the Greek defeat at Chaeronea. Upon viewing the massive Persian army, Charidemus pointedly observed: "[Your magnificent army] gleams with purple and gold; it is resplendent with armour and an opulence so great that those who have not witnessed it simply cannot conceive of it. The Macedonian line is certainly coarse and inelegant, but it protects behind its shields and lances immovable wedges of tough, densely packed soldiers . . . What you need is strength like theirs. You must look for help in the land that produced those men—send off that silver and gold of yours to hire *soldiers* [emphasis added]."[3]

When he heard this shocking assessment, Darius ordered his soldiers to slit the Greek leader's throat—but the kernel of truth that Charidemus had exposed at the cost of his own life would prove hauntingly accurate. Alexander caught the bulk of Darius's army crossing a mountain pass at Issus and once again led the Persians to believe that he would attack from the left, while he personally led his Companion Cavalry to wheel around the right flank. Once he had routed the right wing of the Persian army, Alexander made a beeline for the Persian nerve center, charging into the flank of Darius's center with the Companion Cavalry. Accounts of the battle depict Alexander establishing eye contact with Darius and attempting to strike the Persian king. Whatever did happen in the general melee, Darius quickly decided that Alexander was too much and fled the field in his chariot, leaving behind 110,000 Persian and allied dead. Alexander pursued Darius until nightfall but, delayed by the huge swaths of the retreating Persians, could not reach his quarry.

The battle of Issus cemented Alexander's hold over the western crescent of the Persian Empire, confirming the fact that his first victory at the Granicus was no fluke and that the Macedonian army could accomplish its lofty goal of defeating Persia. The victory also provided the first glimpse into Alexander's post-conquest strategy. Instead of the ruthless spirit he had shown at the Granicus by ordering the execution of all Greek prisoners, Alexander treated the captured wives and concubines of King Darius with deep respect. Not only did he promise that the women could keep their titles and belongings, but he allowed them to join his Macedonian court. Eventually Alexander would marry a Persian princess and incorporate units of the Persian army into his own.

At the Granicus and Issus, Alexander had shown Darius that he wasn't afraid of the much larger Persian force, and that his tactical genius and personal courage could offset the numerical superiority of the Persian army. But he still only occupied half of the Persian Empire. The other half, home to Darius's capital and immense wealth, still lay untouched in modern-day Iran and Iraq. And so instead of accepting the increasingly frantic offers of peace from Darius, Alexander set out for the Persian nest, convinced that he could once again meet and defeat Darius. After years of being tormented by the Persians, Alexander could feel that the advantage was finally swinging in favor of the underdogs. But the Persians had not given up, and, after learning two bitter lessons at the Granicus and Issus, were eager to show the world that they were no pushovers. Alexander was only too willing to oblige.

THE FINAL SHOWDOWN: GAUGAMELA

Here we are, then, the morning of October 1, 331 BC, three years after Alexander stepped foot on the Asian mainland. Waiting on a plain carefully chosen for its favorable terrain, Darius has control over the largest army ever assembled in the ancient world. Not to be outdone a third time, Darius cleared the plain of obstacles so that he could deploy his scythed chariots against the Macedonian infantry. He even brought elephants, imported from India, to add terror and firepower to his army. Altogether the Persian army was even more powerful than the one mustered at Issus. Its total numbers were estimated to be as high as one million by ancient scholars like Plutarch, but the most likely number was closer to 200,000, including a vast cavalry contingent perhaps numbering as many as 40,000. For his part, Alexander was relying on the same troops that had performed so brilliantly at the Granicus and Issus—augmented by fresh infantry and cavalry and hardened by two years of constant marching and fighting. Darius had arrayed his army in solid squares, confident that Alexander would not break through a tight defense.

Seeing the bulk of the Persian army, Alexander's senior general, the influential Parmenion, suggested a night attack to surprise Darius. But Alexander, perhaps because of pride or out of his belief in the prophesy that he would become master of the known world, revealed to him at the Temple of Amon in Egypt, simply told Parmenion, "I will not steal victory." Alexander's strategy for winning the day was again bold and compelling: he would feint an advance with his left and right wings, enticing Darius to reinforce his defenses away from his center, and lead a cavalry charge into the nexus of the Persian forces. As the battle began, Alexander used a new ruse: he walked his cavalry across the front of the Macedonian line from left to right, visibly exposing himself and causing Darius to believe that he would launch a cavalry charge on the Persian left flank. To match this perceived threat, Darius ordered his forces to reinforce the left flank, starting the depletion of the Persian center that Alexander desired. The Persian king then ordered a heavy cavalry attack into the Macedonian left, held by Parmenion. As ordered by Alexander, Parmenion refused battle and simply held off the cavalry charge, although the ferocity of the Persian attack came close to buckling the Macedonian line. Elements of the Persian cavalry broke through a gap in the Macedonian ranks, but instead of exploiting this sudden advantage by surrounding Parmenion's left wing, the Persians chose to pillage the Macedonian supply camp, thus wasting their only opportunity to gain the upper hand.

At this turning point in the battle, Alexander saw that the Persian attacks on his left wing and his own feint had drawn off sufficient numbers from Darius's center. The Macedonian phalanx had already dealt with Darius's chariots by letting them through the front lines, encircling them, and killing most of the drivers and horses. Now it was their turn to attack, following Alexander's charge at the head of the Companion Cavalry into the weakened Persian center. The outcome of the main charge was in doubt for some time, with both Darius and Alexander spurring their men forward and the Persians nearly enveloping Alexander. It took an apparent omen—the sight of an eagle gently hovering over Alexander in the middle of the carnage—to restore the confidence of the Macedonians, who finally drove through the main Persian body and came within sight of Darius. With his charioteer dead and his forces beginning to retreat, Darius took the reins and fled for the second and last time as Alexander furiously pursued him.

The price tag for Darius's third and final defeat was horrendous. In the field of Gaugamela lay more than 50,000 Persian dead, along with 5,000 Macedonian dead, a ratio of 10 to 1. The Persian tally would have included Darius himself and the remainder of the fleeing Persians had Parmenion not sent a desperate signal for help, which Alexander received just as he was about to launch a full pursuit of Darius. Having to choose between capturing his main prize and saving the left wing of his army, Alexander turned his cavalry around to come to Parmenion's rescue. The Companion Cavalry quickly turned the tide back in the Macedonians' favor, and the last remnants of the Persian army surrendered or fled. As Victor Davis Hanson astutely writes, this final act showed that "Alexander's revolutionary practice of total pursuit and destruction of the defeated enemy ensured battle casualties unimaginable just a few decades earlier."[4] Alexander didn't seek trophies or personal glory. He wanted to achieve total victory, and he had adopted Greek and Macedonian battle tactics to ensure that his army would not just defeat but annihilate the Persians.

ALEXANDER'S CREATIVE EXECUTION FORMULA

In total, Alexander's destruction of the Persian army at the Granicus, Issus, and Gaugamela resulted in well over 200,000 Persian deaths. Alexander would enter the Persian capital of Babylon to claim its riches and take for himself Darius's throne before stepping into Afghanistan and India. Just how did Alexander, with his compact Macedonian army, manage to not only once, but *three times*, defeat a much superior foe? Starting with his first battle fighting the Greeks at Chaeronea, Alexander began to formulate a strategy for winning against the odds, and from that moment on continually refined his Creative Execution formula. As a result, Gaugamela and the conquest of the Persian Empire was the apotheosis of Greek and Macedonian warfare, and remains unmatched in the annals of antiquity. Only Julius Caesar would match Alexander's reputation as the most accomplished general of the ancient world, yet the forces that Caesar fought in his greatest campaign in Gaul (modern-day France) were puny compared to the vast Persian armies and complex geography that Alexander faced in Asia. Caesar's genius was as much political as it was military, whereas Alexander had only one objective: the complete defeat and conquest of the Persian Empire.

Let's take a look at how Alexander's Persian campaign fits into the Creative Execution formula, and thereby shares the same qualities that were wielded centuries later by the U.S. Coast Guard and Thomas Cook.

Unique Strategy

More than any other general in ancient history, Alexander had a clearly articulated view of how he would conquer Asia and fulfill his country-men's wish of bringing down the Achaemenid dynasty. It's important here to understand the difference between motive and strategy. Alexander's motive in conquering Asia was to remove the threat of Persian hegemony and create a harmonious world order. This goal was not new. Greek and Macedonian rulers for 200 years had been bent on eliminating the very real threat that the Persian Empire represented, and, as we saw with the march of the Ten Thousand, some had come close to succeeding. The newness of Alexander's strategy was the way in which he proposed to fight the Persians in order to win total victory—something that had eluded his predecessors and would inspire Western warfare for centuries to come. There were two unique yet simple elements to his strategy:

1. Feint and deny his left wing. In all his battles, Alexander would arrange his forces so that his left wing, usually commanded by his most experienced general, would "refuse" combat by simply standing their ground and deflecting enemy charges. This stratagem allowed Alexander to concentrate his offensive firepower in the center and right wing of his army, while giving the enemy the impression that

his main thrust would come from the left wing. This was an audacious strategy that almost cost Alexander his victory at Gaugamela when Parmenion's left wing buckled as it absorbed the onslaught of the Persian cavalry.

2. Lead a cavalry charge through the enemy center, followed by the bulk of the infantry to cut down enemy forces. At Issus and Gaugamela, Alexander led a charge that was directed at the center of the Persian lines and King Darius himself. Both times he came close to slaying Darius, and changed the tide of the battle by breaking through the enemy's lines and delivering a fatal blow with the combined power of his Companion Cavalry and phalanx.

Alexander's actions bring to life a key concept of Western warfare, which endures today under the name of "center of gravity" operations, where one attacker seeks to disrupt or destroy the opponent's nerve center. The U.S. Joint Staff Officer's Guide describes the center of gravity as "the characteristics, capabilities, or locations from which a military force derives its freedom of action, physical strength, or will to fight." In the case of the Persian army, its will to fight clearly emanated from King Darius himself. Alexander understood that regardless of the size of the Persian army, going after its center—or Darius himself—would be the fastest way to defeat it. And that's the Unique Strategy he pursued at the Granicus, Issus, and finally Gaugamela.

The other unique aspect of Alexander's strategy was his personal commitment to lead the Companion Cavalry into action, and always use the cavalry and the phalanx as reinforcing elements of terror and destruction—what the Pentagon today would call "shock and awe." While the Greeks fought mostly as infantry, Alexander understood the advantage of heavy cavalry on the vast terrain of Asia, and selected his finest warriors to join him in the Companion Cavalry. As Hanson explains, Alexander was the master of delivering "stunning cavalry blows focused on a concentrated spot in the enemy line, horsemen from the rear turning the dazed enemy onto the spears of the advancing phalanx; [and] subsequent pursuit of enemy forces in the field."

He adds that "In all such cases, the overriding agenda was to find the enemy, charge him, and annihilate him in open battle—victory going not to the larger force, but to the one who could maintain rank and break the enemy as a cohesive whole."[5] The fact that Alexander successfully used the same strategy three times in a row to defeat Darius's army is a testament to the Macedonians' battle discipline and to the strategy's near-faultless premises.

Candid Dialogue

The ubiquity of Candid Dialogue in Alexander's leadership stands in stark contrast to the Persian way. At the onset of his campaign, looking for ways to motivate his troops, Alexander delivered a powerful speech reminding the Greeks and Macedonians fighting under his banner that they were "free men." He referred to Persians as "slaves" who had no personal or political freedom. Accordingly, men in Alexander's army were free to associate, hold assemblies, and sometimes vote on important issues. This familiarity and openness was replicated at the royal court, where Alexander often invited and recognized common soldiers and commanders. As Partha Bose reports, "Alexander studied Aristotle's subtle framing—the way he would phrase a question, the way he would elongate or emphasize certain words, where he would pause in the asking. . . . He could frame a question in a certain way and, based on the response he got, be persuaded whether he could trust the respondent or be wary of him."[6] Alexander used this technique to test his generals' and soldiers' commitment to the Macedonian cause, and as a result clearly understood his troops' mental state and readiness for battle.

Alexander's unceremonious and inclusive style built a strong esprit de corps in his army, and inspired respect from his friends and enemies alike. He spoke plainly in explaining his aims and strategy, and in showing his pleasure or displeasure. In a disagreement with Parmenion, who was pushing him to accept the peace terms offered by Darius before Gaugamela, Alexander simply replied that he would accept, too, were he Parmenion. The concept of free men fighting for a noble cause, Alexander's direct approach, and his use of fast couriers to relay information on the battlefield all contributed to his stunning victories. The *Cambridge Illustrated History of Warfare* explains that "the superiority of western military practice derives in part from its tradition of free speech, unbridled investigation, and continual controversy, relatively free from state censorship or religious stricture."[7] Unlike Alexander's open and inclusive style, King Darius behaved like an imperious monarch, and paid the price in battle. Instead of encouraging Candid Dialogue and listening to his commanders' advice for fighting Alexander, he ordered the execution of Charidemus, the only leader in his entourage courageous enough to tell him the truth about his ineffective army.

Clear Roles and Accountabilities

Alexander showed true genius with the training and organization of his army, which he kept to a manageable size and focused on specific tasks and skills. He organized his army into three corps of specialized warriors: the Thessalian cavalry, which included the small group of Companion Cavalry that Alexander personally led, and which acted as the shock troops; the powerful phalanx, with its rows of *sarissai* that worked as a unit to mow down enemy infantry; and the javeliners who harassed enemy cavalry. Alexander kept his army purposely small in order to maintain effective control and wield these three groups in unison. Hanson observes that the "coordination between infantry and horsemen was an entirely new development in the history of Western warfare, and was designed to make numbers superfluous." He explains that the battles of the Macedonians "were not to be huge shoving matches between phalanxes, but sudden Napoleonic blasts to particular spots, which when exploited would collapse and thereby ruin the morale of the others."[8]

Reflecting this organizing philosophy, all of Alexander's generals and soldiers knew their exact role and place on the battlefield. Unlike

Darius, whose decision making was tightly centralized, and whose army didn't follow a clearly established battle plan, Alexander's field commanders didn't need specific orders to understand what Alexander intended to do, or to follow him into battle once he launched his cavalry charge. "[Alexander's commanders] were so tightly linked in their sense of purpose and ambition that they were certain every one of them would know exactly what to do," writes Partha Bose. "The Companions had been trained to work independently or together as a group. They knew their role here, which was to charge into the Persian center at any cost. In pursuit of that single objective they kept adapting themselves as needed."[9]

Perhaps the most impressive illustration of Alexander's approach to dividing roles and responsibilities was the discipline of the troops that were to hold back and deny the left flank. Although Parmenion sent for help at Gaugamela, he never buckled or questioned his orders. The Persian cavalry, which for a fleeting moment had the opportunity to roll up the Macedonian left wing, in contrast, had no clear design and decided to sack the Macedonian camp. This single difference between the Macedonian and Persian war machines meant that the Persian army fought for the sake of fighting itself, rather than pursuing a clear goal. The greatest achievement sought by Persian leaders was to challenge and kill individual foes in man-to-man battles, a macho and entertaining, but otherwise futile, gesture. Macedonian leaders did not seek individual combat or glory but focused on fulfilling their part of Alexander's battle plan—even if it meant just standing their ground and refusing combat, as Parmenion was instructed.

Bold Action

Alexander was all about decisive, bold action to bring about a swift victory. This usually meant waiting for the right time to unleash the Companion Cavalry against the Persian center. The concentrated, decisive action that the Macedonians perfected with the Companion Cavalry was a Hellenic tradition unique to Western warfare. Greeks and Macedonians practiced the art of synchronized movement and reinforcing maneuvers, which ensured that no part of the army would fight alone. At the battle of Thermopylae, King Leonidas only had 300 Spartans to block off the entire Persian army—because he knew that his soldiers would stick together and form a defensive shield that the Persians could not break. It took a Greek traitor, who showed Xerxes a way around the pass, for the Persians to finally overcome the Spartan defense after three days of stubborn resistance. Likewise in his first major battle at Chaeronea, Alexander waited until the left wing was under attack to launch the Macedonian main cavalry attack and surround the Athenians and Thebans.

Bold Action was a trademark of Alexander. He was an ardent admirer of Achilles, whose tomb he visited after landing in Asia. "I wish I could see Achilles' lyre, which he played when he sang of the glorious deeds of brave men," he exclaimed after anointing his hero's grave with sacred oil.[10] At the Granicus, he plunged into the river despite Parmenion's warning that it was late in the day and that the opposite bank seemed rough and uneven. His love of Bold Action was made famous in the tale of the Gordian Knot, which takes place in the city of Gordium where Alexander set down his winter quarters in 333 BC. Unable to untie the thick rope because he could not find the ends, Alexander cut the knot in two with his sword, and produced the required result. This Bold Action earned him the favor of the local oracle, who declared that Alexander would become master of all Asia. To this day, the cutting of the Gordian Knot remains a symbol of Alexander's untamed spirit and ability to make instant difficult decisions.

Alexander made three bold decisions during the Persian campaign, and each one impacted the ultimate outcome:

1. He decided to attack the Persians as soon as he reached the Granicus, rather than wait until the next morning to assess the situation—as conventional wisdom would suggest. This decision took the Persians by surprise and gave Alexander the advantage by allowing him to deploy his troops in the formation he desired.

2. Again ignoring the advice of Parmenion, who advocated a night attack in order to avoid fighting the massed Persian army at Gaugamela, Alexander chose to wait until morning so that Darius could muster his entire army. He wanted to provoke Darius into a full-fledged battle, and didn't want a nighttime skirmish that would result in a confusing battle. This decision had a positive unintended consequence: expecting a night attack, Darius had kept his troops awake all night. As a result, the Persians who fought at Gaugamela did so without the benefit of a full night's sleep.

3. Perhaps the boldest decision Alexander ever made was to stop the pursuit of Darius when he realized that Parmenion was in an imminent state of collapse at Gaugamela. He put aside his personal need for vengeance and closure, and wheeled the Companion Cavalry back to save the Macedonian troops under Parmenion's command. It was a bold decision that sealed the Macedonian victory and effectively ended the reign of King Darius, who fled into the Persian countryside and was ultimately killed by one of his own officers.

Visible Leadership

Charging at the head of the Companion Cavalry with his distinctive white plumed helmet, there is no question that Alexander not only felt exalted about leading his army into battle but also believed that his place as a leader and conqueror was at the front of his line of battle. Alexander's determination and blind belief in his ability to overcome the odds presented by the Persian army was a huge contributor to his success on the battlefield. As Steve Forbes and John Prevas write, "Alexander's leadership style reflected his conviction that a man of ability and determination could inspire and direct others to accomplish anything he set his mind to . . . His willingness to remain at the forefront of every operation, never asking more from those he led than he himself was willing to give, is what enabled him to keep his army behind him for so long."[11] He was first to cross the Granicus, followed by 13 squadrons of cavalry, despite waist-high waters and the fact that the Persian army was waiting for him on the opposite bank. He was wounded twice at Granicus and Issus, had several horses killed under him, but never withdrew from the field. As John Keegan wrote of Alexander's victory at Issus, "Outnumbered three to one, Alexander once again chose to attack on the strongest sector . . . crossing the enemy's missile zone at speed, and so braving what ought to have been a disabling barrage from the arrows of the Persian composite bowmen, he led the cavalry directly against the flank where Darius stood."[12]

The morning of Gaugamela, Alexander was fast asleep and had to be woken up by Parmenion, his second-in-command. Parmenion remarked that he couldn't fathom how Alexander could sleep undisturbed the morning of such a momentous battle. "Why not?" Alexander retorted. "Do you not see that we have already won the battle, now that we are delivered from roving around these endless devastated plains, and chasing this Darius, who will never stand and fight?"[13] This could be considered boasting, but reflects the calm and confidence that Alexander felt and spread around his army. His direct, energetic leadership was anathema to Darius, who stayed isolated from his troops and demanded blind obedience.

During his 12 years in Asia, from Persia to Afghanistan and India, Alexander stood at the front of his army. Never once did he go home, or send his army into battle without being at the forefront. "[Alexander] was always the first into battle, he always fought in the very thick of it, and he was always the one pushing deeper and farther into the enemy ranks."[14] Even outside of the battle zone, he acted as a visible leader, as he did by sparing the wives of Darius after Issus. By visibly showing restraint and giving his personal protection to the Persian princesses and queens, Alexander began the reconciliation process with the Persians, which ensured that his personal legacy was not just about conquest but also about blending Western and Eastern culture.

Alexander's personal leadership would be tested as his army pushed further east into modern-day Afghanistan and India. While the Greeks and Macedonians in his army had been motivated to fight King Darius and bring down the Persian Empire, they felt no compulsion to exterminate the dozens of local tribes that opposed their journey eastward, where Alexander hoped to reach the Indian Ocean and embark with his troops for the homeward return. In his most visible act of leadership following Gaugamela, Alexander gathered his discontented commanders and delivered a speech that brought some of them to tears. "If, indeed, there is some cause for reproach regarding the hardship that you have endured up to now, or regarding my leadership, it is pointless for me to continue addressing you," he said. He went on to name the dozens of lands that the Macedonians had conquered, then urged the men to "stand firm . . . for it is toil and danger that lead to glorious achievements, while pleasure lies in a life of courage and in a death that brings undying fame."[15] Eventually Alexander retreated to Persia, yet his visible leadership throughout the campaign from Persia to Afghanistan and India is what kept his Macedonian, Greek, and Persian forces from deserting his cause—or worse, from turning on each other.

FINAL TALLY

Alexander returned to Babylon in the winter of 324 BC, seven years after his victory at Gaugamela. These years were marred by brutal clashes in Afghanistan and India, where his army finally told Alexander that they would go no further. He made a number of unpopular decisions, marrying the ex-wife of a Persian commander, adopting Eastern fashion, and attempting to blend Persian troops into his own. As James Romm writes, Alexander's integration of Persians into his Macedonian army "offended both the pride and the prejudices of his countrymen." While the Macedonians had "accepted, grudgingly, his use of Persians as high officials, his adoptions of Persian dress and court rituals, even the marriages of the king and his top staff to Asian women . . . the integration of the armed forces was a more serious matter."[16] To make matters worse, Alexander had Parmenion put to death on charges of treason, and killed Cleitus, one his best friends, in a fit of drunken rage. In a theme that was as relevant in 330 BC as it is today, Alexander's real troubles lay in managing the peace after his stunning victories over Darius.

Humbled but not discouraged, Alexander planned a fresh campaign against the Arab tribes to the south of his new empire. But he became ill, or was poisoned, and died in June of the following year (323 BC) at age 33. His embalmed body was taken to Alexandria, the Egyptian city he had founded on his outbound journey into Persia, to be entombed in a marble mausoleum. To this day, the actual location of Alexander's tomb remains one of the greatest unsolved mysteries of ancient times. When it is discovered, we may finally learn what killed Alexander.

Despite his reversals and untimely death, one can't argue that Alexander was an ancient master of Creative Execution. He formulated and executed a Unique Strategy to become, as he would be called after Gaugamela, Lord of the World. He carried out his mission with vigor and personal brilliance—in the process killing more than 300,000 Persians, Indians, and Afghans who opposed his eastward march. Alexander's victory was the equivalent of the United States invading the Soviet Union during the Cold War and defeating the Red Army on its own soil—a feat that Napoleon and Hitler both attempted with catastrophic results. Other than Caesar and Napoleon, no other general would come close to achieving such lopsided victories over a vastly superior enemy.

And so from Alexander's early mastery of Creative Execution, we derive some useful glimpses of what it takes to win against the odds, as well as warnings about the dangers of overconfidence. Historians might argue that Alexander's victories at the Granicus, Issus, and Gaugamela were the result of decades of military preparations by his father, King Philip II, which gave the Macedonians an unparalleled edge in fighting the Persians. Likewise, one could argue that King Darius was a fool who overestimated his strength and was an incompetent military commander. A more astute military strategist, well

Battle & Year	Macedonian Losses	Persian Losses	Key Strategy
Granicus— 334 BC	300	10,000 to 20,000 plus 2,500 cavalry and 20,000 Greek mercenaries	Cross the Granicus river and charge the enemy center
Issus—333 BC	500 plus 10,000 wounded	110,000	Refuse left wing, cavalry punch through center
Gaugamela— 331 BC	5,000	50,000	Refuse left wing, cavalry and phalanx punch through center
Totals	*Roughly 6,000**	*At least 170,000*	

* Many more thousands of Macedonian troops died crossing the desert from India back to the Persian heartland in the summer that preceded Alexander's death.

versed in Greek and Macedonian warfare, would surely have prevailed over Alexander with the massive forces and resources available to the Persians. Yet just as in any clash of armies or professional sports teams, it's the final score that counts. And the final score in Alexander's case is overwhelming. From his first clash at the Granicus to the final defeat of King Darius, Alexander put up some impressive numbers.

What we can say with certainty from those numbers is that the combination of a clear and unique Macedonian strategy, precisely practiced and executed over the course of three consecutive battles, resulted in Persian losses roughly 30 times what Alexander's army suffered. While many of the Persian losses were incurred during their retreats, when the Macedonian cavalry easily picked off panicked and disorganized men, Alexander's mastery of the battlefield and his desire for total victory yielded astounding results by ancient—and indeed modern—standards of warfare.

Alexander's personal leadership, charisma, and vision for the inclusion of the Persian Empire into the Western fold, while far-fetched and ultimately impractical, present us with a classic example of Creative Execution in action.

Now let's fast-forward to a time when cavalry charges still dominated the battlefield, but when naval warfare had morphed into a giant gunpowder duel between ships as tightly organized and efficient as Alexander's phalanx. There we shall meet the first master of Creative Execution at sea, who would, through a single action, bring 100 years of peace and prosperity to the European continent.

2

Nelson at Trafalgar

In case signals cannot be clearly seen or understood, no captain can do very wrong if he places his ship alongside that of the enemy.

—Lord Nelson

In early 1805, French emperor Napoleon Bonaparte is at the apex of his power. Unlike Alexander, who had spent his childhood learning the art of Greek and Macedonian warfare in order to lead the conquest of Persia, Napoleon grew up on the remote island of Corsica and embarked on his military career at the age of 15, when he joined the Royal Military Academy in Paris. The following year, the promising second lieutenant was sent to complete his apprenticeship with a French artillery regiment. When the French Revolution broke out in 1789, Napoleon quickly rose through the ranks to assume the posts of general and First Consul. After forging the Grande Armée into a formidable weapon combining the firepower of artillery, cavalry, and infantry, Napoleon started his punishing campaign against a coalition of Prussian, Austrian, and Russian hosts.

To complete his conquest of Europe and beyond, Napoleon has one more enemy to defeat: England. Determined to topple this last domino, he assembles 200,000 of his men at Boulogne on the northern coast of France, waiting for the opportunity to cross the English

Channel. So confident is Napoleon of his success that he orders commemorative medals to be struck to celebrate his victory. The only obstacle between the Grande Armée and London is the British fleet, which controls the Strait of Dover. After two years of delays and false starts (including a plan to dig a tunnel underneath the Channel), Napoleon finally exclaims: "Let us be masters of the Strait for six hours, and we shall be masters of the world."[1]

In a calculated gambit, Napoleon orders Admiral Villeneuve, in charge of the Franco-Spanish fleet bottled up in the Spanish harbor of Cadiz, to break the British blockade and join him off Boulogne. The French fleet is, on paper, more powerful than the British Mediterranean squadron under the command of Admiral Horatio Nelson. For two years Nelson's squadron has pursued Villeneuve's fleet from North Africa to the West Indies and back. Villeneuve has 33 ships of the line under his command, including the Spanish first-rate *Santísima Trinidad*, the world's largest warship with 130 guns. Nelson aboard the *Victory* commands 27 ships of the line and four frigates. Napoleon reasons that the French and Spanish fleets are more than a match for Nelson's squadron, and should prevail—or at least escape capture—if and when they were to run into the pesky English admiral.

When Nelson catches Villeneuve off Cape Trafalgar the morning of October 21, 1805, Napoleon's hopes—and Villeneuve's career—come to a sudden end. In one of history's most vicious naval battles, 18 French ships are sunk or captured, with over 14,000 French and Spanish killed in action, wounded, or captured. Admiral Villeneuve was among those captured as the remnants of the French and Spanish Combined Fleet crawled back into Cadiz. Napoleon never did cross the English Channel, and he finally surrendered—on two occasions he became the master of the island of Saint Helena, where he lived out his life in exile.

How did Nelson achieve such an overwhelming victory, and why did he become an icon both before and after Trafalgar? The answer: like Alexander on land, Nelson was, without question, a master of Creative Execution at sea. Over 10 years, Nelson had conceived a ruthless plan to not just defeat but crush the Combined Fleet. The admiral devised an aggressive strategy to deal with the superior numbers he was facing at Trafalgar—slicing through the center of the Combined Fleet so that English ships could pour fires onto the crowded decks of French and Spanish ships at close range—and spent every waking moment refining its execution with his captains and their crews. Although this strategy had been tested by other English admirals in other naval encounters against the French, no admiral had executed it with such brilliance on the scale that Nelson faced at Trafalgar. Not until D-Day in June 1944 would another military action be so significant in the European theater, and demonstrate the raw power of Creative Execution.

THE NELSON TOUCH

The story of Nelson is one of tactical genius and emotional upheavals, which provides the classic blueprint for Hollywood movies—his young rise to power, his successive defeats of Napoleon's battle fleets, his passionate affair with Emma Hamilton, and his glorified death at Trafalgar. Two hundred years after the battle, more than 100 biographies of Nelson have been written, with more on the way. The battle's bicentennial in 2005 drew no less than 35 navies to the Solent (the strait that separates the Isle of Wight from mainland England), including those of France and Spain, with similar commemorative events taking place in Cadiz and Toulon. Much of this adulation is a result of the fact that Nelson not only delivered England from the threat of French occupation, but also revolutionized British naval doctrine. To put his novel ideas of naval warfare into practice, Nelson openly disregarded the orders of his commander in chief, and published a battle plan for Trafalgar that told everyone—even the French—how he intended to deal with them.

Like Alexander, Nelson was obsessed with total victory—not just a gentle defeat of the enemy. In his 1805 battle orders, which became known as the "Nelson Touch," Nelson wrote that "The Destruction of the Enemys [sic] Armament is the Sole Object" of battle.[2] He then sketched out his revolutionary tactic for overwhelming the Franco-Spanish fleet. Instead of the traditional "line of battle," in which warships approached the enemy in a single straight line—which led to long, drawn-out, and usually inconclusive battles—Nelson decided to break through the enemy line at a 90-degree angle and attack individual ships from close quarters. This aggressive maneuver, first attempted by Admiral Rodney against a smaller French fleet off Dominica in April 1780, would yield much more devastating results than a long-range shoot-out. As Noel Mostert notes, Nelson understood that "Naval actions ruled by line had proved indecisive, with enemy ships neither captured nor sunk. Clear-cut victory had become evasive." Therefore the only sure way to achieve total victory was to achieve "any form of close combat, the melee of old, which could only come through ships breaking away from line to get near or alongside an opponent."[3] On Nelson's copy of the Trafalgar attack plan, you can still see the dark incisions of his quill where he desired the English line to cut through the French and Spanish Combined Fleet. This brilliant, aggressive maneuver remained the tactic of choice for winning naval battles until the appearance of the all-big-gun dreadnoughts in the early twentieth century.

Nelson's trump card was the British rate of fire, which was twice as fast as the French, due mostly to better training and discipline. This meant that in close combat one English ship could unleash two broadsides in quick succession in order to disable an enemy ship. As John Keegan writes, "Nowhere else in the military world of the gunpowder age was such power concentrated, not even in the strongest and most powerful of land fortresses."[4] Thanks to their skillful handling, British ships would unleash their broadside right into the stern of enemy ships, killing and maiming members of the enemy crew often before they could fire their own guns. French gunners, by contrast, were told to aim for the British ships' rigging, sails, and masts—in the hope of dismasting or slowing down their opponents.

Nelson first put his new concepts into practice at the Battle of Cape St. Vincent in 1797. Nelson's commander at the time, Admiral

John Jervis, had ordered the traditional line-ahead formation to confront a Spanish fleet. When he saw a gap in the Spanish formation, Nelson boldly sailed his ship into the middle of the enemy fleet, cutting off the Spanish flagship. "Never in the Royal Navy had any captain ever dared to take such single-minded action upon himself," writes Noel Mostert.[5] The rest of the English fleet followed Nelson into this gap and won the day. Nelson repeated this bravado at the Battle of Copenhagen in 1801. While Nelson was probing the enemy's defenses, the fleet admiral hoisted the signal for general withdrawal. In a gesture that became symbolic of his single-minded focus, Nelson told his officers "I really do not see the signal," and kept his own signal flag for close action up flying at his mainmast. Again the English were victorious. When asked about Nelson's blatant disregard of his orders, Admiral Jervis genially told one of his ship's lieutenants that "if you ever commit such a breach . . . I will forgive you also."[6] The expression "turning a blind eye" emerged from this famous incident where Nelson openly disregarded his superior's orders—and got away with it.

While still a junior commander in the Mediterranean, where he was striving to make a difference in the rapidly escalating conflict between France and her European neighbors, Nelson sailed his ship, the *Agamemnon*, to blockade the town of Genoa, where he thought the French were likely to unload troops ferried from their main base in Toulon. "Here again," writes Mostert, "one prompt, bold, decisive and necessary move upon a huge and complex operational area springs from the remarkable individual that is Horatio Nelson, he the only one who, in a rapidly deteriorating scene of potentially grave consequences, holds a clear image of need and specific action."[7] This clarity of thinking and bold decision making would continue to impress Nelson's friends, officers, and enemies.

When he finally commanded his own fleet at the Battle of the Nile in 1798, Nelson was able to apply his Creative Execution formula unhindered, with breathtaking results. In his first overseas expedition, Napoleon had invaded Egypt and kept his fleet anchored at Aboukir Bay, between Alexandria and the mouth of the Nile. Much like

Alexander at the Granicus, Nelson didn't pause when he sighted the French masts. As dusk settled on the North African coast, he ordered his ships into a pincer attack, bracketing each French ship between two of his own. The French, who didn't expect such a sudden attack, kept their ships at anchor—and paid the ultimate price. Out of 13 ships of the line, the French lost two ships (including the flagship *L'Orient*, whose magazines exploded) and surrendered nine to Nelson. More than 3,000 French sailors were killed in the close-quarter action, versus 218 killed and 677 wounded on the British side. As Roger Knight writes, "Risk-taking seamanship . . . highly skilled crews, a rapid rate of fire and determination by every officer and seaman had devastated French naval power in the Mediterranean in under twenty-four hours."[8]

The Battle of the Nile proved the superiority of Nelson's Creative Execution formula and gave him his first taste of total victory. From that point on, he was firmly committed to aggressive tactics that would result in the Trafalgar onslaught. His reputation was such that, when Villeneuve spotted the English fleet near Trafalgar, he ordered the Franco-Spanish fleet to turn back—too late—toward Cadiz. When this disconcerting order was relayed to him, the commander of the Spanish ships, Cosme de Chucurra, prophetically exclaimed, "The fleet is doomed. . . . The French Admiral does not know his business."[9] Chucurra would lose both his ship and his life in the ensuing battle.

LET EVERY MAN DO HIS DUTY

After spotting the enemy coming out of Cadiz the morning of October 21, Nelson divided his fleet into two columns that would each drive a wedge through the center of the Combined Fleet, isolate the most powerful French and Spanish ships, and let his captains pounce on their victims using superior, concentrated firepower. Due to the very light winds off the cape, the English columns took over 90 minutes to make their way to the center of the Combined Fleet, during which the French and Spanish could fire at will against the oncoming vessels. Amazingly, during this slow creep toward the Combined Fleet, only one English ship, the *Mars*, was put out of action, her masts shot away and her captain beheaded by a stray shot. The *Victory* herself suffered 50 casualties before she could fire her first broadside.

It was during this unsettling barrage that Nelson hoisted his famous message "England expects that every man will do his duty." When Nelson's *Victory* finally sneaked in the gap between the French ships of the line, the effect was devastating. The *Victory*'s first broadside raked the *Bucentaure* through her stern and killed 197 French sailors and wounded 85, instantly taking the French flagship out of the battle. The *Redoutable* suffered a worse fate, and eventually surrendered with only 99 men fit out of a total complement of 643. The second English column, led by Admiral Collingwood, overwhelmed a number of French and Spanish rear-guard ships in close-quarter fighting.

With the destruction or capture of more than half the French and Spanish fleet, Trafalgar was a complete vindication of Nelson's Creative Execution formula. Nelson's victory forced Napoleon to cancel his invasion of England and brought the focus of the war back to the European continent. Waterloo would follow less than 10 years later, and the resulting *Pax Britannica* would usher in 100 years of peace in Europe. By denying Napoleon control of the world's oceans, Nelson gave his country and Europe an immense gift of peace through naval supremacy, which the British put to good use by expanding their own empire and becoming the world's dominant trading power.

CREATIVE EXECUTION AT TRAFALGAR

Like Alexander, Nelson excelled in all dimensions of Creative Execution: he designed a Unique Strategy, encouraged Candid Dialogue with his captains, created Clear Roles and Accountabilities, relished Bold Action, and embodied the concept of Visible Leadership. Let's take a look at how these elements played out at Trafalgar.

Unique Strategy

Nelson's choice of strategy and tactics—to force a decisive battle with the Combined Fleet, approach the enemy line at a right angle, and use superior firepower to overwhelm each ship in close-quarter combat—was both unique and compelling. And it was much more practical than the line-ahead tactic that had guided naval warfare before his time. This strategy captured the imagination of the British Admiralty and of Nelson's commanding officers, his captains, and quite certainly his foes. "It was new, it was singular, it was simple,"[10] Nelson wrote to Lady Hamilton before Trafalgar. Nelson also made it clear that the destruction of the enemy fleet was the only thing that mattered—instead of blockading the Franco-Spanish fleet, going after its supply bases across the Mediterranean, and gradually reducing its power through small engagements.

Nelson's directives to his captains were simple: "no captain can do very wrong if he places his ship alongside that of the enemy!"[11] The admiral's single focus on engaging the enemy was so clear and distinct that he needed to issue no orders at Trafalgar—just watch the plan he had conceived seamlessly unfold. Noel Mostert brilliantly summarizes how Nelson drilled his strategy into every captain and seaman's head, and the impact of his leadership on English morale:

> One of the most celebrated features of Nelson's distinction as commander was his intensive instruction to his captains on what he had in mind for any action. Broad strategy and tactical manoeuvre were exhaustively projected upon whatever scene and circumstances could be in prospect. No aspect of a potential action was ignored or overlooked. It was a rigorous drill that left an insight into the genius of that marshalled mind that stayed with those exposed to it perhaps more forcefully than anything else about him . . . In battle itself it was the basis of their confidence and trust.[12]

Nelson not only shared his strategy with each captain, but fervently argued with the powerful Admiralty in London about the value of relinquishing the line-ahead maneuver in favor of his bold approach. As Mostert writes, "Trafalgar had been . . . the first fully planned and meticulously plotted 'breaking the line' battle on the open sea: long deliberated upon, earnestly longed for, and here achieved."[13] By breaking with the old British naval tactics and introducing the promise of total victory, the Nelson Touch created a sense of euphoria and inevitability that permeated the British fleet. As Cuthbert Collingwood, Nelson's second-in-command at Trafalgar, wrote after the battle, "Nelson possessed the zeal of an enthusiast . . . and everything seemed, as if by enchantment, to prosper under his direction. But it was the effect of system, and nice combination, not of chance."[14]

When Nelson shared his plan to split the fleet in two and cut through the French and Spanish line with his captains before Trafalgar, he made it clear what he was after: "I would go at them at once, if I can, about one-third of their line from the leading ship. What do you think of it? . . . I think it will surprise and confound the enemy. They won't know what I am about. I will bring forward a pell-mell battle and that is what I want." He also wrote to the secretary of the Admiralty that "I laid before them the plan that I had previously arranged for attacking the enemy; and it was not only my pleasure to find it generally approved, but clearly perceived and understood."[15] Nelson's ability to clearly articulate his vision and engage his officers in discussing its implementation was key to his success at Trafalgar.

Candid Dialogue

Nelson believed in what he called "creative disobedience," which gave his subordinates the freedom of action to innovate and change tactics as the battle evolved. The heart of the Nelson Touch was in fact Nelson's complete trust in his captains. Once they bought into his plan, Nelson let each captain decide how they would execute the attack, including selecting the enemy ships they would take on. As Roger Knight writes in his biography of Nelson, "The core of Nelson's talent for leadership was that he made his officers and men feel as if he had faith in them and depended upon them, taking his captains into his confidence, not only engendering personal loyalty quickly and permanently but also creating an atmosphere of trust and cooperation."[16] This abundance of trust, when contrasted with the often pedantic style of the older, tradition-oriented admirals that ruled most of the fleet during the eighteenth century, had the effect of energizing Nelson's men.

Nelson developed such a positive attitude and eagerness to fight the coming battle that all of his captains not only followed him into the fray but also felt inspired by his genius. After briefing his captains before the battle, Nelson recorded this emotional assessment: "When I came to explain to them the 'Nelson Touch', it was like an electric shock. Some shed tears, all approved . . . and, from admirals downwards, it was repeated—'It must succeed, if ever they will allow us to get at them! You are, my Lord, surrounded by friends whom you inspire with confidence.'"[17] Not many of us can claim to have brought our audience to tears after a PowerPoint presentation!

The openness with which Nelson dealt with his peers and superiors was a hallmark of his personality. Nelson understood that if he was to achieve the tactical breakthrough he was so fervently seeking, he would need to face down the Royal Navy's tradition of silent disagreement and encourage his captains to take the initiative and break established norms. In an establishment ruled by iron discipline and fear, with ruthless figures like Captain Bligh of the *Bounty* as his peers (incidentally, Bligh served under Nelson at the Battle of Copenhagen, and gave a good account of himself), Nelson's trust and openness with officers and enlisted men was a breath of fresh air. "One of the most remarkable features in the transaction," said Earl Howe of the Battle of the Nile, "consists in the eminently distinguished conduct of *each* of the captains of [Nelson's] squadron."[18] The freedom of action that Nelson's captains possessed was an entirely new development in the rigid war plans of the navy. The fact that Nelson's captains "were so demonstrably able to exercise their own individuality was totally new," writes Noel Mostert.[19]

Clear Roles and Accountabilities

Once Nelson crafted and shared his unique strategy, he trusted that his captains would make it their own and make the right decisions during the course of a battle. This belief in individual action was central to Nelson's new concept of naval warfare, and to the unleashing of Creative Execution. The "liberation of individual energies to ensure victory," as Nelson's approach to naval warfare is described by Adam Nicolson, "is directly attributable to Nelson's vision of complete victory and the strategy England would use to destroy the Franco-Spanish fleet at Trafalgar."[20]

Nelson didn't stop with his captains. He had the Nelson Touch document published for all, with clear instructions as to where and how each of his two attacking lines was to proceed in case of flagging wind or a change in the enemy's dispositions. Ships' lieutenants (each ship carried three to five) were told how to press the attack should their captain be killed in the action. In one ship, the *Bellerophon*, the ship's master reviewed Nelson's orders and, when asked if he understood them, replied that the instructions "were so distinct and explicit, that it was quite impossible they should be misunderstood."[21]

To allow his ships to achieve the superior firepower necessary to quickly overcome enemy ships in close combat, Nelson drilled the fleet mercilessly in its rate of fire. Whereas the French and Spanish ships, which spent more time in their protective harbors than at sea, could fire one full broadside every two minutes, the English fleet could fire three broadsides in three and a half minutes. This capability showed its deadly effectiveness when Nelson's ships were able to rake French or Spanish vessels from the stern, reload their guns, and fire again before the enemy ship had time to recover. As the French observer Jurien de la Gravière wrote after the battle, "Instead of frittering away this irresistible force [a ship's broadside] as we used to do, in the hope of cutting some ropes . . . [or] destroying some important rigging or wounding a mast, the English better taught, concentrated it upon a more certain object, the enemy's batteries. They heaped our decks with slain while our shot passed over their ships."[22] Nelson used this unique advantage to achieve dramatic results in the opening salvos of the battle, when the *Victory* decimated Villeneuve's flagship with two quick broadsides. Collingwood, aboard *Royal Sovereign*, delivered a fatal blow to the Spanish flagship *Santa Ana* with her first broadside.

Bold Action

Just like Alexander, Nelson believed in total victory, not distracting skirmishes. He first demonstrated this thirst for Bold Action at the Battle of St Vincent when he wore off the line to attack two Spanish ships, in spite of his commander in chief's orders. Nelson didn't perceive his action as disobeying orders. Rather, he seized the moment, which, as captain of a first-rate ship, he believed was his duty to do—especially when it meant closing with the enemy.

At the Nile and Trafalgar, Nelson went for the jugular, destroying the French fleet in two separate engagements. At the Battle of the Nile, he annihilated the French anchored in Aboukir Bay when no other fleet had previously fought at night. His reputation for decisive action was so magnified after the Nile that the cautious Villeneuve "sensed he was fighting not just an enormously gifted and bold opponent but an entire institution built on excellence and precision, overloading the odds from the start."[23] As a symbol of his determination and boldness, Nelson had the *Victory* painted in a yellow and black checkered scheme to make her stand out from French and Spanish ships. After Trafalgar, the British Admiralty ordered all its ships to adopt the same pattern.

Visible Leadership

By the time of Trafalgar, Nelson had become such a powerful image that his sheer presence became a decisive factor. "Lord Nelson is arrived," wrote one of the captains when Nelson took command of the blockading British squadron off Cadiz. "A sort of general joy has been the consequence."[24] Nelson's men, as is typical with great leaders, sensed that they were in the presence of a special human being.

During the battle, Nelson refused to remove his decorations or cover his admiral's uniform while pacing the *Victory*'s open deck. He was convinced that his visible presence would encourage his sailors to fight harder. He had already put this belief into practice at the Battle of the Nile, when an iron fragment gashed his forehead and temporarily blinded him in one eye. When Nelson realized that the wound wasn't lethal, he got up to witness the rest of the fight and write his account for the British Admiralty. In an earlier skirmish in the Canary Islands, Nelson had been in the first boat to attack a Spanish stronghold and was struck in his right arm by grapeshot. Without the aid of anesthetics, the ship's surgeon removed the arm—and within the hour Nelson was giving orders again.

At Trafalgar, Nelson would pay for his leadership with his life. The *Redoutable*, commanded by one of the few aggressive French captains, Jean Lucas, had been specifically set up as a sniper vessel with two full companies of French marines deployed on her topmasts. When the *Victory* came within range of the sharpshooters, Nelson became one of the first casualties, receiving a bullet that entered his chest and severed his spine. He would lie in agony for four hours while the battle raged on, and die after hearing from Captain Hardy that 17 enemy ships had surrendered. His last words, other than random thoughts about Lady Hamilton, his illicit paramour, were typical Nelson: "Thank God I did my duty!"[25] Earlier that morning, Nelson had told one of his officers that "I shall not be satisfied with anything less than twenty [captured ships]."[26] Nelson's death is remembered to this day as one of the most poignant vignettes in British history, and the admiral's leadership provided Britain with an incredible sense of hope during dangerous times. As the *Economist*, a news magazine not known for hyperboles, writes of Nelson, "Only Churchill has shaped the British national sense of unity more."[27]

NELSON'S THUNDEROUS LEGACY

Nelson's state funeral in January 1806 was a solemn event that drew England together when the country needed it most. After three days of public viewing, Nelson's casket was taken to St Paul's Cathedral, where 180 naval officers and "mourners, Nelson's family, the royal family, peers of the realm, government and opposition politicians, the alderman and sheriffs of the City of London" attended his funeral service, along with thousands of mourners outside the cathedral.[28]

Benjamin West, who was commissioned to paint the *Death of Nelson* in 1808, captured the public's adoration for Nelson when he explained that "There was no other way of representing the death of a hero but by an Epic representation of it. It must . . . excite awe and veneration . . . His feelings must be roused and his mind inflamed by a scene great and extraordinary."[29]

West's painting shows Nelson lying on the *Victory*'s deck, surrounded by officers and sailors, shrouded by a ray of light that penetrates through the fog of battle. In fact, Nelson was immediately taken to the orlop, the lowest deck on the ship, which housed the infirmary, and died an agonizing death. The *Victory*'s sailors had no time to gather around Nelson's body, busy as they were fighting the French flagship *Bucentaure* on one side, and the deadly *Redoutable* on the other. But West's depiction of Nelson in a saintly pose on the *Victory*'s upper deck sums up the British feeling about the victorious admiral.

Nelson's victory completed the systematic destruction of French naval power that had begun at the Battle of the Nile. The murderous tally from both battles is worth summarizing:

From this assessment, we can see that Nelson's Touch led to a ratio of 10 to 1 killed in action at the Battle of the Nile, and a slightly lower ratio of 6 to 1 at Trafalgar. Given the number of enemy crews wounded or captured at Trafalgar, however, Nelson's ultimate victory against the French and Spanish Combined Fleet was even more spectacular than the results he achieved at the Nile.

There are some powerful similarities between Nelson's battle tactics and leadership leading to the Trafalgar showdown and Alexander the Great's conquest of Persia, which reinforce how each leader wielded the principles of Creative Execution. For instance:

- In their first major battles against the enemy, Alexander and Nelson both chose to attack right away, rather than wait until they could better assess the tactical situation. At the Granicus, Alexander plunged straight into the river to face the Persians. At the Battle of the Nile, Nelson ordered his ships to attack the anchored French

Battle	English Ships & Losses	Enemy Ships & Losses	Key Strategy
The Nile— August 1798	13 ships of the line, 1 fourth-rate ship, and 1 sloop Losses: 218 killed, 677 wounded	13 French ships of the line Losses: 8 ships captured, 2 destroyed 2,012 killed, 600 wounded	Nelson attacks French fleet lying at anchor in Aboukir Bay, English ships enter harbor and fire at point-blank range
Trafalgar— October 1805	33 ships, including 27 ships of the line Losses: 458 killed, 1,208 wounded	41 ships (18 French and 15 Spanish) Losses: 21 ships captured, 1 destroyed More than 2,000 French killed, 1,000 Spanish killed, 2,500 wounded, and 8,000 captured crew members	Nelson divides his fleet in two columns and cuts through the center of the French and Spanish line
Totals	*English killed in actions: 676*	*French and Spanish killed in actions: 5,000*	

fleet in the first naval night action of the century. Alexander and Nelson knew exactly what they wanted to do in each case, had total faith in their officers to make the right tactical decisions, and felt confident enough to strike without delay. In both cases, their Bold Action stunned—and defeated—a well-defended enemy.

• At the Battle of Issus and at Gaugamela, Alexander sought out the heart of the Persian defense—and launched his Companion Cavalry directly against Darius and his 10,000 Immortals. Nelson was equally determined to strike at the enemy's center of gravity, changing centuries of established naval warfare by decreeing that his ships would not fight a long-distance duel but break through the enemy line to maximize enemy casualties. Both leaders understood that to achieve total victory, they needed to destroy the enemy's nerve center, which in Nelson's case meant putting the French and Spanish flagships out of commission in the opening salvoes of the battle.

- Each leader had fine-tuned their forces so that they felt confident they could prevail in the face of superior enemy power. Alexander had his crack Companion Cavalry and phalanx, which he could rely on to destroy enemy infantry. Nelson's secret weapon was the English rate of fire and daring seamanship, which provided a crucial advantage when exchanging broadsides from close quarters.

Perhaps the most noteworthy aspect of Nelson's use of Creative Execution was his ability to transform the English rules of engagement—something that Alexander didn't have to contend with. Alexander inherited a well-oiled Macedonian and Greek army, which had already mastered the art of phalanx and cavalry warfare. Nelson faced the more complex challenge of confronting 200 years of English naval tradition and flagrantly disobeying orders in order to implement the close-quarters fighting formula. As Noel Mostert explains, by the middle of the eighteenth century, the line-of-battle approach was "set with an inflexibility that denied any impulsive action."[30]

Although the breaking of the line had been tried before Nelson's time, its acceptance was spotty. When a British admiral, Thomas Mathews, had broken the line during a battle against the French and Spanish fleet in February 1744, he ended up being court-martialed and cashiered. The fact that Mathews "fought with outstanding courage finally counted for nothing against the fact that he had broken the foremost standing instruction of Admiralty, to hold the line."[31] By the time Nelson took his first command in August 1781 (the *Albermale*, a French-built ship of 24 guns), memories of Mathews's dismissal from the navy were still a powerful deterrent. Only one other British admiral, Sir George Rodney, broke the line at the Battle of the Saints during the American War of Independence in 1782. But that action wasn't planned by the admiral, who initially deployed his fleet "as one of the best lines of battle I ever saw," according to Rodney's own flag officer. Nelson, on the other hand, anticipated the need to break the line approach and head straight for the enemy's center, which forever altered the English navy's war-fighting doctrine.

MOVING FORWARD

At Trafalgar, Nelson showed the world how to use Creative Execution to defeat a superior force at sea. He was the first admiral to "value in attack even of the weak against the strong: the principle of a smaller but more efficient force hurling itself against superior numbers and creating sufficient havoc with the opponent to affect an entire campaign and its strategic objectives."[32] Curiously, the British would ignore Nelson's bold ideas in World War I and World War II, when it fought mostly inconclusive battles with the German fleet. As Vincent O'Hara sums up, "despite the Royal Navy's superiority in intelligence, doctrine, technology and resources, London, when it adopted its Mediterranean strategy in the summer of 1940, chose a campaign the navy was unable to win. The Royal Navy's victories were mostly in sea denial, not the sea control victories it required."[33]

With the entire world at war again and the Royal Navy stretched to its limits from 1939 to 1941, it would take a defying act of Creative Execution by a Japanese admiral to rouse the next naval giant, the United States, out of its isolationist cocoon, and once again apply the Creative Execution formula that Nelson had made his own.

Yamamoto at Pearl Harbor

A military man can scarcely pride himself on "having smitten a sleeping enemy"; it is more a matter of shame, simply, for the one smitten.

—Admiral Isoroku Yamamoto

Following his accession to power in 1933, Hitler inherited the task of rebuilding Germany's armed forces. While Hitler, like Napoleon before Trafalgar, doubted that the British could be defeated on the open seas, just like Napoleon was before Trafalgar, he lent his support to an aggressive shipbuilding program in order to provide Germany with highly efficient pocket battleships and submarines. When World War II broke out, German U-boats nearly succeeded in severing the artery between England and the United States, just as they had attempted from 1914 to 1918. Britain managed to contain Hitler's surface fleet, and sank the mighty *Bismarck* off the coast of France—but only after losing the fleet's finest battleship, HMS *Hood*, with all hands. In the aftermath of the Battle of Britain, Hitler gave up on the idea of invading England and the action shifted to the fierce struggle between the Kriegsmarine's U-boats and the British, Canadian, and American corvettes and destroyers that escorted cargo ships to resource-starved England and Russia. While the Battle of the Atlantic dragged on in 1940 and 1941, a remarkably prescient Japanese figure, Admiral Isoroku Yamamoto, was busy conceiving his own Creative Execution formula to deal a massive blow to the only naval force in the world that could stand up to the combined threat of the Axis powers: the U.S. Pacific Fleet.

The devastation the Japanese attack caused on the morning of December 7, 1941, was stunning by naval warfare standards. On that Sunday morning, the Japanese task force comprising six fleet carriers—the *Akagi, Kaga, Hiryu, Soryu, Shokaku*, and *Zuikaku*—launched two successive waves of torpedo bombers, dive-bombers, and Zero fighters against the U.S. Pacific Fleet anchored at Pearl Harbor. The Japanese planes caught the fleet—and the United States—unaware. Despite the absence of the U.S. Navy's aircraft carriers and the decision not to launch a third strike against the naval base's oil facilities and repair shops, which Japan would later regret, the attack on Pearl Harbor was a daring piece of Creative Execution. The Japanese destroyed 75 percent of U.S. aircraft parked in neat rows on the island's airfields, and destroyed eight battleships, three cruisers, and three destroyers.

Because the raid on Pearl Harbor was conceived as a "sneak attack," and the Americans—and Japanese diplomats—made much of the fact that the Japanese declaration of war was delivered in Washington, DC, 30 minutes after the attack began, the raid's complexity and magnitude are sometimes discounted by historians and the public. To fully understand the obstacles Yamamoto had to overcome, and the bold decisions that went into conceiving and executing the Pearl Harbor raid, it's critical to uncover the mindset of the Japanese and American leaders who took their countries down the path of the Pacific War, as well as the huge tactical challenges that the Imperial Japanese Navy had to face in order to create the total surprise that was key to success. Whether or not the Japanese declaration of war was received on time had in fact no bearing on the success of the attack. By the time the Japanese news would have traveled back to Hawaii and other U.S. naval commands, the Japanese attack would already be in full swing, leaving the fleet at Pearl Harbor just as vulnerable as it would have been a half hour earlier. As President Roosevelt himself admitted during a radio address he gave just two days after the attack on Pearl Harbor, "Our enemies have performed a brilliant feat of deception, perfectly timed and executed with great skill."[1] The bottom line is that the United States never thought that the Japanese would have the audacity or the skill to launch an attack of such magnitude thousands of miles from its home islands. It took one man's vision to dispel this prejudiced notion.

JAPAN'S GREAT LEAP FORWARD: FROM TSUSHIMA TO PEARL HARBOR

At age 19, Yamamoto was a junior officer on the Japanese cruiser *Nisshin*, which was about to face off with the bulk of the Russian main battle fleet. The year was 1905, and the Russian fleet had sailed halfway around the world—over 18,000 nautical miles—to thwart the Japanese blockade of Russia's main Pacific harbor of Port Arthur (modern-day Lushun in Northeast China). The Russo–Japanese War had erupted the year before when Japan's navy struck the small Russian Pacific Fleet at its anchorage in Port Arthur—a surprise attack that would set the pattern for Pearl Harbor.

The admiral of the Japanese fleet, Heihachiro Togo, had been an astute observer of British naval tactics. The British had all too willingly shared their naval expertise with the Japanese, hoping to leapfrog other European nations in establishing friendly relations with the budding Empire of Japan. Several British observers sailed aboard the Japanese flagship *Mikasa* as the formation of 15 battleships and cruisers sailed between the main Japanese island of Kyushu and the Korean Peninsula, just east of the island of Tsushima. Togo's line of battle, perfectly angled to fire all its main guns against the Russian formation, had never fired its guns in anger. Unlike Nelson's fleet at Trafalgar, which had been fighting the French for years, and had learned to use its superior gunnery in various battles, the Japanese had no deeply rooted belief in their naval supremacy. But on board *Mikasa*, Togo felt confident as he hoisted the Z signal flag, his order to attack. His message to the fleet—"The Empire's fate depends on the result of this battle, let every man do his utmost duty"—was a carbon copy of Nelson's signal at Trafalgar.

When the Japanese line opened fire, its superior accuracy and high explosive shells wreaked havoc on the Russian fleet. The Japanese quickly sank the Russian flagship *Knyaz Suvorov* and three other battleships. One of these, the *Borodino*, was hit in her magazine space and exploded, sinking with all hands. As the carnage continued, even the Japanese were impressed by the Russians' resilience as well as by the extent of their own victory. "It was hard to imagine how any living creature could still find a foothold on that mass of twisted, fireblasted iron," said a Japanese sailor as his ship passed the the *Suvorov*'s sinking hulk.[2]

Only two Russian destroyers escaped the Japanese trap at Tsushima and limped into the safety of Vladivostok—out of a fleet of 50 warships. More than 5,000 Russian sailors went down with their ships, and another 5,000 were taken prisoner when their ships were captured as war prizes. The Japanese losses were ridiculously small by comparison: three torpedo boats sunk, 117 men killed in action, and 500 wounded. Among the wounded was Yamamoto himself, whose index and middle fingers were shorn off by a Russian shot. Yamamoto would from then on be known as "80 Sen" at his favorite geisha house—the regular price for a full manicure being 100 sen.

The Japanese victory at Tsushima shocked the Western world and naval pundits. A modern fleet had been annihilated for the first time since Trafalgar, and a major European power had been defeated by an Asian nation. The Russians surrendered Port Arthur—still filled with ammunition and food—and gave Japan not only a lease over Port Arthur but the entire half of Sakhalin Island. By the late 1930s, with a growing population of 70 million, Japan embarked on an ambitious conquest of Northern China to secure access to raw materials. It built the South Manchurian Railway linking Port Arthur to its protectorate in Manchukuo. The Imperial Japanese Army then went on an unauthorized rampage in Nanking, where its soldiers slaughtered thousands of civilians and unarmed Chinese fighters.

Following Japan's declaration of war against China, and the highly publicized Rape of Nanking, the United States put in place a series of countermeasures that threatened to cripple the Japanese economy to the point where the only option left for Japan became war. The worst of the countermeasures was the decision in July 1941 to freeze all Japanese assets in the United States, ban exports of high-octane gasoline to Japan, and limit the export of other petroleum products. For Japan, the only way out of this economic noose was to plan for the capture of the Dutch and British oil facilities in Borneo and the East Indies (now Indonesia). The staunchest opponent of war with the United States was none other than Admiral Yamamoto, who warned the Japanese prime minister in September 1940 that "if we are ordered to [go to war with America], then I can guarantee to put up a tough fight for the first six months, but I have absolutely no confidence about what would happen if it went on for two or three years."[3] Despite his misgivings, Yamamoto proceeded to plan the Pearl Harbor attack, aware that a surprise dawn attack against the U.S. Pacific Fleet was Japan's best hope to knock out the only regional power capable of thwarting its Asian ambitions. As Paul S. Dull writes, "It was a gambler's decision, but the gambler hoped to alter the odds with a bold plan and new naval concepts."[4]

CREATIVE EXECUTION AT PEARL HARBOR

Just how did Yamamoto conceive, train for, and execute the Pearl Harbor attack? And how did he display the kind of leadership that would turn him into a national hero, despite his vocal opposition to the war?

Yamamoto began planning the attack in 1940, less than a year after being appointed commander in chief of the Combined Fleet. His first task was to convince the Japanese high command of the feasibility of mounting a successful seaborne air attack—something that had never been tried before. Just like Nelson had to convince his peers to change the traditional line-of-battle approach before Trafalgar,

Yamamoto needed to persuade his peers in the Japanese Navy that new tactics based on aircraft carriers, not venerable battleships, would decide the outcome of a future conflict with the United States. As Ian Toll explains, "The raid on Pearl Harbor was an eleventh-hour revolt against more than thirty years of war planning, which had envisioned a decisive fleet battle in the western Pacific."[5] Yamamoto held secret war games to demonstrate the power of torpedo-armed aircraft against stationary targets. Then in November 1940, the British unknowingly strengthened Yamamoto's hand when they mounted a carrier-based raid on the Italian harbor of Taranto. With only 21 planes, the British were able to sink three Italian ships, while losing only two aircrews. After fresh accounts of the Taranto raid reached Yamamoto, he ordered his staff—including Commander Minoru Genda, the leader of Japan's fleet air arm—to conduct a feasibility study for a surprise attack on Pearl Harbor. When Genda presented his findings in January 1941, Yamamoto became convinced that Japan could carry out the attack if his staff could overcome three nagging challenges.

1. *Secrecy.* With the heightened state of tensions between the United States and Japan, and the war raging in Europe between the Axis powers and the British, naval movements were carefully tracked using spies and radio-signal detection. In order to sail from Japan to Hawaii undetected, the fleet would have to maintain full radio silence, while coordinating its movements over 4,000 miles of ocean.
2. *Distance.* It was assumed in the 1940s that the maximum operating range for a modern fleet was under 2,000 miles. Supplying a fleet over longer distances would require access to harbors or oil-supply facilities—which the Japanese didn't have. And even if they did find a facility in the Pacific to refuel from, how would the fleet then avoid detection?
3. *Harbor Depth.* When launched from an aircraft, a torpedo typically dives 80 to 100 feet after hitting the water. It then stabilizes and continues on its course. The water depth at Pearl Harbor was

only 30 feet, which made it too shallow for the use of conventional torpedoes. This well-known fact led many American naval experts to discount the possibility of an aerial attack.

The Japanese naval staff dealt with each obstacle conclusively. To maintain secrecy, the fleet assembled in Hitokappu Bay, away from its main bases, and departed the east coast of Japan on November 26 shrouded in foggy weather. The bad weather continued to shield the task force during its eastward journey, and a string of picket submarines ensured that no American ships or aircraft got in its way. Following a rarely used route in the North Pacific, the Japanese fleet sailed just south of the Great Northern Circle, and managed to stay totally undetected. Some Japanese warships still in Japanese waters sent fake radio signals to divert the attention of American intelligence analysts, who had lost track of the Japanese carriers, but believed they were still in their home waters.

To solve the lack of supply facilities on the route, Yamamoto developed the concept of at-sea refueling. A total of eight tankers and supply ships sailed with the main fleet and resupplied the carriers at sea on December 3. The fleet that struck Pearl Harbor would refuel at sea several times in December and January as it continued to serve as the main strike force for the Japanese advances in the Philippines, Singapore, and Dutch East Indies. (After World War II, the U.S. Navy would perfect the art of underway replenishment as it began to deploy carrier battle groups around the world).

Challenged by Yamamoto, Japan's weapons designers came up with a highly innovative solution to the torpedo dilemma. Instead of developing a lighter, less lethal torpedo that could be used in Pearl Harbor's shallow waters, the Japanese fitted out their existing torpedoes with wooden fins, which would break away on impact and cause the torpedo to run shallow. This elegant solution would have deadly consequences for the U.S. battleships moored side by side at Pearl Harbor—in effect sitting ducks for the Japanese torpedoes.

With these three critical problems solved, Yamamoto felt confident that the attack on Pearl Harbor would achieve total surprise and a swift victory. The only unknown was the location of the three American fleet carriers, which Yamamoto believed would be more crucial to the outcome of the war than the aging battleships of the Pacific Fleet. Without this crucial information, Yamamoto nevertheless sent the fateful signal "Climb Mount Niitaka" to Admiral Nagumo, in charge of the Pearl Harbor task force, on December 1. At 5 a.m. on December 7, Nagumo dispatched floatplanes from his heavy cruisers to assess the weather conditions over Pearl Harbor. When the report came back as favorable, the six Japanese carriers turned into the wind and the first wave of 49 high-level bombers, 40 torpedo bombers carrying the shallow-running models, 51 dive-bombers, and 43 fighters took off from the four carriers' decks. Waiting for them at Pearl Harbor were seven battleships in Battleship Row, one battleship in dry dock, eight cruisers, 29 destroyers, and an assortment of submarines, minesweepers, and auxiliary vessels. The closest American carrier, the *Enterprise*, had been delayed on its journey back delivering aircraft to Wake Island, and would miss the action by a day. Had the *Enterprise* returned to Pearl Harbor on December 6, as she was scheduled to, she would have been the primary target of the Japanese, and surely sunk. As it turned out, not only did the *Enterprise* escape destruction on December 7, but she was the only American carrier to survive the entire conflict in the Pacific from beginning to end.

Using the Creative Execution lens, let's deconstruct the Japanese strategy and attack on the morning of December 7, 1941.

Unique Strategy

The plan for attacking Pearl Harbor was, in retrospect, simple and straightforward. Everything from the timing of the ships' departures from Hitokappu Bay to the actual launch of the first wave aircraft was carefully laid out by Yamamoto and his staff. Little was left to chance. The fleet was kept as a single unit, reducing the complicated pincer maneuvers that would doom later Japanese operations. Submarines were deployed in large numbers to screen the task force and provide eyes and ears around the Hawaiian Islands. Torpedo planes, dive-bombers, and vertical bombers carefully rehearsed their attack runs in Kagoshima Bay—ensuring that they would conduct deadly simultaneous attacks against their packed targets. As Ian Toll writes, "Dive bombers planted their bombs with pinpoint accuracy; the torpedo planes came in low and made textbook drops; the Zeros roared in on the tails of the bombers and made deadly strafing runs. If not for the carnage on the ground and in the harbor, the entire spectacle could have been an air show."[6] Japanese planes did not necessarily attack in the order they had been assigned, but the element of surprise was sufficient to provide for a relatively easy victory. By the end of the morning, Japan had lost just 29 planes to American ground fire.

Even though the American public was outraged by the sneak attack, and later turned on the intelligence community and on President Roosevelt for not putting the fleet on war footing in early December, the Japanese plan was simply brilliant in its concept, and so well executed that few American military leaders could have escaped its consequences. "The attack succeeded not because of American shortcomings but because it was brilliantly conceived, skillfully planned, and carried out with courage and daring," writes Nathan Miller. "Surprise or no surprise, there was no Allied force that could have stopped the fleet that hit Pearl Harbor—and if the Pacific Fleet had tried it would have been destroyed."[7] Several war games designed by the military colleges in the United States have shown that even if the Pacific Fleet battleships had left Pearl Harbor on December 6, on the eve of the Japanese attack, they would have been found and sunk—with much greater loss of lives in the open ocean.

Candid Dialogue

While the Japanese military tradition allowed for little dissent and open dialogue between officers, Yamamoto set a remarkable example when he openly disagreed with the Japanese plans for a war with the United States. Enraged by his stance, Japanese extremist groups issued several assassination threats against Yamamoto, who was appointed commander in chief of the Imperial Japanese Navy to shield him from his enemies on land. As commander in chief, Yamamoto would continue to foster open dialogue within his staff and sailors. This was no easy feat. According to historian Paul Dull, "Junior officers and staff members [in the Imperial Japanese Army and Navy] could and did override the recommendations of generals and admirals. The real decisions were often made by lower-level officials, and if a top official disagreed with them, he might be assassinated."[8]

The second challenge Yamamoto faced was to convince the Japanese military leadership that attacking Pearl Harbor was the best strategy to quickly bring about a negotiated peace with the United States. Although he had opposed war with the United States, "Yamamoto saw it as his duty to put Japan in the best position to win—and to win quickly."[9] Traditional Japanese naval strategy was based on a defensive scheme in the Central Pacific—which Yamamoto discarded in favor of the Pearl Harbor attack. Armed with the evidence from the British raid on Taranto, Yamamoto was able to convince his colleagues that the attack on Pearl Harbor was the best option for Japan.

In contrast to Yamamoto, his Pearl Harbor commander, Admiral Nagumo, was known as a "gruff and uncommunicative officer" who only reluctantly accepted Yamamoto's proposal for a strike on Pearl Harbor—and made the questionable decision to withdraw the task force from Hawaiian waters rather than carry out a third strike.[10] This contrast between Yamamoto and his top commander did not impede the planning and execution of the Pearl Harbor attack, but it did bode poorly for the performance of the Imperial Japanese Navy after Yamamoto's death in April 1943. Instead of the open debate and rational decision making that inspired Yamamoto to conceive Pearl Harbor, his "less imaginative and more conservative" replacement, Admiral Mineichi Koga, made decisions that sent the Imperial Japanese Navy into a frightful graveyard—as we shall see when we look at Operation SHO.[11]

Clear Roles and Accountabilities

While Yamamoto was the Imperial Japanese Navy's mastermind, he devised a clear system of roles and accountabilities for the attack on Pearl Harbor. Yamamoto himself stayed in Japanese waters and received news of the battle aboard his flagship *Nagato*, while Admiral Nagumo personally directed the attack from the deck of the carrier *Akagi*. Yamamoto confined himself to the role of strategist. Admiral Nagumo and the commanders of the Japanese air arm, such as Mitsuo Fuchida, who led the first wave of attacks, were the tactical masters who carried out the plan.

Each element of the Japanese navy had clear roles to play in the operation. Submarines would act as reconnaissance units across the Pacific, and confirm that the U.S. fleet was still at Pearl Harbor. The main actors would be the six carriers and their air crews, which trained as a unit. Zero fighters would provide air cover, while torpedo bombers would carry out low-level attacks and dive-bombers would come in high overhead. Decision making was clearly delegated to the attack leaders who would also conduct a battle damage assessment.

Bold Action

The attack on Pearl Harbor was clearly a decisive action that built on the Japanese tradition of attacking first—as Togo had done in the Russo-Japanese war of 1904 to 1905. There was no hesitation among the Japanese attackers, who chose to go after the eight battleships in the absence of any American aircraft carrier. Nagumo's reluctance to launch a third strike has been criticized as shortsighted, and indeed it was. While his staff argued for a third strike—which would have been aimed at the U.S. repair shops, submarines, and oil depots—Nagumo was supremely concerned about the vulnerability of his aircraft carriers, and chose to withdraw. In hindsight, a well-executed third wave would have had a more significant impact on the outcome of the Pacific War than the first two. With Hawaii's oil and ship-repair facilities destroyed, the U.S. Navy would have had no choice but to redeploy its fleet to San Francisco and give up—albeit temporarily—its only forward base of operations against Japan.

Despite Admiral Nagumo's oversight in launching a third wave, the decisive nature of the Pearl Harbor attack was difficult to deny in 1941, and it remains so today. The *Arizona*, *Oklahoma*, *California*, and *West Virginia* were sunk, beached, or capsized. The other three battleships, the *Maryland*, *Tennessee*, and *Pennsylvania*, were seriously damaged, along with three light cruisers and three destroyers. Out of more than 300 American planes operating from the various airfields on Oahu, only 43 were left untouched.

The decisive action of Pearl Harbor was followed by a series of incredible conquests by the Japanese, who within "twelve hours brought a bewildering series of shocks as [they] executed their plan of coordinated attacks across six thousand miles."[12] The Imperial Japanese Army landed on Guam, Hong Kong, and Malaya. In an attempt to slow down the Japanese conquest of Malaya and Singapore, the British Royal Navy ordered two of its most powerful warships, the *Repulse* and *Prince of Wales*, to intercept a Japanese force at sea. The British ships were located by a scout plane, and a group of Japanese dive-bombers based north of Saigon, in what had been French Indochina, attacked the British formation on December 10. Both British ships were sunk in 45 minutes—another seismic shift in the balance of naval power in the Pacific. On February 15, 1942, the British garrison surrendered Malaya and Singapore to the Japanese—a permanent blow to British prestige in Asia. With the loss of the Pacific Fleet battleships, the sinking of the *Repulse* and *Prince of Wales*, the Japanese eradicated all U.S. and British surface naval forces in the region, as well as two-thirds of U.S. frontline aviation—within the first two weeks of the war. Few actions in military history were as decisive as the attack on Pearl Harbor and the conquest of the Philippines, Dutch East Indies, and Malaya by the Imperial Japanese Navy and Army in the opening salvos of the Pacific campaign.

Visible Leadership

The Imperial Japanese Navy in 1941 counted some rare leaders, including Admiral Yamamoto, Admiral Nagumo, and Commanders

Mitsuo Fuchida, Kosei Maeda, and Minuro Genda—who conducted the training of the aircrews for the attack. Without these senior officers' leadership and enthusiasm, the attack at Pearl Harbor would certainly not have succeeded—and, indeed, without Yamamoto "selling" the plan to his colleagues in the navy and army it would never have been conceived or approved. In addition to their visibility during the long months of preparation and training that preceded the raid, Yamamoto and his commanders found some creative ways to energize Fuchida and his naval aviators when the decision to launch the attack was communicated to the fleet:

- Admiral Yamamoto's battle order, read out to the fleet on December 6, had strong undertones of Nelson's Touch. "The rise and fall of the Empire depends upon this battle," the order read. "Every man will do his duty."[13] After the order was read, Admiral Nagumo raised the same Z signal flag that had been hoisted by Admiral Togo at the battle of Tsushima.

- Fuchida himself wore a blood-red shirt for the attack, meant to hide any injuries he might receive during the raid. He flew the first plane off the deck of the *Akagi* and led the attack group that dropped the single bomb that penetrated the *Arizona*'s forward magazines. It was also Fuchida who radioed the "Tora! Tora! Tora!" (Tiger! Tiger! Tiger!) message back to Nagumo to inform the admiral that the Japanese had achieved total surprise.

REVERSAL AT MIDWAY

Within three months of Pearl Harbor, the Japanese had established the Greater East Asia Co-Prosperity Sphere that, in their war-plan estimates, should have taken twice as long to complete. The sphere included the Philippines, the Malaya Peninsula—including Singapore and its priceless harbor—and the Dutch East Indies. Suddenly Japan had access to the natural and energy resources that it had been denied since its occupation of Manchuria. This period of Japanese expansion was only tempered by the sinking of the small carrier *Shoho* at the Battle of the Coral Sea—the first battle in which the Japanese and American fleets fought each other exclusively from the air. In exchange for the *Shoho* and slight damages to the large carriers *Zuikaku* and *Shokaku* (both Pearl Harbor veterans) the Americans lost the fleet carrier *Lexington*, and the *Yorktown* was badly damaged. The U.S. Navy could hardly afford this rate of exchange—something Yamamoto was keenly aware of. Believing that the balance of naval power (based on his available carriers) was tilted in his favor, Yamamoto decided to roll the dice one more time—and lure the remaining U.S. carriers into a decisive battle at Midway.

Unlike the clean, simple plan for the Pearl Harbor attack, Yamamoto's plan to attack Midway—a small island in the central Pacific—reflected the growing Japanese preference for complex, multi-pronged offenses. As Miller writes, "Yamamoto's plan smacked more of the war-gaming table than reality . . . The Combined Fleet was divided into no fewer than sixteen different groups of warships spread all over the North Pacific."[14] Yamamoto also staged a diversionary attack against the Aleutians, which took a couple of carriers and surface ships away from the Midway operation. The Midway operation thus failed the first principle of Creative Execution: a unique and well-understood strategy.

Unknown to Yamamoto was the fact that American naval intelligence had broken the Japanese naval code, JN25, and was able to read up to 85 percent of Japanese fleet messages. To convince Admiral Nimitz that Midway was the real target of the new Japanese operation, which was consistently identified by the two-letter code AF in Japanese transmissions, Midway was instructed to broadcast a message saying that the island's freshwater plant had failed. When Station Hypo, which decrypted the intercepted Japanese messages, picked up a coded message saying that "AF" was short of water, Nimitz and his staff realized that they had a unique opportunity to set a trap for Yamamoto's fleet. Workers at Pearl Harbor's shipyard worked around the clock to repair the damage to the *Yorktown*, one of the greatest repair jobs in history. There were "hundreds of individual decisions and impromptu ingenuity [by] American welders, riveters, electricians, carpenters, and supply officers who on their own and without written orders turned a nearly ruined ship into a floating arsenal."[15] By contrast, the Japanese carrier *Shokaku* had arrived for repairs in Japan 10 days before the *Yorktown*, but her captain estimated that it would take up to three months to repair her light damages. Yamamoto's self-confidence was so high that he didn't press the issue with *Shokaku's* captain.

With the *Yorktown* out of Pearl Harbor after three days, Admiral Nimitz was able to confront Yamamoto (who had joined the fleet on board the battle cruiser *Yamato*) with three carriers, including *Enterprise* and *Hornet*. Admiral Nagumo flew his flag on the *Akagi*, flanked by the Pearl Harbor veterans *Kaga*, *Hiryu*, and *Soryu*. As the two fleets raced toward each other across the Pacific Ocean, the Americans held the ultimate trump card: thanks to the Station Hypo intercepts, they knew that the target of the Japanese operation was Midway. Based on this intelligence, Nimitz was able to deploy and hold his carriers in the precise location from where he could pounce on the Japanese fleet once it neared the Midway atoll. Whereas the Japanese had approached Hawaii undetected in December 1941, the Midway operation presented the reverse scenario: the Americans knew where the Japanese were going, as well as the number of ships committed to the operation, whereas the Japanese had zero information about the location of the U.S. fleet.

The sequence of events that unfolded starting at 3 a.m. on June 3, 1942, was the first feat of Creative Execution by the U.S. Navy in World War II—as well as the first real breakdown of the Japanese navy since Pearl Harbor. The Japanese debacle was fueled in part by Japan's heightened sense of invincibility since the string of easy victories that followed Pearl Harbor. "The enemy is not aware of our plans,"[16] Nagumo confidently stated to Yamamoto and his flag officers on the eve of the battle. At 4:30 a.m., Nagumo launched 108 planes to strafe the marine positions and airfield at Midway—the opening salvo in the battle. Of these planes, over 60 percent were lost or damaged due to ground fire or American fighters protecting Midway. This should have been a signal for Nagumo that the Americans were not as clueless as he had assumed.

Fate and mechanical intricacies dictated the outcome of the momentous battle that was to unfold next. Still unaware of the presence of the American carriers 200 nautical miles north-northeast of the island, Nagumo decided to launch a second strike against Midway. This required taking all planes below decks (some of which had been pre-armed with torpedoes as a precaution, should the American fleet somehow materialize) and rearming them with gravity bombs. Meanwhile, the surviving planes from the Midway strike were returning to the four carriers, adding to the confusion and delays on the Japanese side. While this landing, refueling, and rearming process took place, Nagumo received the first report that an American task force had been sighted. He absorbed this news with shock and disbelief. When a second report came in confirming the presence of an American carrier, he immediately reversed his decision to launch a follow-up strike against Midway and instructed his crews to reload planes with torpedoes and armor-piercing bombs for an attack on the American fleet. The initial arming, de-arming, and rearming of Nagumo's planes wasted a precious hour and resulted in ordnance and fuel lines strewn across the decks of the Japanese carriers.

While Nagumo was pondering just how large the American fleet was, American scout planes had already sighted the Japanese fleet. Fletcher and his boss, Admiral Spruance, made the decision to launch all available aircraft from the *Yorktown*, *Enterprise*, and *Hornet* against the Japanese. What followed was a medley of determined attacks by American pilots that led to the sinking of all four Japanese carriers. First in was a group of torpedo bombers from the *Hornet*, which launched an independent attack against the main Japanese force. Without their own air support, every single plane in this flight was shot down by Japanese Zeros and antiaircraft fire. The heroism of Torpedo Squadron 8 has become legend. The squadron's leader, Lieutenant Commander John Waldron, told his pilots, "If there is only one plane left to make a final run-in, I want that man to go in and get a hit."[17] Only one squadron member, Ensign George Gay, survived the encounter after ditching his Devastator airplane near the Japanese task force. Gay was picked up the following day by an American PBY (flying boat). For the next few hours following his ditching, however, he witnessed the greatest sea battle since Trafalgar, bobbing on the Pacific current in his Mae West life preserver.

Within minutes of the failed torpedo attack, dive-bombers from the *Enterprise* and *Yorktown* sighted the Japanese fleet and, with the Japanese Zeros still at low altitude, found the skies over the Japanese fleet clear of enemy fighters. This attack, better coordinated and unopposed by enemy fighters, changed the course of the Pacific War. The *Kaga*, hit by four bombs, erupted into flames. *Akagi* suffered a similar fate, her flight deck peeled apart by a 1,000-pound bomb. The *Soryu* was hit by three bombs and caught fire from stern to bow. Fuel lines and ordnance fed the fires and led to massive conflagrations. The three mighty carriers, which had played a central role in the Pearl Harbor attack and conquest of the Philippines, Malaya, and the Dutch East Indies, had become a floating inferno.

Despite the loss of three carriers, Yamamoto didn't give up the fight. He still had one carrier at his disposal, and believed that only one American carrier lay behind the vicious attack. With Nagumo's flagship out of commission, Yamamoto ordered Rear Admiral Abe Hiroaki, now in charge of the Mobile Strike Force aboard the sole surviving carrier, *Hiryu*, to strike back at the Americans. The *Hiryu*'s planes took off unmolested and followed the American dive-bombers back to the *Yorktown*. The American carrier was struck by several bombs and torpedoes and stopped dead in the water, but was able to unload all her crew. Before the attack, however, the *Yorktown* had launched its remaining aircraft against the *Hiryu*. With help from the *Enterprise*'s dive-bombers these pilots sunk the last remaining Japanese carrier. The following morning a Japanese submarine found the *Yorktown* still afloat and torpedoed her, ending a valiant fight to save her by her crew. The *Yorktown*'s pilots had already avenged her by sinking the *Hiryu*, but the loss of a fleet carrier was a further strain on the U.S. Navy's stretched resources.

The tally of this gargantuan struggle was gruesome. In one morning, "four of the carriers that had wreaked havoc upon the Allies from Pearl Harbor to the Bay of Bengal had been lost, along with some 250 aircraft and their crack air groups . . . With a single thrust, Spruance and Fletcher had destroyed the offensive capability of a fleet with far stronger than their own—and inflicted upon the Imperial Japanese Navy its first decisive defeat since 1592."[18] More than 3,000 Japanese sailors perished, as well as 1,000 Americans.

Worse than the defeat was the confused Japanese reaction—including that of Yamamoto, who sent the following message at 7:15 p.m., when four of his carriers had already been sunk: "The enemy fleet, which has practically been destroyed . . . is retiring eastward."[19] When Admiral Nagumo, finally back in action, retorted that the Americans had possibly four or five carriers in the area, Yamamoto dismissed him and put Admiral Kondo in charge of the task force. Finally, in the middle in the night, reality set in and Yamamoto called off the invasion of Midway and withdrew his fleet toward Japan. The Japanese high command was likewise unwilling to have the Candid Dialogue required in the aftermath of the battle, and instead announced on June 18 the loss of a single fleet carrier. Sailors from Nagumo's task force were forced into isolation upon their return to their home ports for fear that they would reveal to the Japanese public the extent of the navy's losses at Midway.

The inability of the Japanese high command to deal with the defeat at Midway was perhaps as significant, in the long term, as the loss of four carriers. It was incomprehensible to most American strategists, as John Keegan writes, that Admiral Yamamoto "did not concentrate [his forces], thereby confronting his enemy with a mass of force that could not possibly be defeated."[20] Had Yamamoto kept his fleet together, scratched the feint offensive against the Aleutians, and shown a sense of urgency in repairing the carriers damaged at the Battle of the Coral Sea, his fleet would have had twice the striking power at Midway—and quite likely would have prevailed. Yet instead of providing a stark reminder of the need for more simple strategies and vigilant leadership, Midway threw Yamamoto and the Imperial Japanese Navy into a pit of despair from which it would never recover.

THE FINAL CURTAIN: OPERATION SHO

By late 1944, the initiative in the Pacific had fully shifted to the United States. Although the Imperial Japanese Navy still presented a credible force, and included the world's two largest battleships, the *Yamato* and her sister ship *Musashi*, each displacing 72,800 tons, the American industrial machine had kicked into full gear and was producing more fleet and escort carriers in a month than Japan could hope to produce in one year. This was exactly what Yamamoto had forecasted, yet the Pearl Harbor mastermind would not live to see his dark premonitions come true. His plane was shot down by American fighters in April 1943 while on a tour of the Japanese Empire's forward bases, and crashed into the jungle. With the empire's fate hanging in the balance, the Japanese fleet, now led by Vice Admiral Kurita Takeo, made one final dash at the American fleet in Operation SHO.

Operation SHO was directed at the American invasion of the Philippines, which General MacArthur had promised to retake from the Japanese. The Japanese plan called for a multitude of strike forces—just like at Midway—to converge on the American beach-head at Leyte Gulf. The Mobile Carrier Force, led by Admiral Ozawa and centered on the last remaining Pearl Harbor carrier, the *Zuikaku*, would be sent as bait to draw the main American naval group, Task Force 38, away from Leyte. With the American fleet chasing the Japanese carriers northward, no less than three separate surface groups would make their way—undetected and unimpeded—through the San Bernardino and Surigao Straits to close in on the American invasion force. The date for all four groups to arrive at Leyte Gulf was set as October 25, 1944—five days after MacArthur had waded ashore to utter his most famous line: "I have returned."

The first event to shatter any hope of success for Operation SHO was the discovery of Kurita's battle force by two American submarines, the *Darter* and *Dace*, the evening of October 23. After trailing the task force and reporting its position, both submarines attacked the largest targets, including Kurita's own flagship, the battleship *Atago*, which sank with the loss of 359 men. Kurita shifted his flag to the super battleship *Yamato* as more torpedoes from the *Dace* and *Darter* struck the heavy cruisers *Takao* and *Maya*. Over the next few days, fierce naval and air battles raged around Leyte Gulf as the four Japanese formations were spotted and dealt with by Task Force 38. The *Yamato* and *Musashi* were both attacked from the air and the latter sunk after being hit by 18 torpedoes—while the rest of the Japanese forces were beaten back by American battleships and bombers. The Japanese losses included two of the four carriers sent as bait, the *Zuikaku* and *Zuiho*.

One could argue that the unraveling of Operation SHO was in fact a feat of Creative Execution by the U.S. Navy—and it almost was. As the battle began to unfold, Admiral Halsey, in charge of the American carrier force known as TF34, steamed north to take the bait presented by the Japanese carriers. This would have been fine, except that Halsey took his entire fleet with him, leaving one of the approaches to Leyte Gulf undefended. After much confusion about Halsey's whereabouts, Admiral Nimitz, monitoring the developments from his headquarters at Pearl Harbor, sent a flash message to Halsey that, deciphered hastily, asked: "Where is, repeat where is, Task Force 34? The world wonders." Even though "the world wonders" was only a random sentence intended to mask the main message, it was included in the formal note shown to Admiral Halsey, with biting effect. Imagine receiving that kind of e-mail from your CEO, and having it read by everyone in your company!

Halsey's slip-up was caused by poor communication between the American commanders—and as a result no one in the U.S. Navy knew who was supposed to cover the San Bernardino Strait. This allowed the remnants of Kurita's surface force to enter Leyte Gulf unopposed and engage the escort carriers protecting the American beachhead, which could have had devastating consequences for the American forces on shore. But Kurita lost his nerve after a heroic defense by U.S. destroyers and land-based aircraft, and after a 20-minute engagement withdrew his fleet. This was a close call that showed that, despite its overwhelming superiority, the U.S. Navy still faced a potent enemy. Had Kurita proceeded further, he would have easily blown his way past the defending escort carriers and destroyers that stubbornly blocked his path, and run straight into the transports and support vessels of the American invasion force.

Operation SHO was doomed to fail due to two fundamental mistakes. First was its unnecessary complexity, with four surface action groups converging on Leyte from the north and south. The likelihood of all four groups entering the battle area at the same time, without the benefit of modern communications, was literally nil. The second was an astonishing detachment from reality by the Japanese naval staff. How could the Americans, who by October 1944 had established naval supremacy and controlled the air space over the Philippines, not notice the entire Imperial Japanese Fleet steaming down for a decisive battle? As Paul Dull observed, "SHO was an exercise in utter stupidity. The Japanese officers knew it, but given their initial programming as Japanese and as naval officers, their orders had to be obeyed."[21] The Imperial Japanese Navy repeated in Operation SHO the same mistakes that had doomed the Midway operation, and therefore completed the circle of self-destruction that had started in June 1942. Without a clear, simple strategy, devoid of the candor and leadership imposed by Yamamoto at Pearl Harbor, and twice bereft of the opportunity to win the decisive battle its leaders sought, the Imperial Japanese Navy limped home from Operation SHO as a broken unit. The Creative Execution balance had shifted permanently to America, whose economic and technological prowess had been correctly foreseen by Yamamoto.

PEARL HARBOR'S LEGACY

Yamamoto's brilliantly conceived attack on Pearl Harbor not only plunged the United States into World War II, but created a lasting impact on the American psyche. To this day, fuel continues to leak from the *Arizona*'s oil bunkers underneath old Battleship Row. Even after the needless sacrifice of the Imperial Japanese Navy's remaining battleships in Operation SHO, Japan pressed on with the war, unleashing kamikaze attacks against the U.S. Navy's carrier battle groups. As newly appointed President Truman met with Joseph Stalin and Winston Churchill in Potsdam in July 1945 to secure Russia's participation in the war against Japan, only one hope remained to avoid a full-scale invasion of the Japanese home islands: the Manhattan Project, the ultra-secret attempt to build the world's first atomic bomb.

When the world's third atomic explosion occurred over Nagasaki on August 9, 1945 (the first had been a test in the New Mexico desert, and the second had been a bomb dropped three days earlier over Hiroshima), Japan's dreams of Asian hegemony came to a brutal end. Ironically, the Nagasaki bomb exploded directly above the Mitsubishi armament factory that had produced the torpedoes for the Pearl Harbor attack. This single bomb killed more than 70,000 Japanese and destroyed 44 percent of the city. A fourth bomb, thankfully never used, was on its way to the Pacific theater, destined for a subsequent attack on Tokyo.

Between the Pacific War's two epicenters—the attack on Pearl Harbor and the destruction of Nagasaki—the human toll of the fighting at sea and on land defies imagination. Out of 50 million soldiers and civilians who died in World War II, a third died in Asia. Japan had 2.65 million killed—of which 2.1 million were military. The war and lower birth rates meant that the population of Japan actually shrank between 1940 and 1945, from 73 million to just over 71 million. On the American side, more than 18,000 U.S. marines died during the war, the vast majority in their heroic efforts to retake islands that the Japanese had seized early in the conflict, from Guadalcanal to Iwo Jima.

More than 31,000 U.S. Navy personnel lost their lives, including the 2,117 killed at Pearl Harbor.

To this day, the U.S. Navy maintains the world's most potent and expensive fleet of nuclear aircraft carriers—aptly named the *Nimitz* class—the last of which, the *George W. Bush*, was commissioned in 2009. Displacing nearly 100,000 tons, these warships embody the notion that the U.S. Navy will never again find itself at a disadvantage when fighting a foe at sea. Several would be on hand in 1991 when the Gulf War erupted and General Norman Schwarzkopf found himself staring across the Saudi desert.

From Desert Storm to Iraqi Freedom

The great duel, the mother of all battles,
has begun.

—Saddam Hussein, January 1991

Between World War II and the collapse of the Soviet Union in 1990, the United States firmly established itself as the world's leading military and economic superpower, in the process taking Creative Execution to new heights. In its direct and indirect confrontations with the Soviet Union, as with the implementation of the Marshall Plan in 1947, the Berlin Crisis of 1948, the Cuban Missile Crisis of 1962, and the moon landing in 1969, the United States consistently demonstrated that its creative spine was stronger and more flexible than that of the ossified Soviet regime. In each case, the United States found creative and decisive ways to overcome what seemed at the time like unsolvable problems: how does one rebuild a Western European continent ravaged by the most savage war in history? Answer: pour $13 billion in economic and technical assistance into 16 countries, as Secretary of State George Marshall did between 1948 and 1952. How does one sustain the population of Berlin once its roads and water supplies get cut off by the Soviet Union? Fly in relief supplies for 13 months, an effort that required 280,000 aircraft missions during the Berlin Airlift.

How does one get to the moon? By building the world's largest rocket engine, the Saturn V, which propelled the Apollo missions and made Sputnik look like child's play. Even when disaster struck, as it did when the Apollo 13 crew lost power on their way to the moon, the Americans recovered with creative solutions—a feat faithfully recreated in the movie *Apollo 13*, where Ed Harris, playing the role of flight director Gene Kranz, announces that "failure is not an option." And indeed "failure is not an option" seemed to be the resolute motto for America in the 1950s and 1960s as it fought the nihilistic forces of communism around the globe.

And yet, not everything was quiet on the American front in this period of post-world-war recovery. First came the Korean War, which threatened to see China enter a no-win conflict with the United States, and the permanent division of North and South Korea. Having largely disbanded its ground and naval forces after World War II, the United States and UN forces charged with liberating South Korea from its northern aggressor found the Korean conflict more reminiscent of World War I trench warfare, and within a few months were barely holding on to a corner of the Korean peninsula. The only decisive action that saved the UN coalition was General MacArthur's landing at Inchon in September 1950, a bold piece of Creative Execution. Despite the Joint Chiefs of Staff's apprehensions, MacArthur landed his troops behind enemy lines and achieved the kind of tactical surprise that distinguished Nelson at the Nile and Trafalgar.

With the Korea stalemate still fresh in the history books, the United States began its third Asian campaign of the twentieth century after the French gave up Indochina. The 10,000-day war in Vietnam took the horrors and frustrations of the Korean War and multiplied them tenfold. Despite superior air power, naval supremacy and battlefield mobility, the United States was unable to prevent the South from being overrun by the communist North. The 55,000 Americans killed in action in Vietnam remains the highest number of casualties suffered by the United States since World War II—and dwarfs the 4,483 U.S. deaths in Iraq between 2003 and 2011. What is more remarkable about the Vietnam War is the fact that the United States could fight a war halfway around the world using only a *fraction* of its military forces. The bulk of its army, air force, and navy were firmly rooted in the European and North Atlantic theaters, ready to blunt an assault by the Warsaw Pact forces, which thankfully never came.

The U.S. withdrawal from Vietnam in 1975 ushered in a decade of soul searching and anti-American sentiments around the world, counterbalanced by the Soviet Union's own blunder in invading Afghanistan in 1979. But this period of healing and rebuilding in the U.S. Armed Forces led to the most productive span of military thinking and development in U.S. history. By the time the Berlin Wall came down in 1989, the United States had essentially doubled or tripled the effectiveness of its military, focusing less on raw firepower and saturation bombing, which it had employed in World War II and Vietnam, and more on precision strikes and stealth technology. Even as the Soviet Union morphed back into Russia in the 1990s, the United States didn't stop fielding new weapons and new tactics—it simply slowed down the procurement pipeline that the Reagan administration had lubricated in the 1980s, and continued to equip the navy, army, and air force with ships, tanks, and aircraft that would ensure U.S. supremacy over any battlefield. Instead of an all-out war with the Soviet Union, the retooled forces of the United States would face its first test not far from where Alexander challenged Darius on the Iraqi plain of Gaugamela: on the Saudi and Iraqi border, where Saddam Hussein stood triumphant after invading Kuwait.

IRAQ'S TORTUOUS DESTINY

Created as a British Mandate in 1921, using the same logic that gave us Yugoslavia at the Treaty of Paris in 1919, where the victors of World War I quilted the world into various ethnic fashions, Iraq has from its humble beginnings been a volatile state. Traditionally ruled by the Ottoman Empire, Iraq consists of three major ethnic groups: Sunni and Shia Muslim Kurds in the north, Sunni Muslim Arabs in the center, and Shia Muslim Arabs in the south. The country's population exploded in the second half of the twentieth century, surging from 5 million to 25 million, with a heavy concentration in the cities of Baghdad, Mosul, and Basra. The British first landed in Iraq during World War I after it declared war on the Ottoman Empire and recognized Kuwait as an independent state. After the armistice was signed in 1918, the British governor in Iraq, Arnold Wilson, declared confidently: "The average Arab . . . sees the future as one of fair dealing and material and moral progress under the aegis of Great Britain . . . The Arabs are content with our occupation."[1] And thus began the West's naive embroilment in Iraqi affairs.

The British occupation led to—you guessed it—a major insurgency. With 133,000 troops in Iraq, the British managed to quell the insurrection, but only after 10 years of bitter fighting that left 20,000 British and Indian troops killed or wounded. The cycle of violence led Colonel T. E. Lawrence (better known as Lawrence of Arabia) to write that "the people of England have been led in Mesopotamia into a trap from which it will be hard to escape with dignity and honour."[2] The British were only too happy to end their occupation in 1932, after which a number of pro-British governments oversaw the growing exploitation of the country's oil reserves, first discovered around Kirkuk in 1927. From then on, oil revenues became the main source of economic development in Iraq—for good and for bad.

During the Cold War, Iraq experienced its own communist-inspired revolution and became a Soviet client, relying on Russia to equip its growing armed forces. The government nationalized the Iraq Petroleum Company, which had been run by the British, and boosted oil revenues from $1 billion in 1973 to $26 billion by 1980. Much of this fresh surplus went to buying Soviet tanks and fighter aircraft, so that by the early 1980s Iraq's army had become the largest in the Middle East, and the fourth largest in the world. Then in September 1980, with Saddam Hussein fresh in power, Iraq declared war against Iran. The motive was shady—Saddam made up a land claim and gave Iran an ultimatum to hand it over—so that, in fact, "Iraq's decision to resort to force was a compound of preventive war, ambition and punishment for a regional rival."[3] The same self-serving reasoning would drive Saddam to invade Kuwait in 1990.

When Iraq's army rolled into Iran, Saddam Hussein expected a mollified Iranian defense and a quick Iraqi victory. Instead, the conflict turned into a protracted series of attacks and counterattacks. After eight years of inconclusive fighting, both sides came to the negotiating table and struck an agreement that restored the pre-war borders, meaning nothing had been gained by either side. The war's toll on both countries, however, wasn't negligible. Iraq had wasted more than $125 billion of its oil revenues ($25 billion of which was spent on importing military hardware from Russia, France, Germany, South Africa, and China), and lost more than 200,000 men killed in action. As a country of 14 million people, Iraq could barely afford the protracted war, and borrowed 10 times its yearly oil revenues in order to meet its military and civilian needs. This financial burden would play a colossal role in leading Saddam down the path of military expansion. As Dilip Hiro writes, "having expanded its military . . . Iraq under Saddam emerged as the most powerful nation in the Middle East, outstripping Turkey and Egypt."[4] The Iran–Iraq War also prompted Saddam to manufacture chemical weapons—which he used in the waning days of the conflict to dislodge Iran from its forward positions.

Although Iraq was financially drained after eight years of conflict, Saddam Hussein didn't give up his dream of asserting a stronger Iraqi presence in the Middle East. The next opportunity to do so arose in August 1990, when the tiny state of Kuwait had the audacity to pump more oil than its OPEC quotas suggested. This decision drove down the price of crude across the Middle East. Kuwait also—quite thoughtlessly—demanded repayment of loans it had made to Iraq during the Iran–Iraq War. Irked by these decisions and his belief that "[Kuwait was] a remnant of imperialism, 'artificially' split off from what became and so legitimately a part of Iraq," Saddam sent his battle-hardened Republican Guard and 130,000 troops into Kuwait, which fell within 24 hours.[5]

The unintended consequence of Saddam's occupation of Kuwait was that it suddenly put Iraq's army on the doorstep of Saudi Arabia's largest oil fields. Saudi Arabia and its Western clients decided that this was an unacceptable threat. Within 24 hours, the United States introduced a UN resolution demanding the restoration of Kuwait and imposing sanctions on Iraq. Within one week, the United States had convinced Saudi Arabia to accept American troops on its soil, and began the buildup of military forces known as Desert Shield. Much like Hitler had gambled in invading Poland in 1939, Saddam had invaded Kuwait thinking the international community would just accept his land grab as a fait accompli. Instead, the United States took the opportunity to demonstrate how its armed forces had gone through a quiet but significant transformation since Korea and Vietnam—and could deliver a hammer blow of Creative Execution anywhere around the world.

SCHWARZKOPF'S GAMBIT

The responsibility for organizing and deploying the coalition forces that contained Iraq directly after the invasion of Kuwait fell to General Norman Schwarzkopf and the recently formed U.S. Central Command, CENTCOM. Schwarzkopf, whose father had served in both world wars, was determined to avoid the mistakes the army had made in Vietnam. He had taken over CENTCOM in November 1988, and rightly anticipated that the aggressor nation in the Middle East would not be the Soviet Union or Iran, but Iraq, whose 900,000-man army was in search of a new victim in the aftermath of the inconclusive Iran–Iraq War. Schwarzkopf backed up his foresight when the U.S. Joint Chiefs drafted a military strategy that discounted the Middle East. The new CENTCOM commander took his concerns straight to Secretary of Defense Dick Cheney, who according to Schwarzkopf "immediately ordered that the Middle East be written in [to the plan]."[6] When Iraq invaded Kuwait in August 1990, Schwarzkopf was in the middle of staging a CENTCOM war game that oddly resembled the unfolding drama.

From the time U.S. troops and combat aircraft landed in Saudi Arabia, on August 7, 1990, as part of Desert Shield, Schwarzkopf had to deal with three significant tasks: first, to organize the coalition forces in order to repel a potential push into Saudi Arabia by the Iraqi Army, which had begun to amass its forces near the border; second was to develop a strategy to liberate Kuwait; and third was to manage the political dynamics between the main Desert Shield partners—the United States, Britain, France, Saudi Arabia, and a host of Arab nations such as Syria and Egypt that felt compelled to participate but didn't want to be seen as subservient to the United States. As he established his headquarters in the Saudi capital, Schwarzkopf articulated the four phases of the campaign, which would address each question and form the basis of his Creative Execution formula:

1. Initiate a strategic air campaign aimed at destroying Iraqi infrastructure and military nerve centers.
2. Eliminate Iraq's air defense in Kuwait.
3. Launch sustained air attacks against Iraq's entrenched army in Kuwait.
4. Launch a coalition ground offensive to dislodge Iraq from Kuwait.

The plan was logical, but necessitated an entirely new concept of integrated ground and air operations, the AirLand Battle, which the army, navy, and air force had labored over since Vietnam as a way to fight future wars. Now that Desert Shield was unfolding, CENTCOM's planners began to juxtapose the army, air force, and navy assets available in the theater in order to achieve the four strategic goals Schwarzkopf had identified—a significant cultural shift for American forces. As a senior air force planner later wrote, "From day one and throughout the war, there were continuous confrontations and serious discussions concerning the assumptions and proposals of the strategy's various operational components . . . [In Vietnam] there were as many as five separate air wars conducted by five separate authorities . . . The air component planners on General Schwarzkopf's staff integrated and synthesized the various tactical and strategic elements into a single joint/coalition air component plan."[7] In other words, this wouldn't be another Vietnam, where the air force, army, and navy independently decided how and where to attack the enemy. As Schwarzkopf himself later wrote, "I would have given my left arm if our Air Force could have had half the capability in Vietnam that it demonstrated in the Gulf."[8]

The early phases of Desert Storm called for sustained air strikes by coalition fighters and bombers, which took out everything from the Baghdad telephone system to the dozen or so Iraqi air bases and Scud mobile launchers inside Iraq and Kuwait. By the time the ground offensive was ready to go, Schwarzkopf had achieved his aim of reducing the Iraqi forces dug in across the Saudi border between southern Iraq and Kuwait—some 540,000 troops, 4,200 battle tanks, 2,800 armored personnel carriers, and 3,000 artillery pieces—by an astounding 50 percent. The air campaign was lethally effective and caught the Iraqi Army completely by surprise. "We used surface forces to cause the 'bad guy' forces to mass and congregate," explained a CENTCOM planner, "and then we used air power to eliminate them . . . it was that simple."[9]

To address the more difficult strategy of how to conduct the ground war, Schwarzkopf came up with a brilliant maneuver: he would reserve his best armored divisions for a "left hook" that would attack Saddam Hussein's three Republican Guard divisions from the west—well inside Iraq—while the U.S. Marines and coalition forces struck north toward Kuwait. Like Nelson and Alexander, Schwarzkopf was determined to not just win the battle but to obliterate Saddam Hussein's main forces. His instructions to his air and ground troop commanders clearly reflected this single purpose. "I want the Republican Guard bombed the very first day, and I want them bombed every day after that," he told his key air planner, Colonel John Warden.[10] When the ground campaign began, he told his commanders: "We need to destroy—not attack, not damage, not surround—I want you to *destroy* the Republican Guard. When we're done with them, I don't want them to be an effective fighting force anymore. I don't want them to exist as a military organization."[11] Goals don't get any clearer than that.

By the middle of January 1991, the forces that Schwarzkopf had asked for were ready to execute his Unique Strategy.

DESERT STORM UNLEASHED

At 2:30 in the morning on January 17, Norman Schwarzkopf walked into a room full of generals and colonels of the U.S. and coalition forces to read a message he had addressed to the troops of Central Command. He noted that the coalition forces were "the most powerful force our country, in coalition with our allies, has ever assembled in a single theater" and concluded by saying that "my confidence in you is total."[12] At 2:47 a.m., the first flash message announcing the destruction of two radar installations across the Iraqi border by U.S. Special Forces reached his headquarters in downtown Riyadh. This was followed by a stream of tactical messages relaying the brutal efficiency and execution of the air war over Iraq:

"0310: PHONES OUT BAG." This meant the telephone and broadcasting facilities in downtown Baghdad had been taken out by F-117 stealth fighters.

"0415: NO FEEDBACK ON AIR TO AIR / NO BEEPERS ON SHOOTDOWN." Meaning that the Iraqi Air Force had been caught by surprise and no coalition planes had been shot down since the opening salvos.[13]

By the afternoon of January 17, the U.S., British, French, and Saudi air attacks had completed 850 missions from Kuwait to Baghdad with only two coalition airplanes lost to enemy action. More importantly, the two armored corps that would deliver the surprise left hook had started their westward deployment. After four weeks of pounding by the U.S. Air Force, the stage was set for the execution of Schwarzkopf's unique strategy. The first units to cross into Kuwait and Iraq were the U.S. Marines—charged with taking on the heavily defended approaches to Kuwait, which Saddam's army had mined and fortified since its August invasion.

Schwarzkopf's plan for the ground offensive was followed almost flawlessly. Despite the slower-than-expected movement of one armored corps, which paused to regroup its forces during the second night of the offensive, the two-front attack against Iraq's forces succeeded beyond even Schwarzkopf's expectations. Instead of the anticipated two-to-three-month "mother of all battles," it was all over in 100 hours. As the two armored corps slammed into the three Republican Guard divisions dug in west of the Kuwaiti border, panic spread among Iraqi forces. As James Dunnigan wrote, "The 7th Corps moved like a huge armored mallet, swinging north, then east, crushing the Iraqi divisions with air, artillery, and tanks . . . The 3rd Armored Division made a 200-kilometer move during the night, with not one of its 320 M1A1s [main battle tanks] breaking down during the long tactical march . . . The Iraqi forces were shattered; the ground war was over."[14]

In fact, the coalition forces had destroyed 27 of the 42 Iraqi divisions arrayed against them in Iraq and Kuwait, and had badly defeated—but not completely destroyed—the three Republican Guard divisions hunkered down in southern Iraq. The ceasefire came into effect at 8 a.m. on February 28. Schwarzkopf had achieved the most lopsided and decisive victory since the German blitzlerieg of 1939 and 1940. Combat casualties for the coalition forces involved in the ground attack were 28 dead, 89 wounded, and 5 missing.

CREATIVE EXECUTION PLAYS ITS PART

At the root of the coalition's overwhelming success was the sheer technological superiority of the U.S. Air Force, Navy, and Army. As Schwarzkopf explained in an interview with the *Guardian*, "Even though they had a large military and probably a very capable one for this part of the world," matched against "the sophistication of the US military, there is no comparison. [The Iraqis] grossly underestimated the type of war they were getting involved with and they paid the price for that."[15] Yet the prowess of U.S. weapons such as the M1A1 Abrams main battle tank, the Patriot antiaircraft missile battery, and air superiority fighters such as the F-15E would have been much degraded had Schwarzkopf and U.S. military commanders not designed a strategy as bold and creative as they did during Desert Storm, and reinforced its execution through Candid Dialogue, Visible Leadership, and Clear Roles and Accountabilities. "I adopted a campaign plan that capitalized on using our strengths against their weaknesses," Schwarzkopf later wrote. "That's good strategy for any business . . . You learn to work with all constituents to build a coalition with a common goal so you all know exactly what you want to do . . . When things come up that are not part of the goal, you put them aside. You stay focused on the goal."[16]

During Desert Shield and Desert Storm, Schwarzkopf effectively wielded the principles of Creative Execution to avoid the confusion of command and control that had plagued U.S. operations in Vietnam. His clarity of purpose, commitment to winning, and careful handling of the coalition forces were key enablers in the success of the air and ground war. As Barry McCaffrey writes, "victory was not secured after only a few days of fighting on land; it was fifteen years in the making. It was rooted in the lessons of Vietnam."[17] Here's how Schwarzkopf's Desert Storm strategy fed off the Creative Execution principles.

Unique Strategy

The four phases of the Gulf War provided a clear and simple framework for the offensive operations that started in January 1991. Schwarzkopf not only shared this strategy with his top commanders, but also briefed the president and the Joint Chiefs of Staff several times, each time stating exactly the types and number of forces he would need to shift from the defense of Saudi Arabia (Desert Shield) to an offensive operation against Iraq. The ultimate left hook through the Iraqi desert, where Schwarzkopf threw in the might of two armored corps, was a masterful strategic gamble. Initially the CENTCOM planners had come up with a riskier offensive plan that included an amphibious assault by the U.S. Marines and a massive drive through Kuwait—which Schwarzkopf rejected. "The offensive lacked any element of surprise," he writes. "It was a straight-up-the-middle charge right into the teeth of the Iraqi defenses. And even assuming things went well, casualties would be substantial."[18]

Schwarzkopf's decision to attack with the left hook through Iraq was certainly on par with Alexander's brilliant strategy of denying the left wing of his army at Gaugamela, or Nelson's decision to break with naval tradition and slice through the middle of the French and Spanish Combined Fleet. In a postwar interview with PBS, Schwarzkopf acknowledged that "it was a very, very aggressive plan . . . to throw forces up against the main lines and hold them, and then to make this very wide—almost a turning movement . . . to go very deep across unknown terrain, to move very rapidly. It was a bold plan. And therefore it required bold planning and it required bold execution."[19] Unlike the long, drawn-out conflict in Vietnam, Schwarzkopf planned a single, integrated masterstroke into the undefended Iraqi flank. His strategy was simple, yet brilliantly effective.

Candid Dialogue

Among the five principles of Creative Execution, Schwarzkopf best personifies the ability to have a candid, no-holds-barred dialogue. Before Desert Storm, he challenged political leaders to provide him with the necessary resources to accomplish his task, and didn't shy away from taking on senior U.S. commanders to get his point across. When the chief of staff of the army, Carl Vuono, paid Schwarzkopf a visit during the early planning phases, Schwarzkopf felt he didn't have enough divisions to mount an offensive drive into Kuwait and Iraq. He told Vuono directly: "Carl, you guys on the Joint Chiefs are supposed to be the President's principal advisors on warfare. Why am I being required to send back an offensive plan I don't believe in? You, the chief of staff of the Army, ought to be telling the President we're in no position to go on the offense unless we have more forces."[20] This got Vuono's attention, and ultimately the president's.

When Schwarzkopf agreed to send his staff for a briefing in Washington, he instructed them to be candid and forward, especially when talking to the President: "One of the things we have going for us is that we don't bullshit the President," he explained. "You should explain our capabilities, but do not tell the President we're capable of something we're not."[21] Schwarzkopf had requested an additional heavy corps (of two armored divisions) to go on the offensive. He would in fact get three more army divisions and one marine division—mostly as a result of his convincing conversations with Carl Vuono, Colin Powell, and Dick Cheney, who supported him. There would be no Vietnam War repeat of the guarded dialogue between the executive branch and the military.

Schwarzkopf also laid it out clearly for his staff and his commanders. He told his two corps commanders responsible for executing the left hook, Tommy Franks and Gary Luck, "I'm going to be drilling you guys unmercifully between now and D-Day to convince me that you are logistically prepared."[22] Schwarzkopf also earned a reputation for being direct and candid with the media. When he stood in front of the podium, or in front of his troops, he was clearly in charge and comfortable handling tough, direct questions.

One of the most famous episodes of the war was Schwarzkopf's criticism of the VII Corps and its commander, General Tommy Franks. Franks led the massive VII Corps wheeling around the Iraqi left flank, but preferred a more deliberate mode of attack than what Schwarzkopf had ordered. When Schwarzkopf woke up on the second morning of the ground attack to find out that Franks had stopped for the night instead of pursuing the Republican Guard, Schwarzkopf became furious and took the unusual step of calling directly the corps's Tactical Operations Center. "I want to keep pushing," Schwarzkopf told the officer in charge. "We got a full court press on . . . Keep moving!"[23] At the end of the war, Schwarzkopf went very public with his disapproval of Franks, who he felt missed the opportunity to destroy the Republican Guard divisions inside Kuwait. Both on and off the court, Schwarzkopf was a direct, candid commander, and his officers knew where they stood with him at all times.

Clear Roles and Accountabilities

The attack plan for Desert Storm clearly spelled out the roles and responsibilities of each army unit, and utilized the unique capabilities of U.S. and allied troops. The French 6th Division, which could travel light and included elements of the French Foreign Legion well suited to desert warfare, took up the task of protecting the left flank of the U.S. VII and XVIII Corps well inside the Iraqi desert. The British 7th Armoured Brigade, called the "Desert Rats," was part of the initial thrust into Iraq, clearing minefields and destroying 300 dug-in Iraqi tanks and armored personnel carriers, while the U.S. Marines kept up the threat of an amphibious landing off the coast of Kuwait. Like any brilliant offensive plan, Schwarzkopf had built into Desert Storm a number of feints to convince the Iraqis that the coalition was attacking—as the Iraqis expected—through the Kuwaiti corridor. Had the Iraqis possessed any kind of satellite imaging capability, they would have seen that the United States had repositioned its main armor 200 miles west of Kuwait. Without this information, and obsessed with the defense of its newly won territory, the Iraqis kept believing that the marine and British divisions attacking the heavily defended Kuwaiti corridor represented the main coalition attack, and were shocked when the bulk of the XVIII and VII Corps smashed into the flanks of the Republican Guard units west of Kuwait.

To ensure that his commanders were clear about their roles and responsibilities, especially the XVIII and VII Corps going up against the Republican Guard, Schwarzkopf reiterated his expectations with amazing candor and clarity: "We need commanders in the lead who absolutely, clearly understand that they *will get through*. And that once they're through they're not going to stop and discuss it. They are going to go up there and destroy the Republican Guard. I cannot afford to have commanders who do not understand that this is attack, attack, attack . . . If you have somebody who doesn't understand it, I would strongly recommend that you consider removing him from command and putting in somebody that can do the job."[24] This kind of unequivocal directive is what allowed Schwarzkopf to ensure the flawless execution of his left hook maneuver, and the successful move of the marine and British divisions into Kuwait.

Bold Action

Moments before the start of the air war, Schwarzkopf recalls walking back to his office and feeling "as if I were standing at a craps table in some kind of dream—I'd bet my fortune, thrown the dice, and now watched as they tumbled through the air in slow motion."[25] Yet even though he felt the heavy burden of unleashing Desert Storm, Schwarzkopf never stopped pushing himself and his generals to deliver bold, decisive results. Unlike the frustrating fighting in Vietnam, Schwarzkopf was determined to bring about a quick, stunning victory using the coalition's air superiority. He instructed the air force planners to use B-52s to target the Republican Guard units from the first day of the air campaign, and to attack them every hour for the balance of the war. This kind of decisive action turned Desert Storm into a highly focused exercise in destroying the Republican Guard, which Schwarzkopf understood was the center of gravity of Saddam Hussein's forces.

Likewise, the wheeling movement of the XVIII and VII Corps was a bold move that led to decisive day and night actions. In one of the most significant armored clashes of the war, the afternoon of February 27, the VII Corps's 1st Armored Division ran into the dug-in elements of the Medina Republican Guard division, equipped with Russian-built T-72 tanks. Choosing to attack from the longest possible range—about 2,500 yards—the American division used its laser range finders to pick off the Iraqi tanks one by one. In less than 45 minutes, the 1st Armored Division had destroyed 69 Iraqi tanks and 38 armored personnel carriers—an impressive tally that demonstrated the total superiority of U.S. equipment and tactics. Had this encounter taken place between Iraqi and Iranian tanks during the Iran–Iraq War, its outcome would have been vastly different as the two forces tentatively felt around each other and refused combat.

Schwarzkopf summarized his approach to taking decisive action: "When in charge, take command. Leaders are often called on to make decisions without adequate information. As a result, they may put off deciding to do anything at all. That's a big mistake . . . The best policy is to decide, monitor the results, and change course if necessary."[26]

Visible Leadership

From the time he landed in Saudi Arabia to set up his headquarters for Desert Shield, Schwarzkopf became one of the most visible military leaders in American history. Although he wasn't leading the main charge against the Iraqi lines as Alexander did at Gaugamela, or standing on the quarterdeck of the *Victory* like Nelson at Trafalgar, Schwarzkopf spent time with the troops at the front lines and made sure that all coalition officers had access to him. When he visited a marine unit from the 7th Marine Expeditionary Brigade holding a defensive position near the Kuwaiti border during the early days of Desert Shield, he was told that the most important item the troops wanted was access to news and radio reports, so he ordered newspapers and radio transmitters set up so that frontline troops could keep up with the unfolding standoff. When Christmas time came around, Schwarzkopf didn't have a fancy dinner with his general staff. Instead, he went to the main mess in the Escan Village in Riyadh, not far from his headquarters, and walked through the huge tents as men and women lined up to shake his hands. After four hours he finally sat down and ate his dinner among them.

Schwarzkopf's passion—for the people serving under him, and for a rapid, decisive victory—was apparent in all his speeches and orders. "If you lead men in battle, they're *your* people," he wrote. " . . . To be a good leader, you have to lead passionately. I'm a passionate person."[27] Schwarzkopf demonstrated this passion by actively explaining and communicating the strategy for Desert Shield and Desert Storm, and making sure that people in Washington understood the difference between a static defense of Saudi Arabia, which Desert

Shield achieved, and the advance into Kuwait and Iraq, which Desert Storm unleashed. His ability to be a visible leader in Washington, in Riyadh, and with the frontline troops lent him credibility with the U.S. political leadership, with the global coalition partners, and with his own CENTCOM staff and soldiers. Schwarzkopf was, after all, the first Western military leader since Alexander to bring an army into Southwest Asia and triumph over a well-entrenched, confident adversary. Yet he showed even stronger leadership skills than Alexander by retaining positive control of his army and skillfully integrating collation elements into the U.S. plan for Desert Storm—a feat that in itself represented a small victory.

The Creative Execution focus of Desert Storm, steeped in the lessons of Vietnam and enabled by the massive technological superiority of the U.S. Armed Forces, was a high mark for the U.S. military. "For the first time in its history," writes Robert Citino, "the [U.S.] army had conceived, planned, and executed an entire campaign on the operational level. The decision to shift to the left the two corps . . . was the most audacious decision in U.S. military history."[28] That decision, coupled with the highly visible leadership of General Schwarzkopf, crystal-clear roles and responsibilities of the coalition forces, and the Candid Dialogue that played out in the political and military spheres, brought about the most lopsided victory since the fall of France to the German *Wehrmacht* in June 1940. With all swept before them, the U.S. armored divisions returned to their training grounds in the United States and Germany, confident in their knowledge that no other conventional army in the world could challenge their supremacy on an open battlefield.

REVERSAL: IRAQI FREEDOM

For 10 years following the coalition victory in Desert Storm, Iraq and the United States fell into an on/off version of the phony war between France and Germany in 1939. Saddam Hussein slowly rebuilt the shattered Republican Guard divisions that had escaped destruction by the XVIII and VII Corps's massive left hook, while the United States enforced a no-fly zone over the southern part of the country and imposed trade restrictions against Iraq. Oil could only be exported under the UN's Oil-for-Food program, which yielded more than $30 billion by the year 2000. Despite its conclusive military outcome, Desert Storm failed to root out the main causes of Iraq's unstable society: entrenched ethnic groups that could be held together under a tight regime led by Saddam Hussein, but that once set loose from a strong center would spin out of control and engender violence, distrust, and the balkanization of Iraq.

The loosening of these forces was to take place in 2003 with the return of U.S. forces, following the Bush administration's faulty assessment that Iraq had acquired or developed weapons of mass destruction. The claim that Iraq possessed biochemical or nuclear weapons wasn't actually far-fetched, since Saddam had used poison gas in the Iran–Iraq War in the 1980s. This perception was reinforced by one of Saddam's brothers, who deserted to Jordan in 1995 and told Western intelligence agencies that Iraq was "cheating" with its weapons program. When the War on Terror was declared in response to the 9/11 attacks and the Taliban routed in Afghanistan, the Bush administration naturally singled out Iraq as the next rogue state on the "axis of evil" list, and began to drum up international support for a fresh military campaign to permanently unseat Saddam Hussein.

The U.S. invasion of Iraq on March 2003, like Desert Storm, was a lightning-fast military operation, although with far fewer forces. Within two weeks, the U.S. offensive had overrun the Iraqi capital, toppled the Saddam government, and casually swept aside the remnants of the Iraqi Army that had chosen not to desert or disband. With another 10 years of technological development under its belt since Desert Storm, the U.S. military was even more surgical in its defeat of the Iraqi Army in 2003. It used remotely piloted vehicles like the Predator to spot and attack targets, flew strike packages with deadly combinations of B-1, B-2, and B-52 bombers, and used a new version of the Patriot missile and Aegis destroyers to shoot down Iraq's surface-to-surface missiles. In total, the United States expended 20,000 precision-guided munitions such as the Maverick laser-guided anti-tank missile fired from aircraft and helicopters, as well as thousands of cluster bombs—and just over 9,000 old-fashioned, unguided weapons. The U.S. onslaught, based on the principles of AirLand joint operations that worked so effectively in Desert Storm, was therefore—on the surface—an unqualified success. President Bush declared the end of combat operations and "mission accomplished" on May 1, 2003, from the deck of the carrier USS *Abraham Lincoln* while the search for Saddam and the purging of the Iraqi government began in earnest.

Within weeks of this shock-and-awe blitzkrieg, however, the tenuous hold of the U.S. Army on the wide expanse of Iraqi countryside bypassed on the way to Baghdad began to show its soft underbelly. According to a professor from Eastern Michigan University, "the campaign was badly flawed . . . It had relied on too few troops, who were now operating at the end of an untenable supply line . . . The campaign, conceived as a rapid, third-wave information- and technology-based blitzkrieg . . . had instead placed too few 'boots on the ground.'"[29] As a result of having too few forces to deal with the rapidly spreading insurgency, looting, and civil unrest, the United States watched in bewilderment as Iraq began its descent into near anarchy. The sudden morphing of Iraqi Freedom into an insurgency campaign—thought to involve around 50,000 Iraqi and foreign fighters by the end of 2004—was a complete shock for the U.S. administration. As retired general Anthony Zinni, who took over as U.S. commander of CENTCOM after Norman Schwarzkopf in 2000, scathingly commented, "I think there was dereliction in insufficient forces being put on the ground and fully understanding the military dimensions of the plan. I think there was dereliction in lack of planning. The president is owed the finest strategic thinking. He is owed the finest operational planning. He is owed the finest tactical execution on the ground . . . He got the latter. He didn't get the first two."[30]

Zinni's criticism of the Pentagon's strategy for occupying and reconstructing Iraq pointed to some fundamental flaws in Operation

Iraqi Freedom. The real problem faced by U.S. forces wasn't the destruction of the Iraqi military—they had already proved unable to resist the one-two punch of U.S. airpower and ground forces in Desert Storm. The real issue was the political rebuilding of Iraq, which the British had already attempted in the 1920s by writing a new constitution and importing a quasi-democracy, and which the Americans now proposed to do using the same political instruments. The only experience the United States had with postwar political reconstruction was the occupation of Japan in 1945, over which General MacArthur presided. However, the rebuilding of Japan came after four years of fighting and the abdication of the Japanese emperor. In Iraq, as with France's rapid conquest by Germany in 1940, the blitzkrieg offensive had succeeded in bringing down the army and the government, but had left pockets of determined resistance. And again, just as the majority of the French people under Nazi occupation perceived the regime of Maréchal Pétain, installed by the Germans, to be illegitimate, so too did the Iraqi people generally refuse to acknowledge the legitimacy of Ahmed Chalabi and Iyad al-Allawi, the designated Iraqi rulers initially put in place by the Americans.

Unlike Desert Storm, which featured a clear strategy backed up by a strong multi-national force with clear roles and visible leaders, Iraqi Freedom failed most of the Creative Execution criteria. Its execution was exacerbated by the following flaws.

- **Inconsistent Strategy:** The strategy for dealing with postwar Iraq was initially entrusted to the Pentagon, which put in place a retired general, Jay Garner, to administer the country. When Paul Bremer replaced Garner after only a month in office, he made the controversial decision to dissolve the Iraqi Army. When half a million Iraqi soldiers went home to find no jobs, no food, and no water, many turned to vandalism and ultimately insurrection to lash out against the occupying forces. At the ideological level, the strategy for dealing with Iraq shifted from unseating Saddam Hussein and finding weapons of mass destruction to fighting the insurgency, restoring democracy, and providing a shield against Iranian influence—all worthy causes, but certainly not all achievable with the forces initially brought into Iraq.

- **Weak Dialogue:** Compared to Desert Storm, which included an array of NATO, Arab, and Asian coalition forces such as Syria, India, and Saudi Arabia, Iraqi Freedom was primarily led and executed by the United States, with Great Britain as a junior partner. Although much of the world was openly or quietly supportive of the U.S. involvement in Afghanistan, which had clear links to the 9/11 attacks, the tactical shift to Iraq was not equally supported even among the close-knit NATO community. When France expressed reservations about the evidence against Iraq and said that it was unwilling to support the U.S. position at the UN Security Council, it was instantly vilified by the U.S. administration. It took the courageous voices of leaders outside the Pentagon, like General Zinni's, to challenge the U.S. strategy.

- **Diluted Roles and Responsibilities:** From the beginning, the Pentagon played a heavy hand in shaping the strategy for invading Iraq, and for rebuilding the country's infrastructure (mostly its oil-producing capability). The U.S. Department of State, which had other views on how to manage postwar Iraq, was mostly sidelined until the pressure of the uprising forced the Pentagon to acknowledge its shortcomings, and Donald Rumsfeld stepped down as secretary of defense. Most flagrantly, the U.S. Armed Forces on the ground in Iraq had no training in the nation building or civil relations that would prove so critical in the aftermath of the military victory.

- **Poor Decisions:** The decision to disband the Iraqi Army, and to entrust the government of Iraq to Ahmad Chalabi, who became discredited by the United States after it was shown that he had supplied false information to the U.S. military and media regarding Iraq's weapons of mass destruction, made a bad situation in Iraq worse. Likewise, the initial decision to billet U.S. troops inside Iraq's major cities led to early demonstrations and fed the resentment of Iraqi civilians, who began to perceive U.S. forces as occupiers rather than liberators.

- **Detached Leadership:** Whereas U.S. ground commanders such as General Tommy Franks, who led Operation Iraqi Freedom, performed as well as Norman Schwarzkopf in Desert Storm, the central leadership role over the conduct of the war and Iraq's reconstruction fell to the Pentagon's civilian authorities, most notably to Secretary Rumsfeld and Paul Bremer. Rumsfeld's leadership qualities were more reminiscent of Secretary McNamara during the Vietnam War than Colin Powell in Desert Storm: dry, numbers driven, sardonic, and seemingly determined to pursue the same strategy despite mounting evidence that the insurgency was growing in intensity. In one televised interview in the days following the capture of Baghdad, Rumsfeld casually explained that the looting going on in Baghdad was a necessary part of the "messy" transition to democracy. As he spoke, Iraqis were pilfering priceless artifacts from the Iraqi National Museum and appropriating weapons from arsenals left unattended by U.S. troops. In particular, a cache of 380 tons of conventional explosives located 30 miles from Baghdad had been left unguarded and was ransacked by Iraqi insurgents in April 2003. Many of these explosives would find their way into the improvised explosive devices (IEDs) that became the weapon of choice against U.S. armored convoys.

THE REPRIEVE OF THE SURGE

Despite the strategic mistakes of Operation Iraqi Freedom, and the great loss of civilian lives (one John Hopkins University study puts the total number of Iraqis killed as a result of the war and insurgency at 650,000 between 2003 and 2006), there are signs that the violent transformation Iraq experienced during the American occupation had a positive side effect. As America showed in the aftermath of World War II with the Marshall Plan and the rebuilding of Japan's institutions, America has a unique ability to pour its creative and economic resources into rebuilding efforts. For the first time in Iraq's history, Iraqis were able to vote for their political representatives under a new constitution—a better omen than what the British experienced after they introduced their version of an Iraqi constitution in 1924. By 2008, many of the Iraqi families that had left Iraq for neighboring countries such as Jordan and Egypt had returned, and kids were attending schools rebuilt by American engineers and contractors. Attacks on U.S. and British forces were down significantly from 2007 to 2008, averaging 20 to 30 killed in action per month rather than the 100 to 135 in 2004 and 2005—mostly as a result of the surge in U.S. forces in 2007, which brought much-needed stability to Baghdad and other major Iraqi cities. By 2010, the U.S. death toll for one year fell to 60, and in 2011, when the last U.S. combat troops left Iraq, a total of 53 U.S. soldiers were killed, compared to 904 in 2007 at the height of the insurgency.

The surge of 2007 to 2008 was in itself a complete reversal of U.S. military and political strategy for dealing with Iraq. After four years of insurgency, the Bush administration and the U.S. military recognized that their methods for putting down the insurrection—which some observers plainly described as "kicking down the doors at two in the morning and lining everyone up against the wall"—were yielding poor results and in many cases turned neutral civilians into al-Qaeda supporters or fighters. By 2006 and 2007, many of the U.S. senior leaders who returned to Iraq saw a level of devastation that was shocking and deflating, given the Washington rhetoric that suggested that the United States was making steady progress. A small group of U.S. colonels and generals, many of whom were excluded from the command hierarchy during Iraqi Freedom, began to rethink the tactics that were used in Iraq, and lobbied the Pentagon and the White House to conduct a complete overhaul of the U.S. military strategy and leadership responsible for the war. This "revolution from within" led to the dismissal of Secretary of Defense Donald Rumsfeld, the chairman of the Joint Chiefs of Staff, and the top military brass at CENTCOM and in Iraq. As Thomas Ricks writes in his account of the surge,

"Almost at the last minute, and over the objections of nearly all relevant leaders of the U.S. military establishment, a few insiders . . . managed to persuade President Bush to adopt a new, more effective strategy built around protecting the Iraqi people."[31]

What were the key elements of this new strategy? When he arrived in Baghdad as the new commander in Iraq, General Petraeus summed up his strategic tasks as follows: "The first is to get the big ideas right. The second is to communicate the big ideas throughout the organization. The third is to ensure proper execution of the big ideas."[32] Almost to a point, he articulated the first three principles of Creative Execution: Unique Strategy (what he calls the "big ideas"), Candid Dialogue (communicate the big ideas), and proper execution, which encapsulates Clear Roles and Accountabilities, Bold Action, and Visible Leadership. Let's take a closer look at how Petraeus implemented his new thinking using Creative Execution.

Unique Strategy

In the years preceding the surge, U.S. forces had retreated to large bases from which they launched massive armored raids against suspected al-Qaeda or insurgent residences. This strategy telegraphed the message to the Iraqi people that U.S. forces cared more about their own protection than they did about protecting Iraqi civilians. Armed with a new counter-insurgency manual that borrowed from the lessons learned in Vietnam and Algeria, the U.S. Army now adopted a completely new strategy. It would deploy its troops into Iraq's main cities, conduct numerous foot patrols to allow its soldiers to connect with the local population, and, most importantly, it would not retreat to its fortified bases at night but stay and live next to the people it sought to protect. As Ricks writes, the U.S. military would "establish scores of small outposts, and patrol almost incessantly, having learned that if you are present in a neighborhood for only two hours a day, the insurgents may well control it for the other twenty-two."[33]

This new strategy was much more compelling since it allowed U.S. forces in major Iraqi cities to do the job it really wanted to do: convince

Iraq's citizens that they could live in peace and security if they collaborated with U.S. forces and stopped passively or actively supporting the insurgency. Even Senator John McCain, who had supported the initial invasion, finally agreed that "We are getting it right because we finally have in place a strategy that can succeed."[34] But although the United States had finally articulated a coherent strategy for winning the war, it still had to deal with the intense opposition to this new strategy from inside its own military.

Candid Dialogue

The lack of Candid Dialogue from the White House and the civilian leadership at the Pentagon was partially responsible for the political and human hemorrhaging that took place in Iraq between 2003 and 2006. It was clear to inside observers that Secretary of Defense Donald Rumsfeld, Chief of Staff General Peter Pace, and General George Casey, who was the senior commander in Iraq, weren't allowing for any dissent. Their bombastic assessments of progress made in Iraq, and obstinacy with the ongoing policy of keeping U.S. forces in remote bases and shifting the responsibility for urban fighting and security to unreliable Iraqi police and army troops, gradually eroded their credibility with the American public and the U.S. Armed Forces. It took a bold statement by President Bush in January 2007, where he acknowledged that "we need to change our strategy in Iraq,"[35] to clear the way for a complete change in tone and leadership that would allow the architects of the new strategy, Generals Petraeus, Odierno, and Keane, to emerge from the woodwork at the Pentagon. When the new secretary of defense, Robert Gates, took office in December 2006, one of his first phone calls was to General Petraeus, asking for his opinion of what he should look for on his trip to Iraq. "The two men shared a preference for candid, even blunt assessments that would lead to strategic clarity," Ricks recalls.[36] In return for accepting the top job in Iraq, Petraeus asked Gates that their "dialogue should be fairly continuous; it should be based on updates of the situation . . . very forthright, brutally honest."[37]

This new candor from the secretary of defense allowed for a very subtle but discernible change in how U.S. officials and military commanders started talking about Iraq in 2007. The United States changed its rhetoric by explaining that its forces were in Iraq to provide some form of stability, and allow its population to resume a normal lifestyle—rather than focusing on the larger goal of bringing democracy to the Middle East. Mistakes were acknowledged. Local commanders began to share their success stories—and frustrations— among each other. The media, which had been kept at arm's length from Iraqi operations, was brought in as a partner in sharing the new strategy and explaining its purpose to the Iraqi and American people. General Petraeus directed his commanders to talk to the media openly and frequently. If they "overdid it," he would let them know. Openness and candor became the first key to managing the execution of the new Iraq strategy.

Clear Roles and Accountabilities

At the heart of the new strategy was the argument, long made by critics of the 2003 invasion, that the United States had committed too few troops to Iraq, and could not establish security in the country's major urban centers without bringing in new troops whose role would be very different from the roles of the troops that were already deployed in-country. This would lead to the deployment of five army brigades and supporting forces—a total of 30,000 more troops—to Iraq between 2007 and 2008. These surge brigades were truly the last reserve forces in the U.S. Army. To use poker terminology, the United States went "all in." If the surge didn't work, or required more troops, it would be game over. There simply weren't any more troops available. To make the point, the active-duty and reserve troops already in Iraq were told that their tour would be extended from 12 months to 18 months. By the time all the surge forces arrived, in mid 2007, there would be a total of 156,000 U.S. troops in Iraq, plus some 180,000 contractors brought in as drivers, mechanics, cooks, and security guards.

What was special about the surge forces was their dedication to the security of Baghdad, and their special role in protecting the Iraqi population. The first two brigades settled inside the Iraqi capital. The other three brigades deployed on the city's outskirts. Altogether, 21 battalions (including army and marine units) were deployed during the surge. These forces had a distinct role: to relieve the pressure on the Iraqi police, who had been unable to secure Baghdad due to a high rate of casualties, desertion, intimidation, and fraternization with the insurgency. Each brigade was assigned an urban area in Baghdad and its surroundings where they physically moved into schools or abandoned public facilities so they could live next to the local population. They also conducted foot patrols so they could get to know the Iraqis in their district, as opposed to riding around in armored Humvees. These critical distinctions made a huge impact on Iraqis who now began to see U.S. forces as their protectors, and shifted from tacit supporters of the insurgency to more active participants of the U.S. effort.

Bold Action

The concept of the surge was in itself a bold, decisive stroke that committed the U.S. Army's reserve forces to a new, difficult mission. But perhaps the boldest decision in the surge was General Petraeus's concession that in order to bring peace to Iraq's cities, he had to strike a deal with members of the insurgency—some of whom had killed Americans, or might in the future should the negotiations break down. The United States began to reach out to some of the largest insurgent groups, including Muqtada al-Sadr, the Shiite cleric whose forces had declared war on the U.S. occupying force in 2004. General Petraeus's adviser, Major General Fastabend (now a Brigadier General), wrote a provocative essay called *How This Ends* in April 2007 that set the tone for these negotiations. "If this is the decisive struggle of our time—*be decisive!*" he advocated.[38] Along with the surge into Baghdad, he set down the requirements to negotiate with tribes and local militias—the same method that Alexander the Great resorted to in order to end the bloody stalemate his Macedonian troops faced in Afghanistan.

The deals with local militia led to the formation of a group called the Sons of Iraq, a collection of Sunni insurgents and former Saddam-era military who started to collaborate with American forces to sta-bilize the disputed districts of Ghazaliya and Fadhil in Baghdad. In return for their collaboration, the United States promised Sons of Iraq members that they would be able to rejoin the mainstream political movement in Iraq and would be given full-time paying jobs in the Iraqi security forces. The new alliances yielded immediate results— from names of Iraqi police officers acting as informants, to vital information about al-Qaeda's communications network and structure across Iraq. "American tactics and practices immediately improved in myriad ways," notes Ricks. "Having former insurgents as guides also meant there was suddenly much more information on which to act, both because the insurgents were talking but also because they were no longer violently preventing civilians from doing so."[39] The nego-tiations led to more 800 ceasefire agreements with local insurgent groups in 2007, and most importantly cut off al-Qaeda from the end-less stream of recruits that would either volunteer information about American forces or join in the violence. Compared to the decision early in the war to disband the Iraqi Army, the decision to create the Sons of Iraq and negotiate with insurgent tribes was probably the sin-gle most effective and bold action the Americans took during the war to restore peace and order to Iraq.

Visible Leadership

The lessons from the 2007 and 2008 surge are as much about the proper use of the military to quell an insurgency as they are about win-ning against the odds. As Ricks writes, "It is extraordinary to consider that the new strategy that would be implemented by the U.S. military in Iraq in 2007 was opposed by the U.S. military in both Baghdad and Washington."[40] The fact that the surge succeeded was a tribute to the leadership of American commanders—in particular Generals Keane, Petraeus, and Odierno—who not only conceived the new strategy to fight the insurgency, but convinced the White House to adopt it. The army's new tactics elevated American leadership in Iraq and empowered its commanders to take and hold critical ground—something the U.S. military had forgotten in its haste to build large fortified bases to protect its troops. When insurgents launched an all-out attack against a newly established American outpost in Tarmiyah, for instance, the members of the 1st Cavalry Division didn't give up the town. After a bloody battle that left two soldiers dead and 29 wounded out of 38, the officer in charge led his troops to a nearby school to rebuild the U.S. presence. This kind of determined, visible leadership showed the Iraqis that the U.S. forces were clearly committed to their protection.

The Visible Leadership showed by the surge's key strategist, General Petraeus, led to his nomination as commander of CENTCOM in 2008, and as Director of the CIA in 2011. As CENTCOM commander, Petraeus had responsibility for the entire U.S. military strategy in the Middle East, including Iraq, Iran, Afghanistan, and Pakistan. Thanks to the positive impact of the surge and the settlement of the country's political cracks, the bulk of the 142,000 U.S. forces left Iraq in 2010, and the balance in 2011. With Iraq in his rearview mirror, General Petraeus refocused his energy on creating a new strategy for winning the war in Afghanistan. While President Obama endorsed his call for a surge-like deployment to take on the increasingly bold Taliban, Petraeus recognized that the same strategy that worked in Iraq wouldn't necessarily give the United States the upper hand in Afghanistan. "You don't move into a village in Afghanistan the way we were able to move into neighborhoods in Iraq," he explained. "It will be very difficult, and you won't see the dramatic turnaround that we have seen in Iraq."[41]

IRAQ'S LEGACY

By the end of the surge in the summer of 2008, insurgent attacks had dramatically fallen in Iraq from a peak of 1,500 per week in the summer of 2007 to fewer than 150 per week in 2009. In April of 2009, Baghdad hosted its first Flower Show in over six years, and the *New York Times* reported that "for the first time in years, Iraqis have been taking a visible pride in their surroundings."[42] This relatively peaceful period was shattered in 2010 when the Iraqi national elections engendered a new round of violence. In one single day, May 10, 2010, suicide bombers killed 100 people and injured another 350 across Iraq, a new record for the number of civilians killed or hurt by al-Qaeda in Iraq.

Much like the Vietnam War in the 1970s, the War on Terror waged in Iraq and Afghanistan forced the United States to reconsider how to use military force to fight an unconventional enemy. Defeating the Iraqi Army, which General Schwarzkopf masterfully accomplished in Desert Storm, was a relatively easy task. Bringing peace and security to Iraq was a completely different matter, for which the U.S. military was wholly unprepared—but adjusted to over time. Despite the unexpected ferocity of the Iraqi insurgency, the U.S. military didn't throw in the towel. General Petraeus and his colleagues invented their own Creative Execution formula—the counterinsurgency strategy used in the surge—in order to regain control of what seemed like a no-win situation in 2006. This essential difference is what prevented Iraq from imploding into a full-scale civil war.

While the United States has taken Creative Execution to the next level by asserting its military might, its apt demonstration of the formula has also fed a global appetite for achieving this type of staggering creativity and innovation. In the process, it paved the way for companies like Toyota, Four Seasons, and Google to emerge as the new champions of Creative Execution.

5

Creative Execution Marches East

In battle, one engages with the orthodox and gains victory through the unorthodox.

—Sun Tzu

If you weren't one of the approximately one billion people watching the opening ceremonies of the 2008 Summer Olympics in Beijing, where more than 10,000 performers put together a show that took seven years to orchestrate, or if you haven't walked the streets of Shanghai's bustling financial district, or watched Andre Agassi and Roger Federer duke it out on the helipad of the Burj Al Arab hotel in Dubai, you might still think that Creative Execution is a purely Western concept, and that the Japanese use of Creative Execution at Pearl Harbor was a historical fluke. But make no mistake: Creative Execution is making its way East, South, and parts in between. There may be creative energy bursts in the West, such as the construction of the new Cunard liner *Queen Elizabeth*, which an Italian shipyard launched in a remarkable six months, but to see truly gargantuan feats of Creative Execution, you'll be better advised to walk the streets of Dubai, which surpassed New York and Hong Kong as the city with the largest number of buildings taller than 200 meters, including the spanking new Burj Khalifa, the tallest building on the planet. Yes, Dubai had to cancel nine construction projects between 2009 and 2011, but it was still building 15 new towers and had another 18 to 20 in the works when this book went to print. And among the 42 buildings still under construction, you'll find the world's second-tallest residential building and the tallest twin towers in the region, the Emirates Park Towers.

Clearly, the global appetite for supersize development and creative projects has found a new epicenter, which doesn't run through New York or London. The new Freedom Tower in New York, for example, is expected to take an agonizing seven years to build, from 2006 to 2013. With a symbolic height of 1,776 meters, the Freedom Tower will be the world's tallest office building, which will give the United States something to brag about. But let's see: how long did it take to build the Empire State Building in 1931, which held for several decades the honor of being the world's tallest office building? A single year. Granted, the technical challenges of erecting a modern skyscraper are far greater today than they were in the 1930s, and the Freedom Tower was delayed by complex contracts and revisions to its original plan. Yet the Freedom Tower remains one of the few large-scale building projects in the United States.

To find a construction project in the East that will require more than seven years to complete, we need only move slightly south of Dubai, to the Emirates' capital of Abu Dhabi. With more than $1 trillion in global investments concentrated in Abu Dhabi, a city of less than a million people, it can afford to splash on a few big infrastructure projects. Yet instead of a flashy building, the city's most interesting and challenging project is the development of a high-tech, zero-carbon-emission *city* called Masdar, or "source" in Arabic. Masdar will rely exclusively on solar energy and renewable energy sources to power its 50,000 houses and 1,500 businesses. The city will be completed between 2020 and 2025, and the tab for its construction will be roughly $19 billion. Even the global credit crunch won't stop Abu Dhabi from completing this massive project, since the government is funding $15 billion out of its own pocket.

In order to keep the city cool and minimize energy requirements, Masdar will be walled, and its streets will be narrow and shaded.

What's more stunning, in a country that holds 8 percent of the world's oil reserves, is that there will be no cars allowed on the streets. To make this work, the United Arab Emirates is investing in partnerships with several Western renewable energy companies: an offshore windfarm in the UK, three solar-thermal power plants in Spain, and machinery for its two solar panel plants manufactured in Germany. The architectural plans for the city are being drawn up by a British firm, Foster & Partners, and Credit Suisse is investing $100 million in a clean-tech fund to help develop some of the technology for the new city. As *Fortune* wrote, "the city will act as a laboratory to test carbon-free products and prove that alternative energy can be deployed on a massive scale."[1] To cap this environmental accomplishment, the city has struck a partnership with MIT in order to create a Masdar Institute of Science and Technology, or MIST, which is attracting talent from great universities such as Cornell, MIT, and Princeton.

These feats of Creative Execution in the Middle East are being matched, as it was in the heyday of the European Renaissance, with a growing appetite for arts and culture. The Qatar Museum of Islamic Arts, designed by I.M. Pei, opened its doors in November 2008. Not to be outdone, Abu Dhabi signed a $1.6-billion agreement with the French national museum agency to help build a new branch of the Louvre, which will be the centerpiece of a $27-billion development project on the island of Saadiyat, off the coast of Abu Dhabi, scheduled to open in 2015. The island's Cultural District will also feature a 450,000-square-foot Guggenheim museum built by Frank Gehry—set to open in 2017, while Japanese architect Tadao Ando is at work on a maritime museum and arch.

I'm sure if you look around your company, or talk to people involved in the arts in your city or community, you will find that Abu Dhabi, Dubai, or another city in the Emirates is hijacking someone you know to help build up their green buildings, art collections, luxury hotels, or new shopping complexes. Abu Dhabi even asked my mother, Colette Juilliard, who obtained her Ph.D. in French literature from the City University of New York, to help edit some of its cultural magazines as the emirate builds up its collections. "The aim of the Emirate is to become a bridge between East and West," she explains. "To create an intense melting pot that allows both westerners and easterners to soak in each other's culture." By the end of this decade, the Creative Execution burst under way in Abu Dhabi will present us with another version of Dubai that, seemingly, grew out of nothing to become a world-class megalopolis.

Just like the Middle East, China and India are waking up to the fact that they cannot just imitate, but must overtake the West in critical industries. We have become accustomed to thinking of China in the same way we viewed Japan in the 1960s: as a slowly awakening economic giant that mostly produces cheap manufactured goods. But just as Japan learned the art of naval warfare from the West before building its own fleet in the first half of the twentieth century, China is busy building its advanced technological and industrial base to rival that of the West. Take the new 787 Dreamliner, for instance, Boeing's sleek carbon-composite aircraft. Over 70 percent of the aircraft's design and manufacturing is outsourced to countries like China, Russia, and India, which would have been unheard of in the past. Not only are Chinese workers bending sheet metal for the Dreamliner, but Chinese and Indian designers are putting together the specs for the aircraft. Likewise, European aircraft maker Airbus opened its first plant outside Europe in September 2008 in—you guessed it—China, where it will employ up to 600 Chinese workers to assemble its A320 airplane.

China is also taking the lead in the development of a high-speed railway network that may one day link Beijing to Moscow and the rest of Europe. The first track was opened in June 2011, one year ahead of schedule, between Beijing and Shanghai. The $33-billion project cuts down the travel time between the two cities from ten hours to less than five, and is expected to see 180,000 passengers per year. That's roughly the same as the distance between New York and Chicago, which on an Amtrak train will set you back 18 or 19 hours. Despite some public outcry over high fares and the fact that the trains are limited to lower speeds for the first year or two of operations, the bold Chinese plan is paying off: already 90 trains are making the journey between Beijing and Shanghai on a daily basis. Don't be surprised if, over the next decade, China's high-speed trains make their appearance in the United States, Russia, and other countries. While the United States is planning to spend $13 billion on high-speed rail between 2012 and 2015, China is planning to spend $300 billion. Chinese officials have already visited California, and are offering not just technology but hard cash to help finance new projects.

FIVE POISON PILLS

While the East slams together its own Creative Execution formula, the West wallows in self-doubt. As Dambisa Moyo, a specialist in emerging markets at Goldman Sachs pungently explains, "For the past 500 years, Western economic dominance has been a story of ruthlessness and self-interest. Its military power, its global hold, its influence on the world, have been the history of its trade, or rather the history of its single-minded ability to extract from other countries, other continents, other peoples, the material, land and people that would drive its economy forward . . . be it Venice or Holland, Spain, France, Great Britain or the United States . . . the West maintained its iron grip—implacable in its determination to extract from the rest whatever it wanted."[2] In other words, the West used its Creative Execution powers to conquer, dominate, and lead the world. We are now at a turning point in history where the West is more concerned about its survival than it is about extracting what it wants from the rest of the world.

Broadly speaking, there are five poison pills that are contributing to the malaise that seems to have gripped the West, and to some extent the world at large, in the waking hours of the twenty-first century. Those five are: 1) economic uncertainty, 2) global demographic changes, 3) the semi-paralysis of democratic governments, 4) war and terrorism, and 5) climate change. Put together, these trends are like a massive iceberg drifting across the North Atlantic. Unless we can steer clear or reverse course, the decline of the West is a certainty, and we'll find ourselves in a semi-permanent crisis mode. Let's take a quick look at these five poison pills that made their way, inadvertently, into our system.

1. Economic Uncertainty

The financial meltdown of 2008 and the high unemployment that followed are the evil twins that we can't seem to shake off. The United States lost 2 million construction jobs between 2008 and 2011—with California, Nevada, Florida, and Arizona hit hardest. Other industries have been impacted, but none more than manufacturing, which in the United States used to represent 28 percent of all jobs in 1970. Today it's down to a meager 18 percent, and falling fast. Unemployment is as high as 20 percent in some of the Iberian countries in Europe. Half the population of Africa lives in poverty. Other than the sputtering growth in China, India, and Brazil, the world economy is getting by on life support. The Conference Board's Consumer Confidence Index fell back to 2008 levels at the end of 2011, dropping sharply from 46.4 to 39.8 in just one month. The Measure of CEO Confidence fell into negative territory in the third quarter of 2011. The Occupy Wall Street protests are a bleak reminder that many people in North America are feeling left out of the ecosystem that has benefitted the top wage earners. According to Thomson Reuters ASSET4 data, the average CEO earns 142 times what an employee earns in the United States—compared to 69 times in the UK, and a more tolerable 34 times in Sweden.

There are a thousand data points that support the catastrophic decline of the North American and European economies since 2008—but of those chronic unemployment is the most worrisome, particularly for the younger population. The United States is in an uproar with 9 percent unemployment. In Europe, approximately 23 million men and women are unemployed, with countries such as Spain,

Greece, and Latvia topping the chart at 22 percent, 17 percent, and 16 percent respectively. Youth unemployment stood at 21 percent in the euro area in 2011, but this is where it gets scary: youth unemployment is at 48 percent in Spain and 43 percent in Greece. In other words, roughly half of Spain's young, educated people under the age of 25 are unable to find jobs. In the United States, youth unemployment shot up from 11 percent in 2008 to 18 percent in 2011, according to the U.S. Bureau of Labor Statistics. These unemployment trends are feeding the malaise that we feel. How can you feel good about yourself when you see that a quarter or half of your peers are on the street, with no decent prospects for employment? As Michael Lewis wrote in his book on the global financial crisis, *Boomerang*, the United States "might organize itself increasingly into zones of financial security and zones of financial crisis."[3]

The problem, as we see in the unemployment data, is that the recovery that started in July 2009 was mostly a jobless recovery. Without housing construction and manufacturing to stimulate an upturn in the United States, and with the eurozone in a state of shock, there is a real possibility that the West will face the same "lost decade" that afflicted Japan in the 1990s—when the country experienced anemic growth after the implosion of its banking sector and bad debts.

2. Demographic Shifts

Manufacturing and housing bubbles and unemployment come and go, but population growth—or the lack thereof—is more difficult to control. Take the Chinese, who in 1979 implemented the one-child policy to slow down population growth. In 1960, when the world's population was just 3 billion, China had a population of 650 million. This grew to 1 billion in the 1980s, and to 1.3 billion in 2011—a doubling of the country's population in those 50 years. Now that the one-child policy is paying off, China's birth rate is slowing down and India is set to become the world's most populous country by 2040. Let's try to simplify this by comparing the world in 2050, barring any global plague, famine, or military catastrophe, to what we have in 2011:

The World in 2011	The World in 2050
Total population: 7 billion	Total population: 9 billion
Asia's population: 4 billion: -China: 1.3 billion -India: 1.2 billion -Japan: 126 million	Asia's population: 5.2 billion: -China: 1.4 billion -India: 1.6 billion -Japan: 101 million
North America: 351 million	North America: 448 million
Europe: 733 million	Europe: 691 million
Russia: 140 million	Russia: 116 million
Africa: 1 billion	Africa: 2 billion
Brazil: 195 million	Brazil: 218 million

You might have done the math already, but what this tells us is a staggering fact: over the next 40 years, only 3 percent of global population growth will come from the West. The extra 2 billion souls will come almost exclusively from Asia and Africa. North America and Europe will be increasingly populated by older people, whereas Asia and Africa will be dancing to the beat of a younger generation. Already 50 percent of Africans are under the age of 18. When we watch the soccer World Cup in 2050 (which is the actual year it will be played), Asia and Africa will be drawing from a talent pool of 1.75 billion people aged between 20 and 29—which will be more than the total combined population of Europe *and* North America. Now if you were running Adidas or Nike, where would you set up shop over the next four decades?

If you peel the onion back a little more on North America and Europe, you quickly realize that there are two big winners in the shrinking population growth pie: the United States, which increases its population from 317 million to 403 million, and the United Kingdom, which tops up by a healthy 10 million, from 62 to 72 million. Germany loses an astonishing 12 million, by contrast, falling from 82 million to 70 million. France, Germany, Spain, and Italy add a few million, but nothing that compares to the wild swings in Britain and Germany. Canada adds another 10 million, growing to 44 million, and Mexico adds a whopping 20 million. The real losers, whose governments are desperately trying to save face, are Russia and Japan, which together lose close to 50 million people. How do you lose 50 million people? By being a relatively closed and chauvinistic society, which doesn't attract significant immigration. For Russia and Japan, national identity has become a noose each country must extricate itself from in order to ensure their own survival.

This massive demographic shift has unleashed a global hunt for talent that, in my estimate, is going to be a hundred-year war. As the nations with the largest pool of young talent—countries such as India, Iran, and China—begin to take advantage of declining trade barriers, the absence of disruptive technology, and their ability to quickly learn about or duplicate what the West has invented, we will be faced with a tidal wave of Creative Execution. Thanks to instant global communications, this new generation will not see the world as a set of nations with competing interests, but as a collaborative workplace. Deepak Ramachandran and Paul Artiuch, two researchers with the Toronto-based New Paradigm Learning Corporation (now part of Moxie Software), wrote in a white paper on harnessing the global N-Gen talent pool that "the world's rising economies represent an unprecedented source of young labor . . . What's more, the main defining characteristics of the global N-Gen make it better qualified than any previous generation . . . it is technologically savvy, globally-minded, and generally very familiar with (and even fond of) rapid change."[4]

If talk of this new generation (also known as Generation Y, or Echo Boomers) leaves you feeling smug, consider this: in North America and Western Europe, this new generation is equal in size to the baby boomer generation that emerged after World War II. There are 94 million baby boomers in the United States and Canada, for instance, who will be replaced by 93 million Gen-Y or N-Gen workers. In Eastern Europe, China, India, and Latin America, the trend is even sharper, with the N-Gen or Gen Y outflanking the baby boomers 1.5 billion to 971 million. This explosion of the younger generation in rising economies means that Western countries such as Germany, Italy, and Russia—which are experiencing an actual population *decline* over the next 50 years—will need to radically change their immigration policies to attract global talent and fuel their future growth. So the talent war is not just a friendly competition between private companies that operate around the world. It's the new battle-ground to ensure the survival of the fittest countries.

This brewing battle is going to be a challenge for Europe, Japan, and Russia, whose population bases are shrinking and aging at the same time. In Europe, for instance, the UN and Eurostat predicted in 2004 that the population of 18 key countries including 15 of the larg-est European Union members plus Norway, Sweden, and Switzerland would drop from roughly 407 million to 400 million between 2030 and 2050. A more recent study by the UN shows that increased immi-gration could reverse the decline until 2050, with the population of Europe's 18 largest countries possibly increasing by 0.7 percent.[5] Even if this postponed decline is true, Europe is still in trouble because of the significant aging of its population, and its inability to attract tal-ented young professionals from abroad as the United States does. The situation is more dire in Japan, whose population has been in actual decline since 2006. The country's current population of about 127 million (including foreign residents) will decline to a meager 90 mil-lion by 2050, according to the latest UN forecast.[6] That's almost half a million people per year dying without replacements in the Japanese economy, or the equivalent of the entire New York and Los Angeles metropolitan areas disappearing in the next 40 years.

3. Political Paralysis
This one isn't pretty. The horrific display of partisan paralysis dis-played by the U.S. Congress during the debt-ceiling debate in 2011

brought home a startling new reality: that democracy, by default, isn't perfect. The system of checks and balances created by the founding fathers of the United States, conceived as an honest bulwark against the despotic powers of a strong executive or legislative body, has led us to a political impasse with humbling consequences. The same reality has been brought home in a number of Western countries where cohabitation governments have tried to work together in utter frustration, or in newly formed democracies like Iraq where creating a national government is like an endless game of chess. To make things worse, economic crisis seems to further divide—as opposed to unite—political parties. The Tea Party movement in the United States has gained so much influence that during the 112th Congress its 62 members made it nearly impossible for the Republican members of the House of Representatives to compromise with President Obama during the debt-ceiling debate. The result: Congress had an abysmal 9 percent approval rating by the end of 2011.

It seems that we have lost our trust in politicians to do the right thing once in office. Former president G. W. Bush left office with an approval rating of 25 percent, the lowest rating since President Truman in 1952. President Obama started on a high, with a giddy 69 percent in January 2009, his first month in office, only to slide precipitously to 38 percent. Even celebrities like Arnold Schwarzenegger aren't immune: the iconic Hollywood star began his term as California governor with an approval rating of 70 percent in 2003, and exited in 2011 with less than 25 percent. The United States is not alone in this democratic funk. Look what happened to the former Greek prime minister, or to Italy's Silvio Berlusconi—both of whom had to resign after their countries' mounting debt crises in 2011. And in Japan, which elected no less than seven prime ministers in the decade starting in 2000, the democratic process has been torpedoed by scandals, misplaced trust, and the absence of any true leader.

We take democracy for granted, along with the joys and disappointments that come with it. But we need to remember that the longest running democracies, in classical Athens and in the United

States (closely followed by France), have only lasted or been around for 200 years. As Donald Kagan reminds us, "Optimists may believe that democracy is the inevitable and final form of human society, but the historical record shows that up to now it has been the rare exception."[7] Indeed, while the Arab Spring protesters were busy overthrowing despotic governments across North Africa, there was an event in Russia that received a lot less media attention. In September 2011, President Dmitry Medvedev announced to a startled audience at the United Russia party's annual congress that Vladimir Putin would once again stand for election as president in 2012, despite the fact that the Russian constitution bars individuals from serving more than two terms as president. This reminds us that democracies are fragile institutions and that newly democratic states in the former Eastern Bloc, the Middle East, South America, and Asia are not guaranteed eternal survival. We are no longer in the post-World War I euphoria of President Wilson's 14 points, or the "new world order" that President George H. W. Bush greeted with much fanfare after the emasculation of the Soviet Union. Our democracies survive, but the political impasses and economic mess we have created on both sides of the Atlantic, and in Japan, have left democratic nations with colossal headaches that need to get fixed if they are to remain credible economic systems.

4. War and Terror

With the last remaining U.S. forces out of Iraq, and NATO's slow retreat from Afghanistan, it seems like the War on Terror has come to a numbing close—leaving behind just as many frustrations and unanswered questions as the 10,000-day Vietnam War. However, there are two main differences between the Vietnam War and the War on Terror: one is the human cost, which was much higher in Vietnam, where the United States lost 55,000 men. By contrast, coalition casualties in Iraq and Afghanistan combined stand at just over 7,000. This is due in large part to the use of smart weapons and counter-insurgency tactics adopted by a small cadre of Pentagon officers who prevailed with radical new ideas in 2006 and 2007, as we saw in the chapter on Iraq and Afghanistan. The second salient difference is that Iraq and Afghanistan cost a combined $1 trillion to the U.S. taxpayer, adding a huge burden to the U.S. national deficit. The political impact is that just like after Vietnam, the United States is entering a postwar lull where it will be reluctant to deploy armed forces abroad—as President Obama demonstrated when he let Europeans take the lead in supporting the Libyan uprising. In the renewed world order, military and financial restraint are in vogue.

Let's get back to the sea power analogy. When HMS *Dreadnought* was commissioned in 1906, she was the most powerful warship ever built, and the most expensive, at £1,850,000. Today the most sophisticated warships aren't surface battleships but nuclear-powered attack submarines. Quiet, reliable, and deadly accurate when hunting their quarry, these submarines can stay submerged for months and reach top speeds of 30 or 40 knots. The latest class of nuclear attack submarines, built in collaboration by Northrop Grumman Newport News and GE's Electric Boat division, is called the *Virginia*. Extremely quiet, the *Virginia* can attack targets at sea or over land with a mix of Tomahawk cruise missiles, advanced capability torpedoes, and mines. The *Virginia* runs on a ninth-generation core reactor that will provide enough power to the ship for 33 years of operations. The *Dreadnought* and the British Grand Fleet that fought one hundred years ago in World War I, by contrast, could only sustain combat operations for less than a week before needing coal and supplies to keep its steam engines going. There's another significant difference: at $2 billion a piece, the *Virginia* is worth roughly 200 times more than the *Dreadnought* cost England in 1906. Technology comes with a hefty price tag.

One important caveat about the changing nature of war: during the twentieth century, we saw large-scale warfare that decimated Europe, Russia, and Japan. The wars of the coming century will be much smaller, and for the most part fought on a new battlefield: the Internet. Already the United States fends off 40,000 computer attacks from China every day. The GhostNet virus, discovered in 2009, has infected thousands of embassy and government computers worldwide. The GhostNet virus, according to major study on cyber espionage conducted by TheSecDev Group and the University of Toronto's Munk Center for International Studies, is "capable of taking full control of infected computers, including searching and downloading files, and covertly operating attached devices, including microphones and web cameras . . . these instances are consistently controlled from commercial Internet access accounts located on the island of Hainan, People's Republic of China."[8] If that doesn't spoil your breakfast, I'm not sure what will! China, of course, isn't the only player in this brewing cyber war. In 2010, the Iranian nuclear program was hobbled when the Stuxnet worm—which the *New York Times* calls "the most sophisticated cyberweapon ever deployed"[9]—was inserted into the Siemens centrifuges used to process uranium in the country's super-secret facilities. Israel and the United States are widely suspected of developing and inserting the virus, although neither country has admitted its role. We may not be fighting another cold war or world war anytime soon, but the cyber war is definitely on.

5. Climate Change, Energy, and Natural Resources

Of the five poison pills, this might be the most costly and difficult to remedy. While governments continue to argue about the validity of the scientific data of climate change, you might notice on the newer atlases that Greenland has a lot more ice-free coastline than it had 10 or 20 years ago. There are 195 countries that are laboring under the United Nations Framework Convention on Climate Change to limit the CO_2 emissions that contribute to global warming. The Kyoto Protocol, if you were wondering, expired in 2012. So the world now needs to negotiate, in the wake of the financial and economic crisis, a follow-up agreement to cover the next 10 to 20 years, and convince countries that they need to invest their dwindling infrastructure budgets in green energy.

The climate-change debate is closely intertwined with the issue of sustainability and the use of the world's natural resources. The total value of the world's natural resources, including all the forests, lakes, oceans, oil, and gas, is about $44 trillion. Of this, $29 trillion belongs to developing nations. There is a global tug-of-war happening right now to figure out who gets to control that $29 trillion. China, of course, is a major energy consumer that is actively pursuing energy markets in Africa. Who do you think is the single largest investor in the post-Gadhafi, Libyan oil market? The Europeans or Americans, who pushed through the UN mandate for military intervention when Gadhafi's forces looked poised to crush Benghazi and the budding revolution? Or China, who opposed the UN resolution? As you might have guessed, China is the answer. Why did Russia, in 2011, announce the formation of two army Arctic brigades? To stake its claim to the large reserves of gas and oil that sit idle under the Arctic Ocean. But we should not worry, because Prime Minister Putin took the opportunity to announce that Russia would ensure that while it is deploying several thousand troops to the Arctic, it would take great care to preserve the region's "vulnerable ecology." This is a bit like an armed bank robber calming the crowds by announcing that he will hand out free cookies.

More frequent droughts, stronger hurricanes, and the melting ice shelf are all warning signals that we're doing too little too late to prevent large-scale climate change. The question is: do we have the wherewithal to manage the world's resources as a global community without getting into a cold war with China or other energy-hungry nations? This race is on too.

FAST-FORWARD

These five bitter challenges may seem insurmountable, but they are not. What is needed—in order to fix economic imbalances, unemployment, climate change, and the financial stagnation that threatens our democratic societies—is a new surge of Creative Execution. We need the collective wisdom and confidence to innovate and find new solutions to problems. Creativity and innovation are the antidotes to the poison coursing through the world's veins, which is why despite the economic uncertainty and austerity measures introduced in Europe and North America, research and development spending on innovation is on the rise. According to a Booz & Company report, the companies they track in their Global Innovation 1000 study increased research and development spending from $521 billion in 2008 to $550 billion in 2010. We might have lost some faith in our governments and banks, but companies are betting that innovation is the key to growth. More importantly, we need new kinds of leaders who won't be afraid to think boldly, collaborate, and embrace the global matrix we find ourselves woven into.

To better understand how Creative Execution started its eastward march, and became the godfather of some of the world's most striking business successes, we'll travel next to Japan, where a man named Toyoda built a company that pushed the United States automobile industry to the brink of extinction.

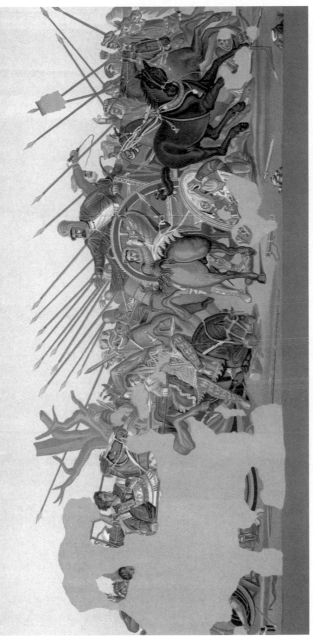

This mosaic from a villa in Pompeii is one of the only ancient depictions of Alexander the Great charging the Persian lines, presumably at the Battle of Issus or perhaps Gaugamela. King Darius is at the right in his royal chariot, under pressure and about to flee the battle.

The Right Hon.ble **ADMIRAL LORD NELSON**, Duke of Bronte, &c.
Who gloriously fell in the Battle of Trafalgar on the 21st of October 1805.

Portrait of Horatio Nelson 1758–1805, English Admiral.

The price of Visible Leadership: Admiral Horatio Nelson is struck by a bullet from a French sharpshooter and collapses on the *Victory*'s deck during the Battle of Trafalgar. Nelson died after learning of the battle's outcome. His penultimate words were "Thank God I did my duty."

Portrait photograph of Japanese Admiral Isoroku Yamamoto, taken during the early 1940s, when he was Commander in Chief, Combined Fleet.

View looking up "Battleship Row" on 7 December 1941, after the Japanese attack. USS *Arizona* (BB-39) is in the center, burning furiously. To the left of her are USS *Tennessee* (BB-43) and the sunken USS *West Virginia* (BB-48).

General Schwarzkopf (right), confers with Chairman of the Joint Chiefs of Staff Colin Powell and Secretary of Defense Dick Cheney during the planning of Operation Desert Storm in February 1991.

Margaret Bourke-White/Getty Images

A Toyota assembly plant in 1952. At the time, American automobile manufacturers reigned supreme. By reducing waste and introducing just-in-time assembly techniques, Toyota would create its own Creative Execution formula to take on GM, Ford and Chrysler in the US and Europe.

Google founders Larry Page (to the left) and Sergey Brin, at ease at their Mountain View headquarters. Larry and Sergey were each worth $16.7 billion by 2011—ten years after they struck up a relationship on the campus of Stanford University.

During his first presidential election campaign, President Obama went to Berlin to make a speech in front of 250,000 Germans, after which he also visited Israel. This bold move showed American voters that he had what it takes to be the leader of the free world. He called on Europeans and Americans to "remake the world once again" —a task that will require many more feats of Creative Execution.

Toyota's Road to Supremacy

*When the decision is made to act, we move fast in execution
because everyone is already fully bought in and in accord.*

—Jim Press, former president of
Toyota Motor North America

No other statistic tells the story of American manufacturing's post–
World War II surge than the automobile industry. In 1950, U.S. car
manufacturers dominated the global market with 80 percent of the
world's automobile production rolling off the assembly lines of Ford,
General Motors (GM), and Chrysler. That's right: eight of every ten
cars manufactured 60 years ago were "Made in USA" beauties, with
classics like the Cadillac Eldorado Brougham (which cost a whopping
$13,000 back in 1957), the envy of every global denizen. In 1955, *Time*
magazine named GM's president, Harlow Curtice, Man of the Year,
touting that his "skill, daring and foresight are forever opening new
frontiers for the expanding American economy."[1]

GM's rise to the top was mirrored by Ford and Chrysler. By 1965,
the Big Three's market share in the United States reached a staggering
90 percent. But as Japanese and other foreign manufacturers got into
the game, the Big Three's iron grip began to give way. By 2010, their
combined market share in the United States fell below 45 percent.

This vertiginous decline saw General Motors, at one time the world's largest company with more than 850,000 employees, go from boom to bust in one critical decade, from about 1997, when it was still flush with cash, to 2009, when CEO Rick Wagoner joined the CEOs of Ford and Chrysler to humbly ask for a $13.4-billion government bailout to keep their companies afloat. As Ron Pinelli, president of the research firm Autodata said in 2007, "The world is changing . . . We were all brought up with the greatness of General Motors, and that these companies were infallible. Times are different today."[2] By the end of 2008, GM and Ford's earnings were so dismal that the two companies' *combined* market valuation was a mere $7.5 billion, while Toyota's market valuation exceeded $100 billion. When GM finally reported its 2008 year-end sales numbers, the last shoe had dropped: for the first time in its history, Toyota had outsold GM. The final 2008 tally saw Toyota sell 8.97 million vehicles worldwide, compared to 8.35 million for GM.

The writing had been on the wall for GM since 1986, when the company reported a $1-billion loss in its first quarter and announced plans to cut 30,000 jobs and close 12 manufacturing plants. GM's parts supplier, Delphi, declared bankruptcy in October 2005—the first serious signal that things were falling off the rails in Detroit. That same year, Ford lost $1.6 billion in its North American operations and had to structure a bailout package for its former parts division, Visteon. In October 2008, GM announced that its oldest factory in the United States, based in Janesville, Wisconsin, was shutting down. At one point Janesville had been the crown jewel of GM's operations, churning out 20,000 SUVs each month. GM had bet on SUVs—and lost to the Prius. Industry observer Alex Taylor, who covered GM for 30 years, wrote a striking cover story on GM for *Fortune* magazine that sounded like an obituary. In the end, he asked, "whether the insular, self-absorbed culture that still dominates GM is up to the job of restructuring the company quickly enough to make it profitable and competitive again."[3] By the time GM reported losses of $38.7 billion for 2008, the stage was set for the curtain to drop. The company filed for bankruptcy in June 2009, and had to rely on the U.S. and Canadian governments to keep its plants open.

While 2008 was the banner year when Toyota overtook GM, the company quickly learned that the art of staying on top is just as difficult as getting there. Hit by the global financial crisis and the spate of defects that forced the company to recall 9 million vehicles worldwide, Toyota went from playing offense to defense in a matter of months. The March 2011 earthquake in Japan and floods in Thailand further impacted the company's production, causing the shutdowns of Toyota's plants worldwide and trimming profits by 19 percent. With car production by the Japanese Big Three (Toyota, Honda, and Nissan) down by one-fifth from April to September 2011, Ford, GM, and Chrysler (the latter now owned by Italian carmaker Fiat) saw their chance to grab back some lost market share. For the first time in over four decades, Ford and GM clawed back market share in 2011. Yet despite Toyota's woes, which we will revisit at the conclusion of this chapter, the company's market valuation remains $100 billion, compared to $34 billion for GM and $38 billion for Ford. And despite GM, Chrysler, and Ford's much-heralded comeback, the bestselling car in North America remains the Toyota Camry as this book goes to print.

Building on Japan's postwar drive to remake itself into an economic powerhouse, Toyota developed new concepts like *kaizen* to embed quality and innovation into its products, earning praise from customers and winning awards that set it apart from its peers. Despite the fact that its design labs are entirely based in Japan (along with 40 percent of its global manufacturing), Toyota seemed better able to anticipate and meet the needs of American consumers than the Big Three companies headquartered in Detroit. Toyota's foresight became evident when oil prices reached $145 a barrel in 2008, and the company was ready to roll out not one but three blockbuster hybrids—the Prius, Camry, and Highlander—whereas GM had to scramble to shut down its SUV production and could not start delivery of its first hybrid car, the Volt, until December 2010.

How did Toyota manage its rise from last to first, and become twice as valuable as America's Big Three companies? Like Charles Dickens's novel of revolutionary France and England, the battle between Toyota and GM is a tale of two hardened cities, Detroit and Toyota City. And an epic tale it is, with players changing sides and placing big bets on technology, people, and markets. Like Japan's conquest of East Asia in 1941, the question remains: will Toyota be able to maintain its leadership position over the next 20 years, or will it experience its own reversal, like Yamamoto did at Midway? Let's take a look at how Toyota mastered Creative Execution, and what the future holds for the Japanese and American automotive juggernauts.

TOYOTA'S RISE TO POWER

The story of Toyota, in many ways, parallels the history of Japan. For centuries, Japan had remained an isolated country that strictly forbade its citizens from trading with the West. Then in 1853, Commodore Matthew Perry led an expedition of five steam-powered ships to Japan with the aim of convincing the Japanese emperor to conduct limited trade with the United States. The Japanese, who had never seen a steam-powered ship, thought Perry's vessels looked like "giant dragons puffing smoke."[4] Perry spent six months anchored in Edo Bay off Tokyo, pressing his demands for Japan to enter into a commercial relationship with the United States and refusing to deal with lesser officials. When the emperor finally sent his personal emissary to meet with this unwanted guest, Perry negotiated the first peace and friend-ship treaty between Japan and a Western power, and more impor-tantly secured access to two Japanese harbors, Shimoda and Hakodate. American ships were allowed to buy coal, water, and other supplies off Japanese merchants, which meant they could sail to Japan loaded with cargo and resupply there for the journey home.

As Japan slowly opened up its market to the United States and Europe, it began a rapid modernization of its economy and infrastruc-ture known as the Meiji era, under the rule of Emperor Mutsuhito.

Suddenly, Japan became obsessed with learning as much as it could from the West. The Meiji charter stated that "Knowledge shall be sought throughout the world so as to strengthen the foundations of imperial rule."[5] More than 3,000 foreign experts called *gaikokujin*, or "hired foreigners," were brought into Japan to teach the fundamentals of engineering, science, languages, and modern warfare. The most visible outcome of this radical period of modernization, as we already saw, was the Japanese mastery of naval warfare culminating in the Battle of Tsushima in 1905, when Japan's navy quickly sent the entire Russian Baltic Fleet to the bottom of the Sea of Japan. In the space of 50 years, the Japanese had gone from kowtowing to Commodore Perry's five "dragon boats" to establishing naval supremacy and taking down one of the world's most advanced navies. This pattern would repeat itself with Japan's manufacturing industry, and with Toyota's challenge to GM.

As Japan modernized its economy in the Meiji era, much like England did during the Industrial Revolution, the main commercial industry that felt an immediate lift was textile manufacturing. In 1894, a young man named Sakichi Toyoda, who grew up in a small farming community outside Nagoya, began to build manual looms, and later bought a steam engine to provide power for his first automatic loom. After a few years of trial and error, Toyoda had refined his invention and in 1926 he founded the Toyoda Automatic Loom Works. Toyoda's inventiveness and willingness to take risks elevated his prestige in Japan, to the point that he earned the nickname "King of Inventors." His power looms, according to one observer, became "as famous as Mikimoto pearls and Suzuki violins."[6]

Sakichi's son, Kiichiro Toyoda, learned the loom-making business from his father. His first task was to travel to England to study the art of spinning and weaving from the leading British company, Platt Brothers. Much like Admiral Togo at the time, and Admiral Yamamoto years later, Toyoda had no qualms about absorbing European technology and improving upon it. And when, in 1930, Platt Brothers offered one million yen (about $20 million in those days) to buy the Japanese company, Kiichiro took the money and founded the Toyota Motor

Corporation. Ironically, given what happened in 2011, Toyoda had witnessed the extensive damage caused to Japan's infrastructure in a large earthquake that struck the Japanese islands in 1923, and yearned to create a Japanese automobile manufacturing company that would hasten the development of the country's road transportation system, much like Ford was doing in the United States. As David Magee writes, "it didn't matter that Loom Works' fortune had been made from the weaving equipment or that Japan had no expertise in high-level machine design and manufacturing; in developing an automobile, the Toyodas saw an opportunity to pursue one of Sakichi Toyoda's business ideals: the betterment of people through creative enterprise."[7]

Toyota made its first car in 1935, using a Chevrolet engine and Chrysler body. Unlike Ford, which had mastered the art of assembly-line manufacturing, Toyota was a low-tech company, with workers hammering body panels together over wooden logs. The company produced trucks for the Japanese army in World War II, and in 1947 produced a new basic car, the Model SA, which became its first mass-produced vehicle. The company's foreign adventures began in the 1950s, when a new president, Eiji Toyoda, took his management team on a 12-week tour of Ford plants in the United States. As Eiji Toyoda visited each plant, he made a number of observations about how Toyota could improve on Ford's formula. As Jeffrey Liker explains, "[Ford's] production system had many inherent flaws . . . they saw lots of equipment making large amounts of products that were stored in inventory, only to be later moved to another department where big equipment processed the product . . . resulting in a lot of overproduction and a very uneven flow, with defects hidden in these large batches that could go undiscovered for weeks."[8] Thus began Toyota's obsession with quality and lean manufacturing. Starting in the 1950s, Toyota developed a manufacturing philosophy that completely eliminated waste, and ensured that no auto parts were produced until they were needed for the next step in a vehicle's assembly. This became the core concept in the Toyota Production System, known by its acronym TPS, which slowly became the envy of European and American carmakers.

Toyota started to manufacture cars for the U.S. market in 1965, with basic small models like the Corona. The company had developed a strong lineup of subcompact cars, but in the United States GM still seemed like an impregnable fortress. In 1985 *Fortune* ran a cover story titled "Will success spoil General Motors?" and showed on its cover four of GM's cars that the company touted as weapons of mass-market domination. Looking for ways to gain a foothold in this lucrative market, Toyota entered into a partnership with—are you ready—GM! Through a joint venture called NUMMI, which stands for New United Motor Manufacturing, Inc., Toyota gave GM the keys to its prized TPS in exchange for the right to start building cars at one of GM's plants in Fremont, California. NUMMI became the proving ground for Toyota in North America, allowing it to run a factory in the United States with the same philosophy and methods it used in Japan. The joint venture was run by an American, Gary Convis, a former Ford executive who was stunned by the efficiency of the Japanese system in operation: "To me, it was like looking at a symphony. Everybody knew their instrument and their music."[9] At NUMMI, Toyota refined its knowledge of American consumers and workforce, in effect turning the small California plant into a beachhead for its U.S. invasion. Its respectful attitude toward the U.S. market and established companies like Ford and GM made it appear unthreatening. Yet once its first beachhead in the United States was established, Toyota became determined to conquer the entire North American continent.

Other than Gary Convis, the other American executive Toyota recruited to help turn its North American vision into reality was Jim Press, who left Ford in 1970 to become president of Toyota Motor North America, and later became the first *gaijin* (foreigner) to be appointed to Toyota's board of directors. After noting that "the people in this company are more selfless. They have less ego and less 'I'm in it for me,'"[10] Jim Press pushed the company to build full-size cars like the Camry that would, in the 1980s and 1990s, start winning the affection of American customers for their reliability, quality finish, and competitive pricing. On the back of his business card, Jim Press had brazenly printed, "If you or anyone you know has had trouble with a Toyota, call me."[11]

On the heels of its success working with GM at NUMMI, where it continued to crank out Corollas and Tacoma trucks for the American market until April 2010 (when the venture finally shut down), Toyota made the bold decision to open a number of plants in the United States. The first—and largest—plant opened in 1984 in Georgetown, Kentucky, with more than 7,500 employees. The Kentucky plant has the capacity to build over 500,000 Camrys, Avalons, Solaras, and Camry Hybrids each year, although its production pace slowed down in 2009 following the global economic downturn. Toyota then made its next big bet in Canada, opening a 5,000-employee plant to manufacture the Lexus RX, Corolla, and Matrix. Whereas it still operates its original 1938 plant on the outskirts of Nagoya, along with 14 other plants throughout Japan, Toyota has now turned itself into a global company. It operates 13 plants in North America, five in South America, eight in Europe, two in Africa, one each in Australia and Bangladesh, four in Thailand, and no fewer than ten plants in China! Out of its 317,000 employees, fewer than 125,000 are based on the Japanese home islands.

TOYOTA'S CREATIVE EXECUTION FORMULA

Toyota's success on the world stage stems from two primary advantages that the Japanese company has nurtured over the past 70 years: one is the Toyota Production System (TPS), which the Toyoda family developed and fine-tuned after its study of Ford's manufacturing facilities in the United States; the second is Toyota's deep listening culture, which has allowed the company to make the right choices for customers while retaining a humble, learning attitude. As Hirotaka Takeuchi, Emi Osono, and Norihiko Shimizu wrote in the *Harvard Business Review* after studying Toyota for six years, "TPS is a 'hard' innovation that allows the company to keep improving the way it manufactures vehicles; in addition, Toyota has mastered a 'soft' innovation that relates to corporate culture . . . The hard and soft innovations work in tandem. Like two wheels on a shaft that bear equal weight, together they move the company forward."[12] Let's take a look at the TPS and Toyota's culture, and see how these two success factors feed into the Creative Execution formula that Alexander the Great first tested 2,000 years ago.

The Toyota Production System

The foundation of Toyota's production system was first laid out by Sakichi Toyoda when he set out to create more efficient looms than his British counterparts. "The ideal conditions for making things are created when machines, facilities, and people work together to add value without generating any waste," he declared.[13] When Toyota started to emulate Ford's manufacturing system in the early 1900s, it did so with a unique lens that aimed at eliminating waste and ensuring that body parts, engines, and other car components only made their way onto the assembly line when needed. These TPS concepts evolved over time so that every Toyota plant around the world now embraces two fundamental TPS practices: one is *jidoka*, which roughly translates into "automation with a human touch," and means that should any defective part or equipment find its way on the assembly line, the machine or process involved automatically stops so that the problem can be addressed. The best example of *jidoka* in action is the andon cord, a cord connected to a light display that indicates the status of each machine. When employees see a defect or problem, they are required to pull the andon cord and stop the entire automation line to which the machine is connected. This ensures that no defect enters the production line and that any problem is immediately recognized and dealt with.

You may think that this would be an embarrassing event for an employee supervising a machine, but at Toyota pulling the andon cord is widely praised and recognized. At Toyota's Kentucky plant, employees pull the andon cord an average of five thousand times a day. As David

Magee explains, "One of the only ways employees can get in trouble . . . is by *not* pulling the andon cord if a problem is spotted or suspected. So important is the andon cord and what it stands for in Toyota's system that using it properly is one of the primary points of being a good employee."[14] Indeed, a Toyota plant manager who boasted to his Japanese boss that his plant had experienced no shutdowns for a month was quickly told that he was "hiding his problems." Under the TPS rules, halting production is a positive sign that problems are being proactively resolved, whereas in GM and Ford plants, machine downtime is widely viewed as undesirable.

The second key element of the TPS is "just-in-time" production, which stipulates that each plant will only produce "what is needed, when it is needed, and in the amount needed."[15] Having seen the stockpiles of unused automotive parts sitting in Ford's plants, and short of the cash required to build large stockpiles, Toyota decided early on that it would only start building a car when it was ordered by a customer—which is why the company doesn't sit on a huge inventory of unsold vehicles. Plants only keep a small amount of parts that are required to start the assembly and order what they need as each car enters the production flow. Toyota's production system is a little bit like going through a MacDonald's drive-through. Once you place your order, worker bees start to make the car so that it's ready exactly when the customer wants it. Fresh components are ordered every day to match the production rhythm. There is little waste of time, energy, and parts. According to Liker, "the power of JIT [just-in-time production] is that it allows you to be responsive to the day-to-day shifts in customer demand, which was exactly what Toyota needed all along."[16]

The "pull" system of production enabled by just-in-time manufacturing has huge advantages. Over the past 30 years, Toyota has been able to eliminate waste and costs while *improving* the quality of its products. And while the principles of *jidoka* and just-in-time are well known to GM through the NUMMI partnership, they have been extremely difficult to emulate. "TPS was revered, studied, and copied throughout the world," notes Magee. But even though several North

American and European companies have embraced lean manufacturing and *kaizen* after looking at Toyota's model, "most companies made only piecemeal efforts" and weren't able to reap the broad benefits inherent in Toyota's system.[17]

Why did companies like Ford, GM, and Chrysler fail to adopt Toyota's production system? The main reason, I believe, is that Toyota's approach to lean manufacturing has been embedded in the company's mindset for generations, starting with the Toyoda loom business. Workers at Toyota plants don't learn about lean manufacturing or *jidoka* as an extracurricular activity. The TPS is built around these concepts, starting with the pull system and the andon cords. You can't work at Toyota without following the "Toyota Way," the company's guiding principles. Ford and GM's roots, by contrast, were seeded around the concept of large-scale assembly and mass-production—in the 1950s and 1960s, for instance, Ford produced 10 times as many cars as Toyota on its assembly lines. So ironically the lesson GM learned from Toyota is the same lesson the United States military taught the Soviet Union and the rest of the world during the Cold War, and made obvious by the success of Desert Storm: it's better to focus on superior quality rather than produce large numbers. While GM was focused on being the world's biggest car company, Toyota was focused on being the best car manufacturer in the world. Likewise, the U.S. military never tried to match the Soviet Union and the Warsaw Pact in quantity of weapons, but instead came up with outstanding designs such as the M1 Abrams tank that outclassed Soviet tanks in everything from speed and protection to accurate firepower. Toyota's TPS, like the constellation of private and public defense labs in the United States, is what ensures that the company retains its edge over time.

Toyota's Deep Listening Culture

It sounds like the TPS might create a rigid, highly controlled environment for Toyota's employees, but in fact the reverse is true. Toyota's culture is one that encourages people to think for themselves, solve problems creatively using *jidoka*, *kaizen*, and continuous improvement, and contribute to the company's overall growth and performance. As Hiroshi Okuda, president of Toyota in the 1990s, carefully explains, Toyota expects its managers to "create energetic workplaces in which younger employees can make their stand without hesitation, fully utilizing their spontaneity, intelligence and senses."[18] There is a sense across Toyota that employees can and do make a difference every day. Or as Magee puts it, "a central element of maintaining the same culture at Toyota year after year is encouraging employees to find different and new ways of contributing."[19]

When explaining the Toyota culture, North American president Jim Lentz simply said: "there is no Toyota dust . . . no hypnotic suggestions . . . no smoke and mirrors. We just work very hard to 'listen' to our customers and then do all we can to help our dealers respond in the showroom."[20] This attitude of constant listening and learning is what propelled Toyota in North America, where it had no presence before the NUMMI experiment.

Toyota's culture was forged in the challenge of starting a car company out of the rubble of World War II, which had decimated Japan's economy and prestige around the world. When you read the Toyota Way, the internal document that describes the company's values and behaviors, you can still feel the brazen hope and sense of desperation that fed Toyota's climb to power. "We accept challenges with a creative spirit and the courage to realize our own dreams without losing drive or energy," the document states. "We strive to decide our own fate. We act with self-reliance, trusting in our own abilities."[21] The idealism of the Toyota Way smacks more like the American Declaration of Independence, or the Charter of Rights written during the French Revolution, than it does a corporate credo. While General Douglas MacArthur and his staff took it upon themselves to write a new constitution for Japan during the U.S. postwar occupation, the Toyota Way became a symbol of Japanese resilience and commitment to regain its status as a legitimate world power. It achieved this not through the arrogant and brutal conquest that was undertaken in 1941, but through a much more humble, customer-focused culture. Through the Creative Execution lens, we shall see that Toyota's culture reinforces its strategy for global growth on all aspects of the spectrum.

Unique Strategy

When Sakichi Toyoda asked his son Kiichiro to take over the Toyota Motor Company, and find ways to emulate or beat Ford, he made it clear that he wanted his son to aim high: "Everyone should tackle some great project at least once in his life," he told him. "I devoted most of my life to inventing new kinds of looms. Now it is your turn."[22] Sakichi didn't hand his son a strategic document that explained how he was supposed to build a car company from scratch. But he infused him with a clear sense of purpose that led Kiichiro to outline a vague but compelling strategy for Toyota's early days: the company would learn what it could from the giant American carmaker, improve its processes, and meet evolving customer demands first at home, in Japan, and later around the world.

This long-term operating philosophy is what has driven Toyota forward since 1938. As Magee writes when he describes Toyota's long march into North America, the company's executives "did not abandon their long-term strategy to chase the next new thing . . . they moved methodically, and executed the plans that had been in place for years."[23] There is indeed a consistency about Toyota's strategic direction since the company entered the U.S. market in the early 1980s that is quite remarkable. Toyota has never wavered from its commitment to build the highest-quality vehicles, at the lowest possible cost, while investing significantly in its North American infrastructure and communities.

Under its new CEO, the grandson of founder Kiichiro Toyoda, Toyota has a crisp global vision, which says that "through our commitment to quality, constant innovation and respect for the planet, we aim to exceed expectations and be rewarded with a smile."[24] While it may sound overly idealistic, this vision is what has allowed Toyota to be forward-looking, getting into hybrid production 10 years ahead of its North American rivals, for instance. As Takeuchi and his colleagues explain, "Toyota tries to cater to every segment because of its belief that a car contributes to making people happy."[25] The focus on meeting customer needs, which change with time, provides a compelling backdrop that sets the company apart from all its rivals.

The other aspect of Toyota's strategy that resembles Alexander's and Nelson's is its simplicity. In fact, as Takeuchi also notes, "it's an unwritten Toyota rule that employees must keep language simple when communicating with each other." There's a special format for business cases used at Toyota that's about one-page long, and includes a brief background, analysis, recommended actions, and expected results. A Unique Strategy, simply communicated and easily understood, is key to the company's Creative Execution formula.

Candid Dialogue

The backbone of Toyota's culture is the fact that managers and employees are direct and honest, and that employees' ideas are actively solicited. As part of its *kaizen*—or continuous improvement—strategy, Toyota encourages employees to make suggestions to their managers about any aspect of their workplace—from the location of the employee cafeteria to the layout of assembly-line tools and machines. More than 600,000 such suggestions are put forward by Toyota employees in Japan alone in any given year, and almost all are accepted and implemented.

Takeuchi, Osono, and Shimizu didn't call it Candid Dialogue, but the fact that Toyota has a strict hierarchy, but gives employees freedom to voice their opinions or question management decisions makes Toyota a unique company. In their article, Takeuchi, Osono, and Shimizu acknowledge that they were "surprised to hear criticism about the company and senior management in our interviews, but employees didn't seem worried. They felt that they were doing the right thing by offering executives constructive criticism."[26] Toyota's culture of contradictions, they found, was based on Candid Dialogue between managers, factory workers, and senior executives. "Toyota deliberately fosters contradictory viewpoints within the organization and challenges employees to find solutions by transcending differences rather than resorting to compromises," they explain.[27] Candid Dialogue, in essence, is the secret sauce that powers the Toyota Production System and the company's ability to continuously improve (*kaizen*). By contrast, *Fortune* writer Alex Taylor notes that "At GM, conformity was everything, and rebellion was frowned upon."[28]

The fact that employees know that they can safely bring up ideas for improvement, and that immediately reporting what's not working or defective is an absolute requirement of *jidoka*, means that Toyota's success is directly related to Candid Dialogue. As Magee writes, "Toyota's culture does not chastise lower-ranking employees for bringing problems to their superiors."[29] He compares Toyota to GM, where an hourly worker "confided that if he didn't show up at work for a month, it would be less of a problem than if he suggested to a superior that a process or decision was hurting the company." The same flaw in Candid Dialogue plagued Alan Mulally when he took over as CEO of Ford in 2006. After finding that the rosy financial picture his executives were presenting didn't add up, he was told by a manager, "we don't share everything."[30]

Clear Roles and Accountabilities

Toyota's culture is a blend of loose matrix structure and a vast informal network of relationships. Whereas every employee knows his or her role in the matrix, there is a clear expectation that listening and teamwork are required of every single employee. To achieve this goal, Toyota has deployed a number of unique concepts. Factory general managers walk the floor of Toyota's assembly plants every day. Dealers are brought into design and operational conversations much more frequently than they would be at, say, Ford and GM. Employees work in *obeya*, large open spaces without partitions, to encourage the sharing of information. Each employee belongs to several committees, study groups, or social networks that link together different parts of the company. When Toyota first opened the doors to its NUMMI partnership with GM, it brought not bosses to the factory but *sensei* (teachers) whose job was to help American workers understand TPS.

Another unique role at Toyota is that of *shusa*, a chief engineer or program manager who has complete responsibility for the development of a new vehicle. The *shusa* isn't a traditional project manager who acts as a coach and tries to influence sales or engineering. As *Fortune* magazine describes it, "The *shusa* is responsible for a program's business success. He defines a vehicle's intended market and is responsible for hitting targets of cost, weight, performance, and quality."[31] The *shusa* is the focal point of a new vehicle's success—or defects—and is clearly accountable for the end product. He provides the leadership direction for everyone from manufacturing to sales.

The Toyota leadership system stands in stark contrast to a traditional company like Ford, where, according to Magee, "those charged with execution were frequently doing one thing while the company leader was saying another." At Toyota, on the other hand, the company's performance is clearly built on "the strength of a management structure that empowers employees, turning managers and leaders more into facilitators and coaches than bosses and autocrats."[32] When Gary Convis joined Toyota as a senior executive for its North American operations, the advice he received from his Japanese mentors was revealing. They instructed him to "manage as if he had no power."[33] This is reflective of Toyota's broader culture of having clear roles and accountabilities, yet pushing decision making down to the lowest possible level and engaging as many people in providing their opinion and advice as possible. As Magee explains, every executive must "remain willing to learn, to leave ego out of the equation, and to maintain a willingness to personally 'go and see' to determine facts and ensure that viable decisions are made."[34]

The decision-making process at Toyota has evolved considerably over the past 20 years to match its global reach and adapt to local markets. As former president Hiroshi Okuda explains, after he took over the company in 1995, "I wanted to create high-speed, flexible car-making with aggressive overseas expansion, ready to pounce on consumer trends, always drawing inspiration from human lifestyles."[35] Under Okuda's leadership, the number of approvals required to make product changes, using Toyota's *ringi* system of escalation, shrank from twenty to just three. Okuda reshaped the company's overall structure to be flatter, brought in younger board members, and began an earnest drive to change the company's promotion system to be merit based, rather than the seniority system most unionized companies are saddled with.

Toyota's emphasis on respect, carefully listening to others' opinions, and the power of teams to influence decisions is not an easy process to navigate. Large Western companies that have embraced matrix management have found that managing the relationship between functional groups and regional operating companies is a difficult task. As Liker explains, "Toyota has established an excellent balance between individual work and group work, and between individual excellence and team effectiveness. While teamwork is critical, having individuals work together in a group does not compensate for a lack of individual excellence or understanding of Toyota's system."[36] This fine balance between individual and team contribution is a key aspect of Toyota's culture, which places emphasis not on formal power and authority but rather on active and selfless contribution to the company's objectives.

Bold Action

From its partnership with NUMMI to its early investment in hybrid vehicles, Toyota has made bold decisions that have allowed the company to expand its market share at the expense of American and European car companies. In 1983, Eiji Toyoda challenged his executive team with a simple question: "Can Toyota create a luxury vehicle to challenge the world's best?" After building 450 prototypes and investing $1 billion in research and development, Toyoda's team produced the Lexus LS400, which was launched in the United States in 1989. Within a few years Lexus became a top luxury brand in North America, with 300,000 vehicles sold annually. As Magee observes, "The 1992 Camry and the development of Lexus validated the company's ability not only to duplicate its success in designing and building for the American market, but also to do so raising the bar to greater heights than ever before in the company's history."[37]

Toyota now has a full lineup of its most popular cars and SUVs, including the Camry, Prius, and Venza crossover, available as hybrids. When the Camry won its first Motor Trend Car of the Year award in 2007, beating out 26 other redesigned vehicles, editor-in-chief Angus MacKenzie made this awe-inspiring comment: "The Camry is the one car rival automakers all wish they could build. It offers something for nearly everyone—performance, efficiency and roominess—at a price point most Americans can afford."[38] In other words, Toyota hit the sweet spot. It was asking more questions, and making bold bets redesigning cars that other manufacturers would leave unchanged for several more years.

While GM, Chrysler, and Ford were placing big bets on their truck and SUV lineups, Toyota anticipated the trend toward smaller and more energy-efficient vehicles. In 1995, it began the design of a brand-new hybrid vehicle, the Prius. As *Fortune* reported when Prius became the hottest selling car in the United States, "Toyota is capable of breaking its own rules when it needs to . . . In rushing the Prius to market, it abandoned its traditional consensus management, as executives resorted to such unusual practices . . . of setting targets and enforcing deadlines that many considered unattainable."[39] The targets Toyota set were indeed lofty: the goal was to design an engine twice as fuel-efficient as the Corolla's, and sell 1-million units a year by the time the third generation Prius came on the market in 2009. Instead of the typical three months required to create design sketches for the first model, the company gave its designers three weeks. In another bold move, the company decided to pre-sell the Prius to U.S. buyers over the Internet, which drew the attention of 37,000 prospective customers.

By the time 2011 came around, Toyota's big bet on the Prius had turned into gold: it had sold 1 million in the United States, and 1 million in Japan. As of this writing, the third-generation Prius has already sold more than a million units.

The bold decision to launch into full-scale hybrid-vehicle production was rewarded as the Prius quickly became, in the words of Jim Press, "the hottest car we've ever had."[40] Did GM take equally bold steps to develop a hybrid? In 2004, GM vice-chairman Bob Lutz called hybrids "an interesting curiosity."[41] By the time GM started designing the Volt, Toyota had already invested $1 billion in hybrid technology and was already working on its next bestseller, the Venza crossover, which made its North American debut in 2008. Jeff Liker sums it up best. Even after the successful launch of the Prius, he says, "Toyota still had a crisis mentality, and Toyota leaders regularly stir the pot even creating a crisis when necessary."[42]

Visible Leadership

From the top down, Toyota's leaders are active participants in the company's day-to-day operations, from the floor plant to dealers' showrooms. Akio Toyoda, the company's very visible new CEO, explained it best in an interview he gave in February 2008: "If I am going to be at the top of the car company, I want to be the owner-chef."[43] Toyota's senior executives, like Akio Toyoda, are expected to be visible, humble, and participative. The Toyoda family, in fact, lives together in a modest compound, despite controlling 40 percent of the company's voting stocks.

Gary Convis, who spent 20 years at Toyota and became one of the company's most senior North American executives, exemplified Visible Leadership every day when he drove his subcompact Corolla into Toyota's Kentucky plant. Instead of an assigned parking spot, he had to fend for himself like a regular employee. Inside the plant, Magee writes, Convis "walks through the assembly plant daily so that hourly workers know he is in the trenches with them, trying to solve problems . . . he tries not to distance himself from workers by displaying any hint of executive arrogance, which can be distracting, if not totally out of place."[44] As further evidence, Toyota's CEO pulls an annual salary of $1 million, with a bonus that brought him to $1.7 million in 2011. The average executive pay at Toyota is a very reasonable $500,000. By contrast, the highest paid CEO among the U.S. Big Three, Alan Mulally of Ford, pulled in $3.34 million in 2011.

LIFE AT THE TOP: TOYOTA'S CREATIVE EXECUTION STRUGGLES

When Toyota finally passed GM as the world's number one carmaker in 2008, the company's former president, Katsuaki Watanabe (now vice chairman), wisely played down the milestone's significance. Instead of fireworks in Toyota City, Watanabe warned his employees that "the change in the world economy is of a magnitude that comes once every hundred years."[45] Toyota was quickly revising sales forecasts as the global recession dampened global car demand, and recorded its first operating loss since opening shop in 1938. Although Toyota subsidiary Daihatsu managed a reasonable 4 percent increase in global sales in 2009, Toyota sales in Japan and around the world dipped by 5 percent. As traffic through Toyota showrooms in North America fell by as much as 60 percent in 2007 and 2008, Toyota's U.S. president, Jim Lentz, reluctantly agreed that "the good times we've been riding for over a decade are temporarily on hiatus."[46] Despite the timely introduction of its hybrid lineup, Toyota wasn't immune to the global financial crisis, which drastically reduced financing options for consumers.

As the financial crisis slowly receded, Toyota started feeling the heat from another unexpected source: faulty car mats. Following the highly publicized death of a California highway patrolman whose Lexus E350 sped out of control and crashed at more than 100 miles per hour, a host of quality issues forced Toyota to recall 7 million cars in the United States alone. After appearing before a special committee of the U.S. Congress, CEO Akio Toyoda declared that Toyota's employees would from then on put their "heart and soul" into every vehicle, "just as mothers make rice bowls for their children."[47] The total financial loss from the recalls in 2009 and 2010 came to more than $5 billion, but more embarrassing was the fact that Toyota admitted to knowing about the faulty floor mats since 2007. Federal regulators in the United States fined Toyota $48.8 million for its slow response, and more importantly Toyota's sterling quality reputation was seriously dented. In 2010, *Consumer Reports* found that 19 percent of respondents rated Toyota as providing the highest quality, compared to 30 percent in 2009. Reeling from this negative publicity, Toyota then found itself hard hit by the March 2011 earthquake. Toyota was the victim of its own just-in-time manufacturing philosophy, with plants in Japan and North America unable to source the parts they needed. For several months, plants in Japan operated at half volume, and those in North America cut production by 75 percent.

Will Toyota rebound and maintain its 15 percent U.S. market share despite its quality and production issues? Automotive experts have revised their forecast for Toyota through 2025, projecting that the company will need that long to rebuild its public image. If you look at what Toyota and its new CEO have done to respond to the crisis, however, an interesting pattern emerges: Toyota is developing a new culture based on the Creative Execution formula to extricate itself from the crisis its previous success created. How? Since the crisis hit, Toyota created a new global vision, Akio Toyoda became a more visible CEO than all his predecessors combined, the company became a lot more candid about admitting past mistakes, it appointed a North American quality executive and gave people in the United States more decision-making powers, and, finally, it took Bold Action by recalling faulty vehicles much more quickly and proactively. All five elements of the Creative Execution formula are present in Toyota's rebirth. Lentz admitted that "We are a totally different company than when this crisis took place."[48]

And so while Toyota has met the Creative Execution challenge set out by Kiichiro Toyoda, and developed into a company that helped rebuild Japan's industrial base and national pride, it is now faced with a new challenge: rebuilding itself, and while doing so re-earning the trust of consumers worldwide. But perhaps Toyota's most important lesson to us is that the company has clearly shown how Creative Execution is open to any start-up or company willing to apply its five principles, regardless of the company's historical or cultural roots. And that's exactly what Issy Sharp, founder of Four Seasons Hotels and Resorts, figured out when he took a look at the luxury hotel industry in 1960.

The Four Seasons Puts On the Ritz

Trust is the unseen and often overlooked determinant of corporate success.

—Issy Sharp, Founder and CEO,
Four Seasons Hotels

From his corporate headquarters in Toronto, Isadore Sharp can look back at his decision to build luxury hotels around the world with confident satisfaction. Better known as Issy, the Canadian hotelier has received every possible accolade, from the first Ruth Hartman Frankel Humanitarian Award to the Order of Canada, the country's highest civilian award. His 86 stunning properties around the world are consistently beating out the bigger heavyweights in the luxury hotel market—the Ritz-Carlton, Mandarin Oriental, and Hyatt—in both profitability and customer service. In its 2011 ranking of the world's top hotels, *Travel + Leisure* magazine gave the Four Seasons 20 of the top spots in the United States alone, and the year before anointed the Four Seasons Resort and Club Dallas at Las Colinas best hotel in the United States. The Four Seasons made *Fortune* magazine's list of 100 Best Companies to Work For in eight different countries in 2008, and continued to grace the list in 2012. Like the British Empire in the nineteenth century, the Four Seasons hotels are omnipresent in every corner of the world—from New York to Hong Kong—and leisure and business travelers are willing to part with $695 for one night at the Four Seasons Hotel New York on East 57th Street, or €790 for one night at the George V Paris, just steps off the Champs-Élysées.

Between 2008 and 2011, the Four Seasons opened more than 10 new hotels, including a refurbished nineteenth-century Ottoman palace in Istanbul, resorts in Bora Bora and Mauritius, and luxury hotels in St. Louis and Seattle. The company has 40 properties under development—and not where you'd expect them. Most are in the Middle East or North Africa, like Beirut and Marrakech, and Latin America and China. You may also be surprised to hear who owns Four Seasons hotels. Michael Dell, star founder of Dell Inc., owns two of the Four Seasons hotels in Hawaii. In 2007, Sharp struck a deal with two of the world's richest men, Bill Gates and Prince al-Waleed bin Talal, to sell them the lion's share of the company. Gates and Prince al-Waleed parted with $3.8 billion in order to each own 47.5 percent of the company, which is now wholly private. Sharp pocketed $289 million from the proceeds of the sale, in addition to $172 million in preferred shares and a 5-percent stake in the new company. Not a bad day to be CEO!

Things weren't always this rosy for Sharp and the Four Seasons. Sharp's family emigrated from Poland to Palestine and then Canada in 1924, with little money. His father, Max Sharp, started a building company where young Issy worked on and off while he completed his architecture degree from Ryerson University. On a trip to California with a university friend when he was just 18, Sharp was briefly arrested—and fined $5—for stealing a pillow from a motel. When he built his first property—a motel for business travelers where you could stay for $9 a night—Sharp had to plead with investors to lend him $1.5 million in financing. He admits that "my vision of the future was to take in enough cash today to pay yesterday's bills . . . ninety-five percent of everything was either borrowed or leased."[1] By the time the Four Seasons Motor Hotel opened its doors in March 1961, however, Sharp was hooked on the concept of building hotels that would increasingly set the standard for customer service in every city. The Four Seasons was first to introduce dual-line telephones, shampoo, and bathrobes in every room. Like Sakichi Toyoda, Sharp took a look at what his big competitors like the Hilton, Sheraton, and Ritz-Carlton were offering business travelers, and designed his own Creative Execution formula to go head-to-head—and win—in the global race to build the world's most successful luxury hotel brand. Let's take a look at how, starting with his Motor Hotel in Toronto, Issy Sharp planted the seeds for the Four Seasons' unlikely domination of the hotel business, which is worth an annual $484 billion on the global monopoly board.

SLEEPLESS IN TORONTO

Although the French first settled in Toronto in 1615, and created a trading post called Fort Rouillé in 1751, Toronto's growth as a major city started under British rule, when it replaced Niagara as the capital of Upper Canada. Despite repeated American invasions during the War of 1812, which led the British to retaliate by burning much of Washington, DC, and the White House in August 1814, Toronto continued to prosper as the Canadian center of commerce and industry. Its population grew from a modest 720 souls in 1814 to 667,500 by the middle of the twentieth century, and in the 1970s it surpassed Montreal as Canada's largest city. Toronto became a beacon for immigrants fleeing the devastated European continent in the aftermath of World War II; today more than half of the city's 2.5 million residents are born outside Canada—this author included.

This expanding metropolis, where 152 languages and dialects are harmoniously spoken, is where Max Sharp & Son received a contract to build a 14-room motel in the mid-1950s. The location of the motel intrigued Sharp. Despite sitting at the corner of two fairly remote highways, the motel was full every night. Sharp decided to strike out on his own to build a motel closer to the city's downtown core, and found a cheap plot of land at the corner of Jarvis and Carlton Streets, in the middle of Toronto's red-light district. Sharp was convinced that he could build a motel with enough class and amenities to attract business travelers, and overcome the negative image of the seedy neighborhood. "There was no vision," he admits. "I was just trying to put one deal together. A concept of combining the informality of a motel with the convenience of a downtown hotel."[2] The key to the hotel's design was the inner courtyard, which Sharp likens to "an oasis in the middle of turmoil."[3] After a successful opening night that included a fund-raising gala for the Toronto Symphony, Sharp watched the 125 rooms in the Four Seasons Motor Hotel fill up instantly, and turn his risky venture into a profitable hit.

Having survived his first hotel launch at age 29, Sharp turned his attention to a new property 15 minutes north of Toronto, where he decided to build a much more ambitious mid-size hotel overlooking 500 acres of parkland. Shaped like a parallelogram, the Inn on the Park became a famous landmark that helped establish Sharp as a bona fide hotel developer. While the Inn on the Park was 20 minutes away from the city's core, its striking architecture and gourmet restaurant became a magnet for business and leisure travelers. Even Soviet foreign minister Alexei Kosygin became a patron. More than his city motel, the Inn on the Park enabled Sharp to stretch the definition of customer service that would set him apart from other hoteliers. "It was a different atmosphere," Sharp recalls, "but the principle was exactly the same. You treated your customers in a manner that made them feel special—as individuals, understanding what their likes and dislikes are."[4] The Four Seasons' corporate head office now stands a few blocks from of the Inn on the Park, although the hotel itself was converted to a Holiday Inn and closed down in 2005.

Having sharpened his skills, Sharp was now ready to place a much larger bet in a city that would truly test his business mettle and architectural prowess. Just as he finished the Inn on the Park in Toronto, the fledgling entrepreneur began a heated round of negotiations with the McAlpine family, which operated the Dorchester Hotel in London where Issy and his wife Rosalie had stayed during a European vacation. While the McAlpines believed that the London market was already saturated with luxury hotels like the Savoy and Grosvenor House, and wanted to build a Holiday Inn-style hotel with 320 rooms, Sharp convinced the British investors to build a mid-size luxury hotel with air conditioning and large rooms, which he believed American travelers would value. "We wanted to be distinct and different," recalls Katie Taylor, who started as a legal counsel with the Four Seasons, became its chief operating officer, and in 2010 replaced Issy as president and CEO. "We knew that American business travelers wanted more personalized service and a support system to meet their needs while they were away."[5]

When the Inn on the Park London opened in 1970, industry watchers were stunned by its immediate success. The hotel was profitable in its first year, and quickly became the preferred hotel for business travelers and celebrities traveling to London. "From the first year it opened," muses Sharp, "that London property has probably been one of the world's most consistently profitable hotels. It made me realize what I really wanted to do, and that was to develop and operate only mid-size hotels of exceptional quality."[6] Even competitors acknowledged the foresight of "that crazy Canadian,"[7] as Sharp was dubbed by his British hosts during the hotel's construction. "The place prints money," concedes Robert Collier, at the time a British hotel manager who went on to become a marketing executive at the Sheraton.[8]

With his Toronto hotels performing well, and his London gambit a success, Sharp catapulted himself into the international limelight, although most other hotel executives discarded him as a wild card. "His outward appearance as an urbane, low-key family man belied a gambler's heart," writes David Olive in his study of Canadian CEOs, *No Guts, No Glory*. "Four Seasons was built on a series of risky propositions beyond the ken of professional managers. Sharp's first three hotels, each ahead of its time in anticipating nascent trends, were initially judged to be a stupendous folly."[9]

What the London Inn on the Park did, however, was clarify Sharp's strategy for competing against luxury brands like the Ritz-Carlton. By relying on his instincts and his training as an architect, Sharp realized that he could lure savvy business travelers away from the 750-room Hiltons and Hyatts by building mid-size hotels and throwing in amenities and levels of customer service that larger hotels could not match. In Sharp's own words, "If we can beat the best hotels in London, why wouldn't it be possible to do it elsewhere? That's when I said, 'From now on, we're going to build and operate hotels only of exceptional quality, and we're going to make each one the best.'"[10] Sharp began to introduce amenities like working desks, large cotton towels, and hair dryers—which we take for granted today but were bold innovations in the 1960s and 1970s. "The principle was to think about it as if you're having guests come to your home," Sharp explains.[11] Sharp would focus on improving the ease of travel, thereby "providing a support system at our hotels to replace the ones left behind at home or at the office."[12]

Sharp's belief in providing superior value, architecture, and service allowed the Four Seasons to charge a premium for staying in London or Toronto. "The traditional belief was that a full-service business traveller hotel needed at least 750 rooms to generate the revenue to pay for its amenities," writes Roger Martin, dean of the Rotman School of Management at the University of Toronto. "Sharp saw a more complex relationship between hotel size and amenity. If he could provide his guests with a higher standard of service, they would pay significantly more per room per night."[13] With this knowledge in hand, Sharp was ready to lay down more tracks in Canada and Europe.

Throughout the 1970s, Sharp led the Four Seasons through a feverish period of building five-star hotels in major Canadian cities and trying to emulate his London success in Europe. Yet his attempts to apply his management philosophy through partnerships with other hotel builders brought more frustration than success. The building of a Four Seasons in Rome took a wrong turn when Italian authorities found that his chosen site held a number of important artifacts, and a project next to Vancouver's Stanley Park was blocked by student activists. Sharp also found himself up against the wall in his hometown of Toronto, where he struck a partnership with ITT Sheraton (now a part of Starwood Hotels) to build a large convention hotel across from city hall. But Sharp was unimpressed by the steely 43-story tower and pulled out his 49-percent stake from the Toronto Sheraton in 1976 to concentrate on expanding his Four Seasons brand, ignoring ITT's offer of a plush executive job. The Sheraton venture put enough cash back into Sharp's pockets that he was able to take the company private in 1977. The move allowed Sharp to guide his own destiny, and he slowly steered a new growth strategy by selling properties in mid-size Canadian cities like Edmonton, Calgary, and Ottawa, and setting his sights on building a luxury hotel in each major U.S. city. As Olive writes, "Sharp was determined to earn a reputation for unrivaled proficiency in managing small-scale luxury hotels. In executing that strategy to near-perfection, Four Seasons eventually found that it could have its pick of the best sites and properties in the world's leading cities."[14]

Having earned his wings in the 1960s, and refined his strategy in Canada and Europe in the 1970s, Sharp's foray into the United States in the 1980s and 1990s turned the Four Seasons into a true powerhouse. His first beachhead was in San Francisco, where he acquired the Clift Hotel and spent $4 million on a renovation. The Clift grabbed first place on *Condé Nast's* list of best hotels in America, which gave Sharp the boost he needed to chart his U.S. expansion. The Four Seasons hit Seattle next, where Sharp took over the Olympic Hotel, and Chicago, where Four Seasons took over a former Ritz-Carlton property in the Water Tower, a high-end complex on the Magnificent Mile.

After the successful projects in Philadelphia and Washington, DC, Sharp was rewarded with the management contract for the Pierre Hotel on New York's Fifth Avenue, which promptly received a $30-million upgrade. With his U.S. expansion in full swing, the last ingredient of Sharp's Creative Execution formula fell into place. Instead of owning hotels and running their day-to-day operations, Four Seasons would focus on developing select properties around the world. The company makes money from what it calls "management fees," sales and marketing fees that are generally calculated as a percentage of a property's revenues. The Four Seasons collects approximately $300 million in fees on an annual basis from its global properties, and acts more as an oversight board that ensures high standards are maintained in architecture and customer service. As Erik Stern explains in *The Value Mindset*, "Four Seasons clearly knows where its competitive advantage lies, and it is not in owning or managing a real estate portfolio . . . Instead of owning hotels and managing them, Four Seasons has measured up its core competencies and stepped back from the standard paradigm."[15] Yet even though his expansion strategy yielded brilliant results, Sharp still felt that he needed another ingredient to sustain his competitive advantage over the Ritz-Carlton and other glitzy hotels. In addition to its unique hotels and luxury amenities, Sharp realized that the Four Seasons needed an operating philosophy to guide the behavior of the company's 35,000 employees. The Golden Rule, as this philosophy came to be known, became the Four Seasons' equivalent of the Toyota Production System, or *kaizen*. It would drive people's behaviors in a way that was consistent with Sharp's desire to become the best in every city where the Four Seasons laid down its red carpet.

THE GOLDEN RULE: SHARP'S SECRET FORMULA

Not until 1982 did Sharp feel the need to lay out a leadership formula. But when he did, it was crystal clear, and has remained the bedrock of how executives and employees treat each other—and customers—at the Four Seasons for the past three decades. "As we expanded," Sharp recalls, "I decided to make our values explicit, to tell everyone how to act. In essence, to deal with others—partners, customers, co-workers, everyone—as we would want them to deal with us." This simple rule is what motivated a Four Seasons bellman to get on a plane to return a piece of luggage to a guest who had accidentally left it behind. "Just put yourself in the other person's shoes and use your common sense," says Sharp. "Business is just a small part of our lives. So go ahead and make the decision—whether you're the housekeeper, the doorman or the waiter. It's no big deal"[16]

Sharp's Golden Rule, even though he believed it was not a big deal, sent ripple waves throughout the company. Nick Mutton, executive vice-president of human resources at Four Seasons, remembers how Sharp asked him to interview hotel management and employees when he first released the company's Goals, Beliefs, and Operating Principles, to help determine who was living the values, and who wasn't. When he got back to Sharp with the results, the CEO took prompt action. "Issy immediately terminated executives who were just paying lip service and not really living up to the values," Mutton recalls. Four Seasons then revised its hiring practices to ensure that only staff that could embrace the Golden Rule would be hired as the company continued on its global expansion. Every hotel general manager was required to meet prospective employees, underscoring that there are no unimportant jobs. "We hire for attitude more than skills," Mutton confesses.[17] The result is that Four Seasons operates with little supervision, with each hotel managed as a small business and with every decision tied to the Golden Rule. This operating philosophy, as Sharp explains, "requires managers who are less bosses than mentors and communicators—whose role is to bring out each individual's best, and coach them to become a winning team."[18]

The Golden Rule wasn't a new amenity or a brilliant architectural stroke, but it provided Four Seasons with a way to win the hearts and minds of its employees around the world. "There is no doubt that people are our most important asset," Sharp told me in our interview. "There isn't a city or a village anywhere in the world that we couldn't go into and pull together a group of people to work by our values and standards. We've done it everywhere . . . because the Golden Rule is universally understood."[19] Sharp introduced a talent-management and feedback system that continually screens managers and employees for their behavior against the Golden Rule. Each year the most senior team at Four Seasons meets to review how hotel managers around the world rate in their direct reports. "It's probably the single most important meeting this company has," Sharp explains. "It preserves what the company stands for." This hands-on talent discussion results in about 30 to 40 executives evaluating the performance of more than 600 key managers—not an exercise for the faint of heart.

The net result of the Golden Rule is that the Four Seasons has been rated by *Fortune* magazine as one of the 100 Best Companies to Work For every year since 1998. One benefit is that the company hires over 30 percent of new employees from internal referrals, and its turnover, at about 23 percent, is one-third lower than the rate of its external competition. When it opened its second Manhattan hotel, the Four Seasons attracted 17,000 people who came to interview for 400 jobs. Like Toyota, which promises employment for life to all employees, Four Seasons found ways to navigate through the post-9/11 downturn and the 2008–9 recession with few employee layoffs. In fact, Sharp approached 2002 and 2003, the worst years on record for the travel and hotel industry, as an opportunity to grow Four Seasons' market share. "We did not want people to arbitrarily lay anybody off," he explains. "We didn't earn the profits we thought we would—but big deal—we still earned a profit!" Sharp's favorite example is the Four Seasons in Istanbul, which lost half of its business overnight after 9/11. Senior managers got together and decided that they would each take a week off per month without pay, which enabled them to keep all hotel staff employed. Some took their holidays ahead of plan. "The politics of decision-making disappear quickly when you use the Golden Rule as your decision-making philosophy," Mutton says. "We demand that our senior leaders and employees get involved in making decisions and act out the values and strategy."[20]

Perhaps the most telling fact about Sharp's reaction to the post-9/11 trauma that seized the travel industry was his decision to keep the emphasis on guests and services exactly the same in every Four Seasons hotel, and to maintain the premium prices that each hotel charged in their respective market. So you would still be paying $395 for a room in Philadelphia, or the standard $595 in Washington, DC. "We decided that we were not going to do anything to jeopardize the integrity of our product," Sharp remembers. "We felt we could hold market share . . . even if our occupancy rate dropped. The pie got a lot smaller for everybody, but our share got bigger." This approach not only upheld the Golden Rule, but also positioned Sharp and the Four

Seasons for its next period of growth—this time beyond the United States and into new markets in the Middle East and China. As it did so, Four Seasons would increasingly find itself facing a revitalized foe in the Ritz-Carlton, whose takeover by the Marriott in 1996 put the venerable firm squarely in Sharp's global path.

SHARP MEETS HIS PRINCE

After his rapid growth in the United States and market-share grab in the aftermath of 9/11, Sharp set out to create a foothold for the Four Seasons beyond its traditional North American and European bases. This was a bit of a gamble, since the Four Seasons' competitive formula of providing a luxury service had only been shown to work, so far, with a North American audience. Katie Taylor explains this risky transition: "In its infancy, our formula for luxury service was a concept proven only in North America," she says. "Even the London hotel catered to North Americans coming to England for business or leisure. So the big question for us was: would the same approach to our culture and our service environment work as well in Tokyo and Istanbul or Singapore as it did in Toronto and London?" With all three hotels a runaway success, the road forward was clear. "At the end of the day, we proved that great leadership and great service could sustain us wherever we went."[21]

Global expansion followed more quickly. Sharp made a huge investment—$188 million, to be exact—buying out the Regent International Hotels luxury hotel group, based in Hong Kong. The Regent gave the Four Seasons 10 prime properties across Asia, and several under development in Europe, Jakarta, and Bali. This new round of expansion came hand in hand with Sharp's vision of developing the Four Seasons' ability to provide management expertise rather than owning hotels outright. "Our vision had now evolved," he notes. "We would create a reputation for service so clear in people's minds that the Four Seasons name would become an asset of far greater value than bricks and mortar."[22] If this sounds like a way to position the company for external investors, you might not be off track. The Regent purchase had ballooned Four Seasons' debt load and forced the firm to record a loss of $119.2 million in 1993. Sharp recovered by selling off a number of properties, but the fuse was lit, and he continued to seek an outside investor to help sustain the company's growth and build newer properties across the globe.

Sharp's search ended when he met Saudi prince al-Waleed bin Talal, at the time the world's fifth richest man, and the prince agreed to take a 25-percent stake in the Four Seasons for $167 million. Sharp retained 68 percent of the voting shares, and al-Waleed committed another $100 million to help finance future Four Seasons expansion. With Asian acquisitions still fresh in his portfolio, Sharp now found himself with a contract to manage the George V hotel in Paris and a host of Middle Eastern properties in Damascus, Dubai, Qatar, Cairo, Amman, and Riyadh. With two strokes of a pen—first the Regent and then the al-Waleed deal—Sharp had, over 10 years, more than doubled the number of properties managed by the Four Seasons, and established a truly global presence. The company's center of gravity, historically in North America and Europe, began an unstoppable eastward shift. In early 2000, over 65 percent of the firm's revenues came from U.S. and Canadian properties. By 2005, that number would fall below 50 percent as Four Seasons opened new hotels in Doha, Alexandria, Kuwait City, and other Middle Eastern destinations. The Middle East also took the pennant as the most profitable region in the Four Seasons' portfolio, achieving profit margins of 48 percent in 2005, compared to a 29-percent global average.

Sharp's ability to maintain a solid brand in any global location, and apply the Golden Rule as his management philosophy, lifted the Four Seasons to new heights. Within six years, Prince al-Waleed's investment in the Four Seasons was worth four times what he had paid. Between 2003 and 2005, Four Seasons growth in earnings per share grew by an astounding 237 percent, while the company's per-share multiple of enterprise value to operating profit, a Wall Street favorite way of calculating enterprise value, reached 47.3 percent, compared to 24.3 percent for its peer group. What did that really mean? That travelers—and investors—were willing to pay Four Seasons a hefty premium for staying at its hotels and owning its shares. A key metric used in the hotel industry is RevPar, which measures revenue per available room across a company's properties. In 2004, when it had recovered from the 2002 to 2003 softening of the travel market, Four Seasons had a RevPar of $244, based on 16,378 total available rooms across its brand. Its closest competitor, the Ritz-Carlton, had a RevPar of $178. People were willing to pay an additional $66, on average, to stay at the Four Seasons over the Ritz-Carlton.

As the Middle East expansion continued in full swing, Sharp's instinctive assertion that business travelers would be willing to pay more for excellent customer service, and that people anywhere in the world could live up to the Golden Rule, was fully vindicated. Sharp summed it up in a speech he gave to the Canadian Club in Toronto: "We have built an economic engine of exceptional service by understanding our customers' needs, and we've made it the best in the world. And we maintain and perfect it through a culture based on the deeply-felt core values embodied in the Golden Rule."[23] With his Creative Execution formula fully formed, Sharp was ready to take the next leap in the company's development. He struck the deal with al-Waleed and Bill Gates that took the company private for the second time in its history in November 2006, which lifted the public shares in the company to $82—an overnight premium of 28 percent. "Now that we've gone from public to private," says Sharp, "there is a certainty of stability. If ownership never changes, and management has got a clear look to the future, the company's legacy is almost assured."[24]

The deal with Gates and al-Waleed freed up Sharp to do what he does best—scout the world for the best properties and spread the Golden Rule—and create new growth in the Four Seasons portfolio. This new vein is coming from condo properties in places like Toronto, Miami, and New York, where starting at just $1 million you can buy yourself a Four Seasons Residence, or if times are tough a Four Seasons Residence Club in Carlsbad, California. With more than 40 Four

Seasons hotels and residences in the works, Sharp has ensured that the Four Seasons brand is now larger than the sum of its parts, and that people around the world are willing to stay—and live—in Four Seasons properties despite the condo and hotel saturation of most large cities. Sharp also learned to keep things small. For instance, in 2006 Four Seasons opened what it calls a Tented Camp in the Golden Triangle region where Thailand meets Laos and Burma (Myanmar). The camp only accommodates 30 guests at a time, and gives visitors the opportunity to get involved in the rescue of baby elephants from Thai cities. Not surprisingly, this risky enterprise landed the Four Seasons Tented Camp on top of the *Condé Nast Traveller*'s Best of the Best category in its 2008 Annual Reader's Choice Awards. Sharp's formula for success had taken the Four Seasons from a modest motel in Toronto's red-light district to the jungles of Asia. Like Alexander and Nelson, Issy Sharp demonstrated that a uniquely compelling, well-executed strategy and the right leadership can propel any novice into a position of global prominence.

HOW CREATIVE EXECUTION POWERS FOUR SEASONS

As we retrace Isadore Sharp's rise from humble motel builder to CEO of the largest luxury hotel chain in the world, it's clear that, like Sakichi Toyoda with his car company, Sharp built a unique formula to lift the Four Seasons to a place where it could win the battle for luxury travel in any city in the world. There were false starts and disappointments, such as being kicked out of his chosen sites in Vancouver and Rome, but like the other Creative Execution leaders in this book, Sharp was able to quickly learn from his mistakes and fine-tune his formula. His own assessment of his professional success tells it all: "Years back, I didn't know where we were going. Today it's easy to look at the future. I see the next decade as the most exciting in the company's history. We will double the number of hotels . . . and the majority will be next-generation, five-star hotels—the kind that we're opening now in Budapest, Prague, New York City."[25] So now that we know—

and Sharp knows—how he became a stellar hotelier, let's decode his growth strategy against our Creative Execution formula.

Unique Strategy

After the success of the London Inn on the Park and the frustration of the ITT Sheraton in Toronto, Sharp knew exactly what his strategy should be, and he made it clear to his employees, shareholders, and competitors: build mid-size luxury hotels, and create a customer-service experience that would set the standard for hotels around the world. "Sharp's genius was to attune himself to the postmodern era of innkeeping where the goal was to satisfy a new craving for a sort of ascetic hedonism," explains Olive.[26] His strategy to operate hotels of exceptional quality, and only manage the hotels, rather than own them outright, has stayed remarkably consistent over 40 years. He explains that since he finished work on the London Inn on the Park, and real-ized that a 250-room luxury hotel could dethrone well-established brands like the Savoy, "We will no longer be all things to all people. We will offer only mid-size hotels of exceptional quality, hotels that wherever located will be recognized as the best."[27] By sticking to his guns and convincing investors to back him up as he expanded around the world, Sharp created a unique, simple strategy to build Four Seasons as a very distinct brand.

Sharp's Unique Strategy was really a combination of architectural prowess, like his parallelogram design for the first Inn on the Park in Toronto, room amenities, and luxury service. "We knew we had to set ourselves apart," he says. After the success of the London hotel, he set the company on a relentless course to "be the best wherever we locate: a goal and a purpose beyond making money that all our people could relate to." Throughout his career, Sharp maintained a highly consistent approach to providing the highest luxury standards for his guests. As Olive writes, "In one recession after another, Sharp had continued to replace fading curtains and to experiment with food and fitness innovations, enabling some of his hotels to boast of patrons who logged 100 repeat stays in a property's first five years of operations . . . It's a product of a culture that can't be copied or bought, only created through collective enthusiasm and belief over many years."[28] Walking into a Four Seasons in New York, Cairo, or Hong Kong, one can see the results of Sharp's compelling strategy at work every day: large rooms, soft towels, quiet plumbing, and decor that fits perfectly in its environment. Each hotel is unique, yet connected to the Four Seasons by its prized location, comfortable large rooms, and outstanding service. The guests don't balk at the extra $100 per night compared to the Ritz-Carlton because they rightly perceive that the Four Seasons offers a unique value, which large brands such as Hilton or Sheraton simply can't compete with.

Candid Dialogue

When he created the Golden Rule, Sharp laid out his expectations for managers and employees to relate to each other, and with customers. Treating other people the way you want to be treated meant that honest and candid conversations had to take place at every level of the company. "I became an evangelist," Sharp recalls, "preaching the gospel of service every hour of every day on every trip to every hotel. Continuously restating it. Getting it down to the bottom: bellmen, waiters, chambermaids, dishwashers, the lowest paid and traditionally our least motivated people, but the ones who can make or break a five-star reputation."[29] Sharp made it a point to visit all his hotels to communicate the Golden Rule, and engage in direct dialogue with his employees about what it meant. He didn't spend much time writing memos—although he did so after 9/11 to remind all employees that the company was going to maintain its high standards and would not discount its prices—but traveled furiously around the world to connect with as many hotel managers and employees as possible.

What's remarkable about Sharp is his ability to make people feel comfortable—which is perhaps as difficult as being candid. When he expanded in Japan, he agreed to put a Japanese banker on the Four

Seasons board as a way to give Japan some visibility. Years later, a Japanese business colleague asked Sharp why he was still keeping the individual on the board, even though he no longer worked at the bank. Sharp knew this was true, but also understood enough about Japanese culture to know that keeping the board member would play in the company's favor. At another time, one of Sharp's in-house lawyers made a few mistakes as she worked on a challenging case. As they tried to fix the problem, she said to Sharp: "It's remarkable. Not once have you ever asked me who's responsible [for this mess]. You never started playing the blame game." Sharp told the lawyer that when you know you've made a mistake, there's no point dwelling on it. "There is no sense being a Monday morning quarterback," he explains. "We can't get people to use their common sense if we're going to second guess people every time something doesn't work out."[30] How many CEOs do you know who would take that positive attitude when things go wrong?

Clear Roles and Accountabilities

Four Seasons is a fairly flat organization of 36,000 employees—among whom roughly 450 work at the corporate head office in Toronto. The flat structure allows people to focus less on internal politics and more on doing the right thing for guests. "Four Seasons has no separate customer service department," quips Roger Martin. "Everyone at the Four Seasons is not just a member of the customer service department, but in charge of it."[31] Every role in the hotel, whatever the functional area, is subservient to the need to make guests feel at home. And whereas the hotel industry is religious about measuring RevPar (the average revenue per available room), Four Seasons cherishes data from employees and customers, which are forward-looking indicators of the hotel's performance. Before measuring employee engagement became fashionable in large companies, Sharp insisted on running an annual survey of all employees to see how they would rank senior executives and their experiences as Four Seasons employees.

While Sharp and his senior team carefully review monthly metrics like RevPar, the focus on people is what makes the business tick. "The reason we've been able to keep talent is because everyone sees that the top people have emerged from their own ranks," says Sharp. "I believe the best talent we've got will always be better than anyone we could get from outside."[32] Yet the Four Seasons also maintains a unique program, called "People in the Marketplace," which is how the company tracks the key talent in competing luxury hotels like the Ritz-Carlton, Mandarin Oriental, and Peninsula Hotels. Even someone who leaves the Four Seasons, CEO Katie Taylor explains, is thought of as an alumnus and tracked carefully until they return to work for the company. She insists that "each one of our 40,000 employees believes in personally caring for and providing an extraordinary experience for our guests."[33]

In a sense, Sharp's emphasis on having everyone in the company focus on making guests feel special, and applying the Golden Rule, is the equivalent of Nelson's advice to his captains before Trafalgar, when he bluntly declared that no captain could do wrong by putting his ship alongside that of the enemy. Everyone at Four Seasons knows that this is their key accountability.

Bold Action

From his insistence on building mid-size luxury hotels in the face of larger competitors to his brilliant decision to offer free bathroom accessories in every hotel room, Sharp made a number of smart bets to get the Four Seasons established, and to finance its global growth. Perhaps his most decisive action was the purchase of the Regent chain in Hong Kong, which gave the Four Seasons instant reach in Asia. Although he knew the company would lose money in 1991 as a result of the purchase, Sharp was determined to seize the opportunity to expand—he knew profits would follow. He was equally decisive in the aftermath of 9/11 when he decided that Four Seasons, despite the precipitous drop in business travel worldwide, would not reduce its rates or lay off large numbers of employees. Sharp made it clear that he would maintain the Four Seasons' high standards, rather than cave in to the temptation of discounting prices. Boosted by their CEO's bold decision, employees around the world stepped up to the challenge and ensured that Four Seasons increased its market share.

Sharp made it clear once he coined the Golden Rule that all employees—regardless of their position in the hierarchy or their functional expertise—were empowered to use their common sense to make every guest feel special. And Sharp backed this up by firing senior executives who didn't live up to this role: "It was a painful process," he recalls. "And perhaps the hardest thing I ever did. But the fastest way for management to destroy its credibility is to say employees come first and be seen putting them last." Sharp had to fire managers who had been with the company since the early days—one of the most difficult decisions of his career. Yet he understood that if he did not take decisive action, the Golden Rule would just fritter away. "The message you give by management actions is how you build enormous loyalty," he explains. "Principles only count in the tough and rough days, so if you really believe them you need to go for it."[34]

Visible Leadership

By striking a deal with al-Waleed and Bill Gates, and retaining the CEO role, Sharp ensured that he remained the central character in the Four Seasons cast. "What I wanted was Sharp himself," said al-Waleed after his first deal to acquire a quarter of Four Seasons, "his expertise, the brainpower within Four Seasons."[35] From the wheeling and dealing aboard the prince's yacht *Kingdom* to the opening of new hotels in the Middle East and Europe, Sharp is always visible to his employees and owners, while constantly maintaining a humble attitude. The billionaire founder maintains a low profile and doesn't mingle with his famous guests, preferring to stay quiet even when, according to his recollection, he rode in an elevator with Joan Collins.

From his early days as a builder with his dad, Sharp was always in the trenches, sharing the burden of digging and doing the hard physical labor that comes with construction. "I worked side by side with my crew," he explains, "digging ditches, pouring concrete in the rain. And when I had to leave they would go on working as if I were there. That was the attitude of fairness and mutual respect I wanted to establish within Four Seasons."[36] This visible yet humble leadership style is reminiscent of Admiral Nelson. Sharp's quiet confidence and clarity of vision is precisely what attracted the McAlpines to Sharp when he struck his deal for the London Inn on the Park, and why al-Waleed and Gates, 30 years later, agreed to keep Sharp in the driver's seat when they bought out the company.

Sharp isn't the only Four Seasons executive who's learned to be visible. Katie Taylor now visits 25 to 30 hotels each year, which helps ensure that she sees every single Four Seasons location at least once every three years. Not only does she meet with employees and all department heads (a total of 30 to 40 people in each hotel), but she also spends private time with each general manager and their family to show her appreciation for their commitment to the company. When I asked if she had ever been made to feel awkward as a female executive visiting the new Four Seasons hotels in the Middle East, she beamed and answered that by far her best employee meetings took place in Riyadh, where the only woman employee was a wedding planner. "It was one of the more emotional visits I've ever done," she says. "My Q&A with managers and employees—all men—lasted longer than any meeting I've had in my entire career. The coffee afterwards never ended. I've never felt more welcomed or more warmly received."[37] That's a great display of visible leadership.

THE FINAL SHOWDOWN

As hotels contend with the impact of the global recession, which knocked 10 to 20 percent off RevPar across all hotel brands between 2008 and 2010, the Four Seasons, the Ritz-Carlton, and other brands like Fairmont and Oberoi are dueling in China and India, the latest frontier in the luxury hotel wars. Most of the 6 percent annual growth expected in the global hotel industry between 2012 and 2015 is taking place in cities like Hainan, Pudong, and Guangzhou, where Taylor and her team are working on building the majority of the new Four Seasons hotels. With more than 100 cities of a million residents each, China remains an untapped market for Sharp and his competitors. "The dynamics and demographics in this part of the world are going to overwhelm what the future will be in our industry," he told *China Business Weekly* in 2008.[38] Since opening its first mainland hotel in Shanghai in 2002, Four Seasons has aggressively sought opportunities in China. The Macau Four Seasons, which opened in 2009, features the very best of Sharp's 40-year experience in building luxury hotels, with about a third of its 360 rooms turned into suites, 14 spa suites, and retail outlets. When the company held a recruitment campaign in November 2008, 4,000 people immediately registered for a total of 800 available jobs.

The Four Seasons isn't alone in ogling the Chinese mainland. Hyatt, the world's largest private hotel company, opened its first hotel in Shanghai in 2008, and is planning new hotels in Beijing and Guangzhou. Carlson Hotels, which manages brands like Regent and Radisson, doubled the number of its management contracts in Asia from 2007 to 2008. The Ritz-Carlton, which followed the Four Seasons' moves in the Middle East by opening hotels in Cairo and Dubai, and which is also developing its own brands of residences and clubs, is looking at new properties in Sanya, a resort island off Hainan, and Shenzhen. "The challenge is both about staying the course and placing hotels in places where guests want us to be," says Ritz-Carlton president Simon Cooper.[39] Not only did Ritz-Carlton, which plans to operate 100 hotels worldwide by 2016, follow in the Four Seasons' global footsteps, but it is also mirroring Sharp's efforts to win the hearts and minds of employees through what the company calls the "Gold Standard" with its credo, "Ladies and Gentlemen serving Ladies and Gentlemen," and its ruthlessly demanding service standards. Like at Four Seasons, Ritz-Carlton staff are completely imbued with the Gold Standard, to the point where, as Joseph Michelli writes, "leaders and frontline staff alike can appear, from an outsider's perspective, to be teetering toward the fanatical."[40] As both hotels go head-to-head, it's a case of the Four Seasons' Golden Rule against the Ritz-Carlton's Gold Standards, with Asia and the Middle East as the fighting ring.

Will Sharp's 40 years of Creative Execution brilliance allow the company to succeed in China, with Taylor as its new CEO? During the Great Depression, all of the Ritz-Carlton's hotels in the United States—except one in Boston—were forced to shut down. The Ritz-Carlton's advantage is that its parent company, Marriott International, has become a massive global player with 19 brands like the Marriott, Renaissance Hotels, and Courtyard. The company already operates more than 30 hotels in China, six in India, and nine in Thailand. Former Marriott CEO J. W. Marriott Jr. learned a few lessons from Sharp in providing the ultimate luxury and convenience for guests. Every guest room in the Marriott's properties in the United States, for instance, is being equipped with a flat-screen HD television. You can connect your iPod, digital camera, or laptop directly to the TV. Marriott's mighty goal is to invest $2 billion in new Ritz-Carlton properties over four years, starting with new hotels in Moscow, Tokyo, and Beijing. In 2013, Marriott will also take on the Four Seasons in New York by opening the city's tallest lodging facility, a 600-room glass monolith at the corner of Broadway and Fifty-Fourth Street.

CREATING THE NEW FOUR SEASONS

As the global economy continues to stutter, the competition between the Four Seasons and the Ritz-Carlton and Marriott will heat up and expand. Boutique hotels, which only make up 3 percent of the U.S. hotel industry, are quickly becoming trendier and more appealing than large luxury hotels. Already half the new hotels under construction in Manhattan are boutique types. And while RevPar grew in 2010 and 2011 (at around 7 percent both years, according to PricewaterhouseCoopers), the largest growth is coming from Asian destinations like China and Singapore. Other than the recent reopening of the Four Seasons London at Park Lane, the Four Seasons opened four new hotels in 2011: Guangzhou (China), Marrakesh, Baku, and St. Petersburg. Just like Creative Execution made its way East, so too, it seems, did the Four Seasons.

While Issy Sharp built the Four Seasons from the ground up, starting with his Toronto motel, it is now Katie Taylor's job to shape the Creative Execution formula that will dictate the company's fortunes over the next decade. When I asked her what she learned from Issy Sharp, Taylor didn't hesitate: "When structuring hotel management contracts, Issy would always let people walk away thinking that they had won," she says. "Issy is an eternal optimist. He taught me that you have to work in a way you believe is right. You can't ever compromise your values."[41] Her Creative Execution formula is quickly evolving, blending the best of what she learned from Sharp with her own reading of global trends. In her first year as CEO, she went around the company's properties asking people what they should be doing better. She came back with five themes that her team is working from. She also clarified the strategy for the business: to be the first choice for guests, to be the first choice for employees, and to provide the best return for the owners.

While she will stay focused on Sharp's formula of building mid-size luxury hotels and providing an outstanding guest experience, Taylor knows that she needs to evolve the Four Seasons' culture to match its global footprint and avoid the complacency and quality mistakes that plagued Toyota after it reached the top. "I want to make sure people look forward, not backward," she explains. "My job is to make sure people are thinking about the next phase of growth, and feel accountable for the next fifty years. What will the guest experience of the future look like?" One of the most interesting projects Taylor is pushing is the development of service standards for the Chinese population. A great guest experience in Shanghai or Macao, for instance, might be quite different from the guest experience in Vail, Colorado, where the Four Seasons recently opened. To reinforce this focus on regional differences, Taylor appointed a president to run the Asia Pacific region, and another to run the Americas operations. What will emerge from this new structure and culture, in my view, will be a fresh Creative Execution formula for Asia, where Four Seasons will go head-to-head with the other luxury brands.

Whether the Four Seasons wins the race in Asia and reaches its goal of doubling its size is difficult to predict. What's clear is that Issy Sharp showed us that, by sticking to a consistent, unique strategy of building mid-size luxury hotels, and following his Golden Rule, he was able to tap into the creative capabilities of employees and Four Seasons guests on a global scale. As he explains, "There has been a consistent thread—the commitment to service and to the employees who deliver the service product every day. It is what propels us forward today as we continue to grow globally. Increasingly, it is something that matters greatly to every business and every brand, not just hoteliers."[42] Sharp's formula propelled him from humble motel operator to global hotel tycoon.

But whereas Sharp built his global empire the old-fashioned way— brick by brick—another company in California, led by two young entrepreneurs, was planning to take over the world online. In its own way, Google redefined the online search experience in the same way Sharp redefined luxury standards in the hotel industry. And that's our next stop on the road to deciphering the art of Creative Execution.

8

Google Ogles Microsoft

Google is not a conventional company, and we don't intend to become one.

—Google statement on its "Jobs" website

While you're busy searching the Internet for the latest information on Lady Gaga or the history of sugarcane, one company is busy making money off your online wandering: Google. Even when the global economy slumps, Google thrives. The Internet-search giant doubled its earnings from 2009 to 2011, with revenues soaring to $38 billion. Do you know a lot of companies that doubled their revenues in the past two years? Or a company that has had more than 10 years of double- or triple-digit revenue growth? I didn't think so.

It helps that Google has monetized the fastest-growing industry of the twenty-first century, and can by itself claim 41 percent of the $31-billion U.S. online-advertising market. In a down economy, that allows you to give all your employees (31,300 at the time) a 10-percent raise, which is what Google did in the middle of 2011. That's right, every single employee. Google lives around the corner from Facebook in Palo Alto, California, you see, and the talent competition is fierce.

The ascendancy of Google is mesmerizing, and the company's mastery of Creative Execution, Silicon Valley–style, even more so.

Google achieved world domination of the Internet-search market at speeds that make Toyota's conquest of North America and the Four Seasons' surge in Asia look like a walk in the park. By the end of 2011, according to comScore, Google commanded 65 percent of the total U.S. Internet-search market, followed distantly by Yahoo! and Microsoft, each with a 15-percent share. "To Google" is now a common verb, and, as Jeff Jarvis writes, "Once upon a time, all roads led to Rome. Today, all roads lead from Google."[1]

Google's strategy appears chaotic, yet the company inexorably moves forward, building and acquiring with a zest reminiscent of Alexander's conquest of Persia. Despite fiascos like Orkut (a social-networking site that only took off in Brazil and Iran), Google continues to move at light speed. In 2011, the company introduced a potential rival to Facebook called Google+, which it hopes will add a powerful social-networking dimension to its business. Its Android mobile devices are becoming increasingly popular, with 500,000 activations a day during 2011. The company gobbled up 48 acquisitions in 2010, followed by a record 57 in 2011, including a $12.5-billion cash deal for Motorola Mobility—a bold move into the hardware space.

From space elevators to self-driven cars, there is little that Google won't contemplate. The Googleplex head office in Mountain View, California, has become somewhat of a mecca for engineering and computing divas who park their surfboards by the main entrance and, according to Google's website, "share an obsessive commitment to creating search perfection and having a great time doing it." Like eBay, Google not only survived the dot-com meltdown of 2000 but grew into one of the most reputable and trusted companies in the world.

Besides the lava lamps, exercise balls, and free food courts dotting the Googleplex, you can find the odd hint of a business in the making, like a live projection of search queries from around the world, or a three-dimensional image of the earth with Internet traffic patterns and real-time searches (color-coded by language) on the second floor. And so the 31,000 Googlers in Mountain View and at Google's newer facility in New York, like the benevolent Whos in Dr. Seuss's classic *How the Grinch Stole Christmas!*, merrily find ways to scan the Bodleian Library or map the surface of Mars between games of foosball and meals of buttermilk fried chicken, recipe courtesy of Google's former executive chef Charlie Ayers (who once worked as chef for the Grateful Dead).

This does not sit well with Microsoft.

Until Google came along, Microsoft thought its ubiquitous applications like Internet Explorer and Microsoft Outlook would allow it to comfortably benefit from the growth of the Internet. The feud was exacerbated in 2004, when Google poached one too many executives out of Microsoft's Redmond, Washington, headquarters, and Steve Ballmer, Microsoft's CEO, allegedly threw a chair across the room and exclaimed "I'm going to *fucking* kill Google!"[2] In 2007, Google released a suite of products called Google Docs that includes word-processing and spreadsheet programs, which it piloted with large companies like General Electric and Procter & Gamble, moving straight into Microsoft Office territory.

Google strongly objected to Microsoft's plan to buy rival search service Yahoo! in 2008, and in 2009 joined a lawsuit in the European Union similar to the antitrust case the U.S. Justice Department unleashed against Microsoft in the 1990s, accusing the software manufacturer of unfairly embedding its Internet Explorer browser in Windows. Google's new web browser, Chrome, was released in 2008 to compete against Internet Explorer, hard on the heels of Google Desktop Search, which allowed people to quickly search their PC for files from Microsoft Word, Outlook, PowerPoint, or Excel. This turned a guerilla war into a full-out assault. Microsoft reacted by trying to block Google's acquisition of DoubleClick in 2008, and after thwarting Google's plans to enter into an advertising pact with Yahoo! decided in 2009 to strike its own 10-year partnership with the company.

And so the stage is set for one of the twenty-first century's most-watched corporate battles, and for the ultimate feat of Creative Execution. Will Google, with its two boyish, irreverent founders, manage to upset Microsoft's plans to dominate the web, and succeed in its "audacious plan to organize everything we know," as one writer put it?[3] Or will the combination of Microsoft and Yahoo!, or Facebook's massive social-networking power, send Google packing? Let's make our way back to Google's infancy to better understand how the company devised its own Creative Execution formula to take over the Internet and reshape the battle for global search supremacy.

HOW GOOGLE GOT ITS GROOVE

When Larry Page and Sergey Brin met in the summer of 1995, the Internet was still rather inchoate. But for the two PhD students from Stanford University, it was an enigma to be cracked. The rapidly growing number of web pages were connected to each other through links that were difficult to organize in order of importance, and made Internet search a tedious, unpredictable proposition. As Randall Stross explains, searching the web for accurate results "was considered by almost everyone in the business to be uninteresting, a behind-the-scenes service that could be obtained from any of a number of fungible suppliers."[4] The leading search engine at the time, AltaVista, had just over 50 percent of the Internet-search market, but could hardly keep up with the exponential growth of the Internet. Like Yahoo!, it tried to manage Internet search by hiring teams of editors who handpicked websites and organized them alphabetically, a costly process that wasn't sustainable as millions of pages were added daily to the web. Page and Brin, who both studied computer engineering and mathematics, felt that they could come up with a search methodology that would better tag the relevance of each web page, and be scalable as the Internet grew. They hoped that, if they succeeded in developing this new algorithm, which they called PageRank, an established player like AltaVista might be willing to pony up $1 million to own the software.

The PageRank algorithm that Page and Brin designed remains the backbone of Google's performance today, and the reason why, 10 years after its founding, Google controls the Internet-search market. Its premise is simple: using the principle of academic citations, which holds that the more a particular dissertation or reference book is cited by other academics, the more relevant it is, Page and Brin designed a web crawler that analyzes links to and from all the websites on the Internet, and determines how important each website is based on the number of links that refer *back* to it. As the company explains, "By analyzing the full structure of the web, Google is able to determine which sites have been 'voted' the best sources of information by those most interested in the information they offer."[5] Instead of giving search results based on keywords, which, if you were searching "white house," for example, would give you all web pages that have the words "white" and "house," Google knows that the most relevant website people seek when they type these two words is the White House in Washington, DC. And that's the first website that pops up in your search, instead of tips on how to paint your house white.

Confident that they had a superior method for searching the ever-expanding web, Page and Brin released the beta version of their search engine, which they called Google after misspelling "googol"—the number 1 followed by 100 zeroes—on the Stanford University website in August 1996. As David Vise writes, "Without intending to . . . [Page and Brin] had devised a ranking system for the Internet, and in the process had inadvertently solved one of the core problems of searching for information on the Web."[6] The website was an instant hit, but sucked up so much of Stanford's computing capacity that the two students were asked to take their project off campus.

Google's recipe for success was unique in the burgeoning Internet industry of the late 1990s. At the time, tech companies were either focused on developing web browsers, like Netscape, which went public in August 1995 and at the time commanded an 80-percent market share, or e-mail services inside a gated space filled with news and entertainment, which is what AOL offered its subscribers. Unlike these content-heavy sites, Google kept its home page clean of clutter, and offered one seemingly mundane service: Internet search. Brin and Page made a bold bet, assuming that as the Internet grew, e-mail services and content would become more open and eventually commoditized, whereas search would increase in relevance. As Vise explains, "Single minded and focused, Page and Brin remained convinced that Internet search was the most important long-term problem they could solve, and that doing so would bring new users in droves . . . They had a target in mind: becoming dominant in search, at the exact time that others were abandoning it."[7]

Forced out of their dorm, the duo moved into a Palo Alto apartment (rent $1,700 a month) and transformed their garage into Google central. Google required dozens of computers and hard drives in order to scan the roughly 10 million web pages in existence at the time, using its web-crawler software. The year before, Page had shocked his thesis supervisor at Stanford by casually informing him that, in order to perform the PageRank algorithm, he was going to download the entire Internet on the university's computers. This remains true today. In order to unleash PageRank's algorithm, Google downloads a carbon copy of the entire Internet on its servers every day. When you perform a Google search, you're not searching live content but only the most recent version of the Internet, which Google has stored on its computers. Google remains secretive about the number of data centers it maintains in the United States to perform this magical feat, but it's safe to say that it no longer depends on the dozen or so motherboards that Page and Brin assembled in their Palo Alto garage back in 1998. Randall Stross writes that Google "decided to build its own machines, a path without precedent in the software industry. By using the same standard components that are the heart of a personal computer and building the machines from the start, Google has been able to add capacity cheaply, effectively, and limitlessly."[8] Eric Schmidt, who joined Google in 2001 to help manage the fast-growing company (Larry Page took over as CEO in April 2011), made a telling remark about the company's reliance on mega-servers at a press conference in 2004, when he said that "All our data centers have gone bankrupt. Because we use so much power and we negotiate such low rates."[9] More recently, Schmidt revealed the existence of a 30-acre Google server facility in Oregon.

One year after they moved into their Palo Alto apartment, Page and Brin saw a huge increase in Google traffic. The number of queries on Google's site rose from 10,000 a day in 1998 to 100,000 a day in 1999, each one taking three to three and a half seconds to process. The company had successfully indexed 60 million web pages, but was still lagging behind AltaVista, which had ranked a total of 150 million pages. Page and Brin set an audacious goal to index one billion web pages, and hired Urs Hölzle, who taught computer science at the University of California, to build the huge computing architecture that the company would need as it let PageRank loose. But Page and Brin had another problem: as the company expanded, and its computer needs grew exponentially, so did its need for funding. Google had received some early seed money from small investors—a single luminary, Sun Microsystems co-founder Andy Bechtolsheim, had loaned Page and Brin $100,000 the day they incorporated the company—but after AltaVista declined to pay $1 million for the PageRank algorithm, it became clear that the company would need some financial backing. They approached two separate Silicon Valley venture capital firms, Kleiner Perkins Caufield & Byers and Sequoia Capital, and convinced them to each invest $12.5 million into Google.

The unusual pairing of the two venture capital firms, so soon after the implosion of the dot-com market, combined with the princely sum of $25 million, caught the eye of many in the industry. As Vise describes it, "Sergey Brin and Larry Page were a breath of fresh air. Instead of a PowerPoint presentation, they came marching in with a working search engine technology that was superior to anything that Doerr [partner at Kleiner Perkins] or Moritz [partner at Sequoia Capital] had ever seen . . . Unlike ordinary people with good ideas who might not be able to see them through, it seemed clear that these guys would do whatever it took to execute."[10] In the press release announcing the capital funding on June 7, 1999, Brin and Page predicted that "a perfect search engine will process and understand all the information in the world."[11] With only one year of experience under their belt, and fewer than 100 employees, that prognosis seemed a little far-fetched. Yet that's exactly what Brin and Page set out to do, with a twist: now that they had perfected the PageRank algorithm, and convinced investors that Google was a player in the race to build the Internet, they had to find a way to turn their search engine into a money-making business.

IS MAKING MONEY EVIL?

When they started the company, Brin and Page chose an unusual motto: "don't be evil." That philosophy permeated Google's approach to the market, ensuring that its search page remained free of clutter and that search results got displayed without being influenced by advertisers or sponsors. As Google grew, it repeatedly turned down offers to incorporate content on its main page or give advertisers more prominent displays on search results. "You can't buy your position in PageRank" became a familiar dictum at Google press conferences and investor meetings. Page and Brin billed themselves as the good guys of the Internet, bent on providing unfiltered, high-quality search, period. The quicker and more relevant the search, the faster Google's visitors were on their way to their final destination. Yet Page and Brin also realized—as did their angels from Sequoia and Kleiner Perkins, that this presented a unique opportunity to position advertising uniquely targeted at a customer's query. As Randall Stross explains, "Google's impersonal, mathematical approach to search . . . provides it with the ability to serve up advertisements that are tailored to a search, rather than to the person submitting the search request," which helps to take the sting out of privacy concerns.[12]

Google's approach to what it calls "Sponsored Links," which appear as a discreet text link on the right side of your search results, was a brilliant coup that allowed Google to make money without appearing to be intrusive. Rooted in its belief that "ads can provide useful information if, and only if, they are relevant to what you wish to find," Google successfully demonstrated that "advertising can be effective without being flashy," as it likes to proclaim.[13] The company now derives

69 percent of its revenues from its sale of Google website advertising, and 27.5 percent from network advertising, according to Gartner research. And it works for small and large companies—you can get started for as little as $5 a day. When users click on the Sponsored Link, Google gets 10 cents, which effectively makes Google a dollars-and-cents company. Yet this low-key, low-cost method of including advertising in search results has propelled Google to grow its advertising revenue by an average of 50 to 60 percent annually since 2000. Its first slowdown occurred in 2008, when the front end of the global recession slowed its advertising growth to *29 percent* over 2007. To think that a 29-percent revenue growth was a disappointing year for Google puts the company's performance in an interesting perspective.

By the time the year 2000 came around, two-year-old Google had shown its mettle by securing $25 million from two competing venture capital firms—both of which eked out a seat on Google's board of directors. The company was starting to make money from its AdWords program, which it launched in 2000 with 350 customers. Despite this respectable growth, Google needed to find a more robust avenue to launch its PageRank algorithm into the big leagues. And so just like Toyota approached GM to form a partnership in the 1970s, Google entered into an agreement in 2000 with one of the largest Internet players at the time: Yahoo!. Through that agreement, Yahoo! basically outsourced its Internet-search business to Google, so that visitors requesting a web search on Yahoo!'s website would in fact be using Google's search engine.

As it finished the year 2000, Google had in place the elements of rapid growth—thanks to its private funding and deal with Yahoo!—that would transform the company from a cool newcomer to an Internet powerhouse. The number of daily searches on Google jumped from 10,000 a day in the company's early days to 100 million by early 2001, and the company reported that it had met its goal of indexing one billion web pages. That number would jump to 8 billion indexed pages by 2004, the last time Google officially reported such trivial numbers. Not only was Google taking over the global search business, but it was doing so without giving anyone else a chance to compete against its easy-to-scale algorithm. The *New Yorker* magazine labeled Google the "search engine of the digital in-crowd,"[14] while Danny Sullivan, an editor at *Search Engine Reports,* observed that "each time I speak, I see more and more people smiling and nodding this way, pleased to have discovered Google."[15]

Amazingly, Google was able to replicate the Yahoo! deal with other premier Internet companies like America Online, EarthLink, and Ask Jeeves, which considerably boosted its reach and scope. AOL alone had 34 million connected subscribers in 2002, when it outsourced its online search business to Google. As Vise writes, "the number of sites with a Google search box would grow to a staggering 25,000, forming a money-generating network that was exceedingly difficult for anyone to replicate."[16] Within two years of inking the Yahoo! and AOL deals, Google surged ahead of its rivals with 47 percent of the global search market, while increasing its advertising revenues from a mere $67,000 in 2001 to $1.4 billion in 2003. By 2004, Yahoo! realized it had made a horrible mistake and terminated the Google arrangement, but the damage was done. Yahoo!'s once mighty market share had dropped to 22 percent in the United States, while Google reigned supreme with over 70 percent.

With its search algorithm vindicated through its lucrative deals with the likes of Yahoo! and AOL, Google was ready for its next bold step: digitizing the roughly 35 million books that were gathering light or dust in over 25,000 libraries around the world. This incredible challenge, which Marissa Mayer, Google's first female engineer, and guardian of the Google home page, called Google's "moon shot," became the first serious test of the company's motto. Google started working with famous libraries—Harvard, Stanford, Oxford, and the New York Public Library—training its staff to use specially modified scanners that didn't injure book spines or long-archived materials. But when the University of Michigan allowed the pilot project to proceed, publishers such as McGraw-Hill and Penguin took offence at the fact that Google was scanning books without seeking the approval of copyright holders. After a couple of embarrassing lawsuits, Google changed the name of the project from Google Print to Google Book Search (now simply Google Books), implying that the purpose of the project wasn't to make all books available online, but instead to create a searchable online index. The controversy openly pitted Google against Microsoft, which had joined the Open Content Alliance (OCA), whose aim was to digitize important books with the assent of copyright holders.

In a preview of how Google would use its speed and Bold Action to get to market ahead of Microsoft and other competitors, Google didn't let the lawsuits slow down its efforts but instead increased its pace. Originally the company had wanted to accomplish the digitizing project in 10 years, but now it was going into warp speed and ratifying protocols with another 30 libraries, ranging from Ivy League universities in the United States to Keio University in Japan and the National Library of Catalonia. As Google explains it, "Our ultimate goal is to work with publishers and libraries to create a comprehensive, searchable, virtual card catalog of all books in all languages."[17] Whereas the OCA project had managed to scan a mere 100,000 books in its second year, the University of Michigan, working with Google, reached the first million-book milestone in February 2008. Microsoft threw in the towel in May 2008 after it had digitized 750,000 books. As Stross sums up, "Google had the chance to jump ahead not only because of its own fiscal boldness but also because others who had tried to digitize the world's books had not gotten very far."[18] Through its bold, determined action working with the world's largest libraries, Google set such high standards and goals that not even Microsoft was willing to put up a fight.

While the book-digitization project got underway, Google spread its wings considerably through new acquisitions and product releases. First it acquired YouTube for $1.65 billion in 2006, along with its 67 employees and co-founders Chad Hurley and Steve Chen, who had, like Google, received some early financial backing from Sequoia Capital. While YouTube was not yet profitable, Google CEO Eric Schmidt was convinced that the uploading of personal videos and images was "the next step in the evolution of the Internet."[19] Google's attempt at launching its own Google Video Store came out flat, and the YouTube acquisition landed one of the most successful Internet start-up companies—where more than 70 million people worldwide watched more than 100 million clips per day at the time of the purchase—into Google's lap. Wonder who the other YouTube suitor was? You guessed right: Microsoft.

Google used the same buy-it-yourself approach to map searches, buying out a small company, Keyhole, whose mapping technology had been showcased by CNN during the invasion of Iraq in 2003. This turned into Google Maps, launched in February 2005. But Google had to make its map product cooler than the competition's, and therefore it added Google Earth, which allows you to zoom in on any part of the planet with satellite imagery, and Street View, which lets you walk down a street in Google Maps viewing continuously recorded pictures at street level.

When I first learned about this feature, I zoomed in on the Paris high school I attended in the 1980s, went to Street View, and was amazed to see a perfect street-level picture of the stately Lycée Racine, still intact and with the same double green doors we used to throw eggs and flour against with exuberant relief the last day of the school year. (I couldn't tell if French kids still practice this quaint method of saying goodbye to their high school, since the picture on Google looked like a wintertime shot.) Using the moving arrows, I virtually walked down the street all the way to the Café Malhesberbes, where we used to escape for an afternoon espresso during breaks—and it was still there too! This trip down memory lane from my basement computer was mind-blowing, but Google Earth and Google Maps had far more serious applications. In the aftermath of Hurricane Katrina, for instance, rescuers used before and after pictures of the devastated Louisiana coastline to pinpoint the likely location of flood victims. Along with the Gmail link, Google Video, Google News, and Google Maps have become the staple of Google's toolbar, offering quick access to anything users want—and retaining the simple, uncluttered home page that set the company apart from content websites.

In early 2004, the last piece of Google's growth strategy fell into place when it decided that it was time to raise money for its upcoming acquisitions and announced its much-anticipated initial public offering (IPO). In the same way that Page and Brin bent the rules with the initial seed funding by asking Sequoia and Kleiner Perkins to join forces, Google set some new rules for the IPO that infuriated Wall Street firms but, to its employees and future shareholders, justifiably epitomized the "don't be evil" motto. First was their decision to only pay half of the usual fee of 7 percent that investment firms were proposing to charge for the IPO. Then they co-selected Credit Suisse First Boston and Morgan Stanley to manage the offering, but also stipulated that, well, they might change their mind at the last minute and cancel the whole thing. As David Vise writes, "In the annals of Wall Street, no business had ever done a successful billion-dollar IPO the way Larry and Sergey wanted to do it . . . If anybody on Wall Street didn't like it, they could sit this one out."[20]

The final straw was the actual stock price itself, which both founders wanted to set at around $125, but eventually settled for $85. The relatively high price made it more difficult for Wall Street traders or investors with an inside track to make some serious money on short-term speculation of the Google stock. The founders also insisted that the minimum number of shares one had to purchase on the day of the IPO would be five—an unusually low number—which allowed almost anyone to buy into the offering. The Google IPO would be an extremely democratic process, stripped of the financial varnish that most Internet IPOs had generated in the 1990s.

In the end, the unconventional logic behind Google's IPO, like the firm's own PageRank algorithm, turned into a bonanza. In its filing, Google revealed that its year-over-year profits in the first half of 2004 were three times those of 2003, and that it was well on its way to earning $3 billion that fiscal year. Page and Brin genially declined to edit out the sections of their IPO filing that the Securities and Exchange Commission found too informal or controversial. Written in the first person, the letter states how "Sergey and I founded Google because we believed we could provide an important service to the world," and that Google wasn't a conventional company, and "we do not intend to become one." The letter also warned that "if opportunities arise that might cause us to sacrifice short-term results but are in the best long-term interest of our shareholders, *we will take those opportunities*," and *requested* (not just suggested) that shareholders take the long-term view.[21] Despite this unusual caveat, and the poor timing of a *Playboy* interview in which the two founders revealed that Google was using its algorithm to "read" Gmail messages and push out related advertising to users, Google's IPO was a resounding success. Within minutes of trading on August 19, 2004, the stock went up to $100, and Page and Brin comfortably raised the $2 billion they had hoped for. A month after trading, Google's stock would break through $130, and in October 2007 reach its peak of $747, then crawl back to $570 by the end of 2011.

THE GOOGLEY SIDE OF CREATIVE EXECUTION

Through its stunning growth and brazen IPO, Google has shown us what it takes to deliver Creative Execution with Silicon Valley gusto. As Adam Lashinsky wrote in *Fortune* after seeing the Googleplex, "this is a company thriving on the edge of chaos."[22] While it has built a $30-plus-billion business on the back of its PageRank algorithm, Google continues to push the boundaries of creative development, whether it's through the breathtaking scenery of Google Mars or clever customization of advertising for its Gmail users. Even in the difficult times of the global recession, the company continued to require that all its engineers spend 20 percent of their time working on independent projects, with no management interference. Let's create our own Street View picture of Google's Creative Execution formula.

Unique Strategy

From the get-go, the unique appeal of Page and Brin's PageRank algorithm is what set Google apart from other Internet-search engines. At a time when other Internet providers like AOL or

Netscape focused on e-mail services and measured their success by keeping users inside their own "walled garden," Google focused on keeping its site simple and letting the logic of PageRank take users out of its site as quickly as possible. What appeared at first blush to be a proposition for losing money on the Internet turned into a scalable gold mine. By sticking to its Unique Strategy, Google not only captured the lion's share of the global Internet-search market but also emerged as "the most formidable challenger that Microsoft has ever faced."[23]

What's even more interesting is that Google's main revenue source, online advertising, "was entirely absent in the original business plans of the founders."[24] Yet Google was able to find a niche for online advertising that provided a much more targeted approach to finding potential customers than the wall-to-wall advertising and pop-ups found on other sites. "Google offered narrowcasting, not broadcasting—it tried to reach the consumer at the point of decision about buying a product, rather than plastering ads in places with the right customer demographics."[25] Google's website remains unique on the Internet—a compelling place to find any type of information, yet without the visual and commercial clutter that's omnipresent on almost every other search engine's site.

A final but important aspect of Google's Unique Strategy is its homemade recipe for assembling thousands of commodity computer-hardware parts to make up its data centers, which allows the company to be a low-cost service provider. As Vise argues, "the most important technological advantage distinguishing Google from would-be competitors is that its employees assemble and customize all of the personal computers the company uses to carry out searches."[26] This unique competency saves Google millions of dollars, and allows its PageRank algorithm to break down any search query in a fraction of a second. The fact that Google maintains a copy of the entire Internet on these computers is a feat that no other company in the world would even attempt to duplicate today, given the terabytes that would be required to make this work from scratch.

Candid Dialogue

Google's culture of Candid Dialogue is rooted in the friendship between Page and Brin. Despite their differences, the pair took an immediate liking to each other. But the binary chemical reaction that took place when the two met for an orientation walk around Stanford's campus in the summer of 1995 meant that Google would emerge as a straight-talking company where people would challenge each other to do no evil. As John Battelle wrote in *Wired*, "Walking up and down the city's hills that day, the two clashed incessantly, debating, among other things, the value of various approaches to urban planning . . . they were clearly drawn together—two swords sharpening one another."[27] This open style of communication is at the epicenter of Google's culture. As David Vise also explains, "Both had grown up in families where intellectual combat was part of the daily diet, especially . . . when it came to issues of computers, mathematics, and the future."[28]

This open communication style can be felt on Google's campus in Mountain View, where discussions about advances in search technology and computer science are as common in the food court as former chef Charlie Ayers's legendary buttermilk fried chicken. As Google's own philosophy states, "Ideas are traded, tested and put into practice with an alacrity that can be dizzying. Meetings that would take hours elsewhere are frequently little more than a conversation in line for lunch and few walls separate those who write the code from those who write the checks."[29] Since the initial IPO in 2004, Brin and Page have upheld their pledge to take turns writing a direct, open letter to shareholders at the beginning of every year, where they explain the company's direction and the success or failure of new products. In his 2007 letter, Page admitted that "advertising is even harder than search . . . Our advertising system works well, but we still have tremendous opportunities to improve it." Their original IPO letter, inspired by Warren Buffet's essays, made it clear that the company would not attempt to "smooth out" its quarterly results to make Google look to be in better financial shape than it really was. This candor and straight talk from Page and Brin, as well as their commitment to keeping PageRank safe from the influence of advertisers, remains fundamental to Google's success.

Clear Roles and Accountabilities

When Eric Schmidt joined Google as CEO in 2001 (he is now the company's executive chairman, after Page took over as CEO in 2011), he provided the business experience that Google needed to balance out the creative energy and technical genius that co-founders Page and Brin brought to the table. The three have been collaborating for so long that, as Brin and Page acknowledge, "decisions are often made by one of us, with the others being briefed later . . . Because of our intense long-term working relationship, we can often predict differences of opinion among the three of us."[30] Both Page and Brin made it clear during Google's IPO that they would retain decision-making rights for the company, and set up a dual-class structure of Google shares that allowed the two founders and the executive team to exercise 61.4 percent of the voting rights. If you're buying Google shares, as Page wrote clearly in the IPO letter in 2004, "you are placing an unusual long-term bet on the team, especially Sergey and me, and on our innovative approach." In the early days of Google, Page and Brin were so close that they actually shared a rectangular workstation in Building 43 of the Googleplex.

Within the company itself, Google employees feel an unusual sense of shared direction and accountability with the top management team, and particularly Page and Brin. As Stross writes, executives at Google "communicate their priorities in unison throughout the company so that even teams at the lowest level of the hierarchy know what principles guide their decision making and what projects will be deemed most helpful in fulfilling Google's mission."[31] Part of this operating philosophy is reflected in Google's structure, which consists of teams without the usual layers of middle management. Schmidt,

Page, and Brin realize that to attract and keep the world's best computer scientists and innovators, they need to keep the structure flat and provide their engineers with space to think creatively. The enduring rule that engineers must spend 20 percent of their time pursuing their own independent projects is a striking example of Google's commitment to Creative Execution.

Bold Action

From the company's inception, Google's founders never shied away from taking bold, decisive action to move the company forward. Page and Brin's first Bold Action was to attempt to download the entire Internet onto their computers. They were so determined to succeed that they rented their first apartment without a single source of revenue. Google takes a bold approach to new-product development, often releasing beta versions of its technology in order to let users get their feet wet and provide critical feedback, as it did with Google+ in 2011. As Stross points out, "the public credits Google as an inspirational achiever for merely trying out new things at a frenetic pace that its rivals cannot match."[32]

One of the boldest decisions Brin and Page made was to digitize books from libraries across the world, an ambitious goal that companies including Microsoft eventually walked away from. The sheer complexity of marshaling the equipment and resources necessary to digitize all the books in a single library would present a sizable challenge for any company. But the idea of digitizing every single book in the world, whether it's written in English, French, or Urdu, seems almost fanatical. Yet that's exactly what Google has been doing since 2002, ignoring the legal quagmire that publishers opened up as soon as the University of Michigan announced its intention to be the pilot site. Google took a similar bold step with its decision to ignore the public backlash about its Gmail product, correctly foreseeing that it could maintain user confidentiality and trust even if it allowed its algorithm to "read" people's mail and display corresponding ads next to their text.

Visible Leadership

From their humble beginnings in their Palo Alto garage to their ringing of the bell on the floor of the New York Stock Exchange in 2004, the day of Google's IPO, co-founders Page and Brin have displayed the kind of Visible Leadership of which Alexander the Great or Issy Sharp would approve. As young, inexperienced entrepreneurs, Page and Brin showed remarkable aplomb when they insisted that their initial capital funding, for instance, be split 50-50 between Sequoia and Kleiner Perkins. Similarly, they stood up to the Securities and Exchange Commission and to Wall Street investment firms when they created the rules for their IPO, insisting that the initial share price be set at $85 and cutting investment firms' fees by half. This is reminiscent of Nelson openly disobeying the orders of his admiral and charging into the Danish fleet at the Battle of Copenhagen.

Page and Brin did not sit back and enjoy their newfound fame in the aftermath of the Google IPO, but instead continued to lead efforts to create new products like Google Earth and win new business. When they found out that AOL Europe had selected Yahoo! to be its exclusive ad provider, for instance, they immediately diverted their plane to land in London in order to meet with Philip Rowley, head of AOL Europe. Even though Rowley told them that the deal was done, and to forget about it, Page and Brin insisted that they meet that same day. After hastily setting up a hotel meeting room, Brin and Page convinced Rowley to reopen the negotiations and hammered out a new deal. As Vise explains, "Brin and Page demonstrated that they not only were visionary founders of a business and technologists but also hands-on managers and aggressive businessmen."[33] This initial deal with AOL Europe blossomed into a broader AOL-Google partnership, in which Google invested $1 billion in AOL in return for easier access to AOL's content. Without Brin and Page's decision to divert their plane and convince AOL to reverse its decision to work with Yahoo!, it's very unlikely that the Google and AOL partnership would have gotten off the ground.

Page and Brin aren't the only Google executives who manage to stay highly visible throughout the company. Take Marissa Mayer, for instance, who joined the company as Google employee number 20. Mayer remains an icon at Google, not only because she was the first female engineer to join the company, but because of her huge impact on the look and feel of Google's home page and new products, which she edits for style, color, and nonsense-free content. In a 2009 front-page article, the *New York Times* described Mayer as "the rare executive who has become—at least in the sometimes cloistered world of computer geeks—a celebrity."[34] By hiring talented executives like Mayer and Eric Schmidt, Page and Brin have created a diversified, highly capable leadership team at Google.

THE FACEBOOK CHALLENGE

After a decade of hotly contested competition for Internet supremacy, the results are in. Through its clever application of Creative Execution, Google has not only become the dominant Internet-search provider, but the quality of its websites like Google Maps and Google News is attracting more visitors than Yahoo!, Microsoft, and AOL. According to comScore, which ranks the Top 50 U.S. Web Properties every month, the market share for Internet search in the United States as of December 2011 stood as follows:

#1—Google, with 65.9 percent
#2—Microsoft sites, with 15.1 percent
#3—Yahoo! sites, with 14.5 percent
#4—Ask Network, with 2.9 percent
#5—AOL, with 1.6 percent

While this makes it clear that Google is the only heavyweight contender for Internet search, there is another fast-growing Internet company, Facebook, which presents perhaps a greater reversal threat to Google than Microsoft does. With only $4.3 billion in revenues in

2011, Facebook isn't the money-generating machine that Google has become. But with 800 million users (on average, Facebook is adding 5 million users a week globally), Facebook is facing the kind of exponential growth that Google enjoyed in its heyday, and is quickly becoming the preferred website for people to share photos and organize everything from company picnics to political campaigns. Facebook's decision to go public in 2012 generated even more hype and buzz than Google's 2004 IPO, suggesting that the company's valuation could easily top the $75-billion target it set when it announced its IPO in February 2012.[35]

Facebook's arrival on the Internet scene is worrisome for Google for several reasons. The first is that Microsoft, which already invested $240 million for a 1.6-percent stake in Facebook in 2007, is its biggest backer, and may well try to increase its stake over time. That would allow Microsoft to gain influence over one billion active Internet users, directing them away from Google sites to places like MSN. The second is that Facebook does to Google what Google has done so often to infuriate Microsoft: it hires away lots of its top talent. In 2007, Sheryl Sandberg left Google to become chief operating officer at Facebook, followed by David Fischer, now Facebook's head of advertising and operations. Sandberg had been vice-president in charge of Google's AdSense program, which allows companies to buy the ad space that runs next to Google searches. In her new job, Sandberg is to CEO Mark Zuckerberg what Schmidt was to Page and Brin: someone who can help bring order out of chaos, and more importantly help Facebook make money. Third is, well, money. While most analysts predict that Google's revenue growth will be capped around $40 billion, the sky is the limit for Facebook. Since Facebook users spend more time on Facebook than anywhere else on the Internet, advertisers are likely to be drawn to Facebook in droves. Already Facebook's display-ad revenue grew by 81 percent in 2011, while Google saw an increase of just 34 percent.

Google's response to the Facebook challenge will test the company's commitment to its values and Creative Execution formula.

The opening salvo was the return of Larry Page to the CEO role, ending the comfy triumvirate that had seen Page, Brin, and Schmidt steer Google through its IPO days. Page masterminded the launch of Google+, which so directly threatened Facebook that Zuckerberg declared a company lockdown to copy into Facebook the Google+ features that users seemed to like. "Google+ is . . . the first test of Page's plan to transform Google into the nimbler, more accountable company it once was . . . [and avoid] the paralysis that grips so many successful companies," Miguel Helft and Jessi Hempel wrote in a *Fortune* cover story.[36] But despite the fact that Google+ drew 25 million users in its first month, not everyone is convinced that Page's new creation can unseat the giant that Facebook has become. As *Forbes* points out, "Google can launch a product that fixes Facebook's issues, and even looks a touch nicer to boot, but its biggest flaw is simply something it can't overcome. It's not Facebook."[37]

Page is changing other things at Google, including reducing the number of small projects, which he felt would distract the company from its monster goals of fending off Microsoft and Yahoo! on the one hand, and taking on Facebook in the social-media sphere on the other. He shut down 25 projects after taking over as CEO in 2011, and streamlined Google's structure to speed up decision making and clarify accountabilities. "Ever since taking over as CEO, I have focused much of my energy on increasing Google's velocity and execution," he explained to analysts. "We have to make tough decisions about what to focus on," he added.[38] Some of the canned projects included megaconcepts like Google Health, Google Labs, and Google PowerMeter. But rest assured: plenty of other lofty Google ventures remain alive, such as the plan to manufacture a driverless car and create the Google Cultural Institute, a Paris-based offshoot of Google Books whose first project was helping the Israel Museum digitize the Dead Sea Scrolls for its new website.

As we race through the second decade of the twenty-first century, Google is no longer the laissez-faire, go-bust-or-go-home company it was when its co-founders hand-assembled motherboards in the garage of their Palo Alto apartment. Through its gargantuan ability to mass-process billions of searches through the magic of PageRank, Google has put its name in the spotlight, and has earned the reputation as one of the most valuable companies on the Internet. Whether or not Google will experience its own reversal—at the hand of Facebook, Microsoft, or a combination of both companies—is a search query that remains unanswered. As Adam Lashinsky put it in *Fortune*, "To believe that Google will find its second act, you have to accept the hubris and the chaos, and that the brainiacs who got lucky once will do so again."[39] Like all masters of Creative Execution, Page and Brin have written their own history by ignoring the old rules and forging ahead with the absolute belief that their cause is just and right, ergo "don't be evil." Luck had nothing to do with it.

9

Creative Execution in Action

There cannot be a crisis next week. My schedule is already full.

—Henry Kissinger

Our journey into Creative Execution has taken us from Gaugamela to California. Yet aside from lopsided military victories and the achievements of visionaries such as Issy Sharp, Larry Page, and Sergey Brin, can we conjure up any more examples of leaders in smaller organizations or in the public sector who have wielded Creative Execution to their advantage? Absolutely! I can think of two in particular who came out of nowhere to lead their party or business to new heights. One of them, Barack Obama, may not seem like a fair example. But before he ran for president in 2008, Obama was a little-known senator who seemed unlikely to take on the likes of Hillary Clinton to win the Democratic Party nomination. Regardless of how you feel about Obama's policies or his presidency, you have to admire the way he pulled himself to the top of the Democratic ticket in one of the most breathless primary battles the United States ever witnessed.

The other example is that of Gary McDonald, who led the turnaround of a small division of the Thomas Cook travel company in North America. While McDonald may feel that his feat of Creative

Execution doesn't fit on the same scale as Obama's, he faced just as many obstacles and challenges, which only his Visible Leadership and mastery of Creative Execution eventually conquered. I'll let you be the judge of which situation was toughest. Let's first start with Obama's come-from-behind victory in 2008, which set a new standard for putting Creative Execution to work in electoral politics.

OBAMA'S SURGE

From the time he declared his candidacy for the Democratic ticket in February 2007 to his election as U.S. president in November 2008, Barack Obama overcame a litany of political, racial, and ideological barriers that finally saw him defeat John McCain by seven percentage points. Not only did Obama become the first African American major-party nominee, but he also became the third sitting senator—after Warren Harding and John F. Kennedy—to be elected president. Most importantly, he had to overcome the powerful stigma of lacking global political experience—a weapon that both Clinton and McCain would wield against him—and provide credible answers to nagging geopolitical issues ranging from the precarious U.S. position in Iraq and Afghanistan to the global financial crisis. His job was not just to convince the American electorate that he should lead the country, but at the same time to convince the rest of the world that he would restore the ethics and moral leadership that the United States had arguably lost in its handling of the War on Terror.

Once Obama became the official Democratic nominee, his campaign outshone McCain's in every possible aspect. As Joe Klein wrote in a *Fortune* essay called "Study McCain and Do the Opposite," Obama "ran the smoothest campaign I've ever seen . . . being himself—preternaturally calm, mature, reasonable—was exactly what the public was looking for."[1] From the get-go, Obama surrounded himself with bright advisers, including David Plouffe as his campaign manager, and Facebook co-founder Chris Hughes, who put together a social-networking strategy that created a tidal wave of community support for the Democrats. Let's take a look at the other aspects of Obama's campaign, using the Creative Execution formula, to understand how the junior senator from Illinois redefined the rules of presidential campaigning.

Unique Strategy

The main strategy Obama followed, given the shaky global climate created by the Bush administration's sloppy handling of the War on Terror (even the success of the surge in 2007 to 2008 couldn't overcome the negative press born out of the U.S.-sanctioned use of torture at Guantanamo Bay and Abu Ghraib), was therefore to portray himself as the remedy to the Bush administration, and to shift focus from the War on Terror to the economy and the rebuilding of relations with America's allies around the world. This singular strategy, wrote Ryan Lizza in the *New Yorker*, "allowed Obama to finesse the perpetual problem of Presidential politics: having one message to win over a party's most ardent supporters and another when trying to capture independents and U.F.G.s [Up For Grabs]—the voters who decide a general election."[2] The main Obama message—and indeed his motto—became "change we can believe in," which would serve to differentiate his campaign from both that of Clinton, a well-established political figure, and McCain, who despite his contrarian views would continue to be saddled with the Bush legacy.

Another, more subtle aspect of Obama's strategy was his emphasis on preaching unity, and using his personal history to convince voters that he was the right person to pull the country back from the brink, both economically and politically. Hints of this powerful strategy first emerged when Obama made his political debut on the national stage at the 2004 Democratic National Convention. His speech, which many already saw as a harbinger of the party's future platform, cautioned against "the spin masters and negative ad peddlers who embrace the politics of anything goes . . . There's not a black America and white America and Latino America and Asian America; there's the United

States of America." Obama went on to make the case that the concept of blue and red states was also anathema to his politics, and that there are people who "coach Little League in the blue states and have gay friends in the red states."[3] Combined with his family background— a father who grew up in a small village in Kenya and made a living herding goats before receiving a scholarship to study in the United States—Obama would come across as a leader who could bridge the social and emotional divide that had so deeply splintered America, and its allies, since the beginning of the War on Terror. The vision of the future that he put out seemed both pragmatic and healing. Moreover, as Joe Klein points out, "it also seems rather amazing that he has been absolutely intent on enacting every one of his campaign promises."[4]

Candid Dialogue

Obama encouraged Candid Dialogue not only with the electorate, which he did through his campaign rallies and online touch points, but also with his own staff. As Barry Libert and Rick Faulk write in *Barack, Inc.*, "Obama praised good work publicly, thanking local organizers at his rallies just as enthusiastically as he thanked the mayor or the governor of the state, and he gave his staff straight, blunt feedback."[5] Libert and Faulk recall a particular case in December 2007, when Obama placed a phone call to Alice Isenberg, a volunteer on Obama's New England Steering Committee. Isenberg had introduced Obama at a Fenway Park fundraiser in December 2007, feeling slightly nervous. A couple of days later, she got a phone call from Obama to thank her for her kind words. She was startled to hear personally from Obama, and momentarily thought the call was a prank, but then recognized the voice. This personal touch from Obama is a rarity among politicians, most of who would have forgotten about Isenberg after two days of running a hard campaign.

The other tool Obama used to foster Candid Dialogue with a broader audience is the Internet. Early in his campaign, Obama saw the potential for the Internet, particularly social websites like Facebook and MySpace, to help garner support and create a multi-way dialogue with the electorate. "There's no more powerful tool for grassroots organizing than the Internet," he declared, and with the help of former Facebook executive Chris Hughes, launched My.Obama.com, a website that helped him raise more than 2 million donations. Visitors to MyBo, as the website came to be called, were asked to record their fundraising progress online, and get in touch with potential voters in their area. Hughes also created an iPhone application called Obama 08 that organized the user's address book by key battleground states, so that people could reach out to their friends in key electoral battlegrounds. Finally, the sponsors of an "Obama for President" user group on Second Life set out to raise donations for Obama's campaign by sponsoring a virtual musical festival.

The Facebook application that Chris Hughes designed also helped draw millions of viewers to watch Obama's speeches, blogs, and press releases. As Libert and Faulk conclude, "his image and message were everywhere on the Internet."[6] More than 21 million viewers have flocked to Obama's channel on YouTube, which hosts more than 1,800 of the president's videos and speeches, both pre- and post-election. The most frequently viewed video of Obama on YouTube during his first presidential campaign, incidentally, wasn't his swearing-in ceremony or victory speech, but rather his debut appearance on the *Ellen DeGeneres Show*, when he walks in to the tune of "Crazy in Love" by Beyoncé. During the show, Obama makes a live phone call to a woman in Richmond, Virginia, who asks him to describe how he would balance work and family life as president. Through the skillful use of traditional media such as the *Ellen* show and new media, Obama got his message across and connected millions of people who flocked to Facebook on election day to show their friends that they had voted by clicking a specially designed box on their profile page.

Obama's use of Candid Dialogue was also highlighted during the selection process for his vice-president, which he announced the last week in August 2008. During the gruesome discussions, report Libert and Faulk, "he brought up tiny details from the massive briefing reports on the candidates, and worked the room for feedback . . . But he never gave the slightest signal of his own preference down to the final choice . . . As a result, the advice was candid and the discussion probed all the pros and cons."[7] Not surprisingly, the announcement of the Biden selection was done through an e-mail message from Obama to his support base, rather than through the media. Obama's insistence on connecting with people directly continues to this day. He launched a new feature on the website www.whitehouse.gov called "Open for Question," where he conducted his first presidential online town hall in March 2009. Through this experiment, President Obama gathered more than 100,000 questions such as this popular one: "The Founding Fathers believed that there is no difference between a free society and an educated society. Our educational system, however, is woefully inadequate. How do you plan to restore education as a right and core cultural value in America?" Although Obama will be hard-pressed to maintain the open access he created with millions of online users, he's clearly determined to do his part so that the social networks and websites he created are ready to swing into action again in 2012.

Clear Roles and Accountabilities

Obama's campaign hinged on the performance of a tightly woven team of young, ambitious individuals. In addition to Hughes, Obama recruited a number of quiet but determined costars. One such costar was David Plouffe, a partner with media firm AKPD who had managed Obama's Illinois senatorial campaign and who *Esquire* magazine described as "modest champion, puppy-loyal, and wholly inoffensive."[8] Later on, Obama would refer to Plouffe as the one who "built the best political organization in the country,"[9] and culled more than 13 million e-mail addresses of Obama supporters across America. After Obama won the election, Plouffe used the famous e-mail list to organize "house parties" across the United States to debate President Obama's proposed legislation. Another of Obama's costars was David

Axelrod, a former reporter for the *Chicago Tribune* who had run John Edwards's unsuccessful 2004 presidential bid, and who in 2006 had played a key role in helping the Democratic Party regain its congressional majority.

When Obama finally wrapped up the Democratic nomination in June 2007, he assembled everyone on his team to tell them that "When I started this campaign . . . what I was absolutely positive of was that there was the possibility of creating the best organization. The way great things happen is when people are willing to submerge their own egos and focus on a common task."[10] The motto for the campaign staff became "no drama Obama," meaning that staffers focused on their tasks and resolved any conflict privately, rather than by leaking their complaints to the *Washington Post* or *New York Times*. Contrast this to Hillary Clinton's campaign, which Tim Dickinson, writing in *Rolling Stone*, described as "beset by leaks and infighting among factions of overbearing strategists, know-it-all advisers, egotistical flacks and self-important campaign managers who battled noisily—and publicly—over message, budget, access to the candidate and prestige."[11]

Another special aspect of the Obama campaign was the use of volunteers on a national scale to canvas and report on the electorate's tendencies. In every battleground state, Obama volunteers knocked on doors to seek out information on who was voting for Obama, McCain, or undecided. At the end of every working day, these volunteers would enter the data into their laptops and e-mail it to the Obama headquarters. This composite daily sketch of how voters were leaning allowed Obama to see the impact of his speeches or campaign activities in a particular state almost overnight. Likewise on election day, handpicked teams of Obama volunteers fanned out in key states such as Ohio to encourage voters to come out, and monitored the activity at key polling stations. As Jon Carson, who recruited and organized 1,400 teams across Ohio, told Libert and Faulk, "We've taken the best of these volunteers, and they're giving us 40, 50, 60 hours a week. They're empowered, and we made them accountable."[12] This spirit of accountability, selfless devotion to the cause, and hard work became the hallmarks of the Obama campaign, starting at the top with Plouffe and Axelrod, and reaching all the way down to field volunteers.

Obama's organizing genius carried over to the White House. Instead of needing to tightly control the government bureaucracy, Obama made it clear that his role was to set the broad agenda and tone for U.S. policy, and then to empower his staff to implement various strategies. As *BusinessWeek* observed before the November 2008 election, Obama was convinced that he would "do the chief executive's job by focusing completely on providing leadership vision, judgment, and inspiration . . . He pledges to stay above the managerial fray and, instead, hold agency heads fully accountable for the performance of the bureaucracies in their charge."[13] Once elected, Obama appointed Rahm Emanuel, the fourth-highest-ranking Democrat in Congress, as his chief of staff (Rahm later quit his White House job to become mayor of Chicago). This choice was widely acclaimed due to Emanuel's reputation as a tough negotiator and people manager. Emanuel was so intent on getting Obama's $700-billion bailout package through Congress in early 2009 that he sought a special dispensation from his rabbi to work through Rosh Hashanah. To emphasize the importance of Pakistan, Afghanistan, and the Middle East, Obama also made two new appointments: that of Richard Holbrooke as U.S. special envoy to Pakistan and Afghanistan, and George Mitchell as special envoy to the Middle East. With these two key appointments, Obama showed that he continued to value the importance of Clear Roles and Accountabilities inside his administration, and that he would do what it takes to get the right people working on the right problem.

Bold Action

The first example of Bold Action was Obama's decision to give up public financing for his presidential bid, and instead rely on his independent fundraising activities. This move caught everyone by surprise, since it meant that Obama would give up the $84 million that, as a major-party candidate, he was entitled to take to the bank. Through his website and fundraising events, Obama built up a war chest of $750 million, compared to John McCain's $360 million. This gap became significant in the last few weeks of the campaign, when Obama outspent McCain three to one, and had the leisure of spending $39 million on a single key state—Florida—while McCain, operating under the tight rules of public funding, could only spend a combined total of $84 million *across all 50 states* in September and October 2008. This bold decision showed Obama's confidence in his team's ability to organize a great fundraising campaign, and it consequently made the Republicans look like yesterday's party. Not only was Obama relying on social-networking sites, YouTube, and iPhones to get his message out, but he was also collecting millions of dollars—mostly in amounts of $25 to $200—from the MyBo website. Of the $750 million the Obama campaign raised, a whopping $500 million came from these online donations. McCain's website lagged well behind that of Obama—according to Nielsen Online, 3.3 million unique visitors went to the MyBo website in August 2008 alone, compared to 1.6 million for McCain's site.

Once he was elected, Obama quickly made another bold decision. He nominated Hillary Clinton, who had fought him tooth and nail in the Democratic primaries, to be his secretary of state. He also retained Robert Gates, who had succeeded Donald Rumsfeld as secretary of defense in November 2006, in order to provide continuity for the ongoing wars in Iraq and Afghanistan. As Libert and Faulk write, the nomination of Clinton "was an act of supreme self-confidence, and one that brought into the Obama administration a world-class intellect and well-known global emissary."[14] Faced with what the *New York Times* called "The Great Depression," Obama also made some rapid, bold decisions about the economy, introducing an $825-billion stimulus package to top the $700-billion bailout plan already signed into law by President Bush. Obama himself pointed this out in his inaugural address, when he said "the state of our economy calls for action, bold and swift."

Visible Leadership

Obama's ability to maintain his cool during the campaign, and to portray himself as the way forward for the world and the United States, in terms of both political and racial unity, created instant prestige and visibility. As Jabari Asim writes, "Thanks to Obama's convincing, thorough demonstration of intelligence and verve . . . the idea that one should govern by speaking softly and carrying a big stick—an African proverb made famous by a white American president—has now been dynamically embodied by an African American head of state."[15] Obama's Visible Leadership had been in evidence for several years before his White House run, as he had shown during his various trips to Africa, where he was often greeted as a returning prodigy, and at the Democratic National Convention in 2004, where his positive speech was felt by many to be more awe-inspiring than the over-staged performance by Democratic nominee John Kerry.

During the 2008 campaign, Obama's visible leadership was forged and tested on several occasions. First was a YouTube debate with Clinton in July 2007, which would influence much of Obama's campaign plan for the next 12 months. When asked by the interviewer whether they would be willing to meet with the vilified leaders of North Korea, Syria, Venezuela, Cuba, and Iran, Clinton remained cautious while Obama simply responded "I would." This deceivingly casual answer shocked the audience. Sensing this to be a key moment, Clinton pounced on Obama, lecturing him about his lack of global political experience. How could the president of the United States casually agree to meet with the leaders of what previous presidents had labeled the axis of evil? The next morning, Obama's campaign staff gathered to discuss how to retract Obama's comment, fully expecting a media onslaught. The mood was gloomy. When he entered the room and heard what people were struggling with, Obama cut in with a remarkable observation: "We met with Stalin," he said. "We met with Mao. The idea that we can't meet with Ahmadinejad is ridiculous. This is a bunch of Washington-insider conventional wisdom that makes no sense. We should not run from this debate. We should have it." And so instead of deflecting questions about Obama's answer, his galvanized staff went on the offensive, stressing how Clinton's approach reflected a stilted way of dealing with the issues confronting America abroad, and how Obama offered a fresh, wise alternative to dealing with the world. In this one fell swoop, Obama positioned himself as an agent of change in American politics.

Obama had another opportunity to turn a potentially embarrassing situation into a leadership moment when his former pastor, Rev. Jeremiah Wright Jr., was shown accusing the United States of murdering innocent Japanese at Hiroshima and Nagasaki, and shouting "God damn America!" as he vented anger about the way African Americans had been treated in the United States. As the pastor who had been a close family friend, officiated Obama's wedding to Michelle, and baptized their two daughters, Wright's vitriolic attacks on U.S. values could not be ignored by the Obama campaign. Just like he had in handling his comments on meeting with the leaders of Iran and North Korea, Obama chose to step into the controversy and told Axelrod that he wanted to deliver a speech on race—a topic the Obama campaign had carefully avoided. It took three days for the writers to craft the speech, which Obama delivered in Philadelphia. Blunt and direct, Obama acknowledged the racial fears that had played out in the United States over 200 years, but finally outlined his choice: "We can play Reverend Wright's sermons on every channel, every day . . . We can pounce on some gaffe by a Hillary supporter as evidence that she's playing the race card, or we can speculate on whether white men will all flock to John McCain." If we did that, he warned, "in the next election, we'll be talking about some other distraction . . . and then nothing will change." And so once again, prodded into the limelight, Obama stepped up and addressed a difficult issue head-on. "Obama demonstrated that there is no gain to be had by putting your head in the sand and pretending the problem doesn't exist," write Libert and Faulk.[16] This became a turning point in the primary campaign, which further positioned Obama as a levelheaded leader who could tackle difficult issues with aplomb.

Once Obama wrapped up the Democratic nomination, he had established himself as a credible leader with strong convictions about the economy and how the United States should end the war in Iraq and refocus on Afghanistan. Yet even though he had managed to edge out Hillary Clinton and turn her years of insider politics experience into a liability, Obama still needed to convince undecided voters across the United States that he would effectively represent American interests and values abroad. In July 2008, Obama decided to visit Israel and Europe, following in the footsteps of John McCain, who had gone to meet with Israeli prime minister Ehud Olmert in March of the same year. Unlike McCain, however, Obama stepped into the limelight of Middle Eastern politics by not only meeting with Israeli officials but by visiting the occupied territories in the West Bank and meeting with the president of the Palestinian National Authority, Mahmoud Abbas, and deliberately stating his opposition to Hamas. Obama's visit had an electrifying effect in both Israel and the occupied territories. As Itamar Eichner wrote in the *Yedioth Ahronoth* newspaper, "Barack Obama landed at Ben-Gurion Airport, and out of the plane stepped Barack Obama, like a rock star, into a particularly emotional reception."[17]

Obama bested his performance in Israel by delivering an emotionally charged speech a few days later in Berlin, where he spoke in front of 200,000 jubilant Germans. Obama's speech was loaded with positive messages such as "we will reject torture" and "now is the time to build new bridges, listen to each other, learn from each other and, most of all, trust each other." Obama's speech in Berlin had echoes of Ronald Reagan's visit there in the 1980s, when he challenged then Soviet president Gorbachev to "bring down this wall," as well as John F. Kennedy's June 1963 speech where he famously declared "Ich bin ein Berliner." This supreme act of visible leadership by Barack Obama, four months before the U.S. presidential election, not only transfixed audiences in Israel and Germany, but sent a powerful message back to the American electorate about Obama's credibility on the world stage. How did McCain respond? The day Obama delivered his speech in Berlin, McCain visited a German restaurant in Ohio to have lunch with a group of small-business owners, and evaded questions about Obama's Berlin presence by declaring that he would "love to give a speech to the German people," but would only do so once elected president of the United States. In the end, Obama's decision to head to Israel and Germany provided U.S. voters with an early opportunity to see the kind of leadership he would act out on the global stage, whereas McCain's visit to Ohio received the same treatment as a visit to a local 7–Eleven.

Early in his tenure as president, Obama was asked by a *New York Times* reporter if he was trying to accomplish too much too quickly. Obama gave a typical Creative Execution answer: "Now is the time for us to make some tough, big decisions," he said. "There's nothing inherent in our political process that should prevent us from making these difficult decisions now, as opposed to 10 years or 20 years from now . . . It will depend on leadership."[18] Obama's leadership was certainly tested—from the financial crisis to the BP oil spill and health care reform, he dealt with more controversial issues in his first two years in office than most presidents have during their entire term. What will stand out to most historians looking back on his presidency 10 or 20 years from now may have much to do with his unique election campaign, which will resonate through the ages as a distinctive example of Creative Execution.

THOMAS COOK'S NORTH AMERICAN TURNAROUND

Now that we've looked at Barack Obama's election campaign, let's return to the business sphere and explore the turnaround of Thomas Cook Americas. Unlike Issy Sharp, Kiichiro Toyoda, or the Google co-founders, Gary McDonald wasn't asking himself how he could start a new company when he took over as CEO of Thomas Cook Americas in the late 1990s. Instead, McDonald was staring at a business that had lost $5 million the previous year and needed a radical shift in direction. He had just finished a two-year stint at Thomas Cook's head office in the United Kingdom, where he had developed a strategy to transform the travel company into a technology-driven market leader. At the time, Thomas Cook was the world's largest travel and foreign-exchange company, which served more than 20 million customers annually and generated gross sales of more than $40 billion. The company made money by selling travelers checks, using the interest on the float between the time when a customer purchased the checks and the time when the customer cashed them to make handsome profits. This formula worked well when interest rates soared above 13 percent in the early 1990s. But by the end of the decade, when interest rates dropped below 5 percent, Thomas Cook stopped earning the relatively easy money that came from investing its mighty float.

McDonald and his peers in the UK dealt with the looming crisis by hiring the Boston Consulting Group (BCG), a high-end strategy consulting firm, to determine how to better leverage Thomas Cook's unique competence: managing money and people on the move. One net result of this new thinking was the decision to offer banks around the world the opportunity to outsource their foreign-exchange business to Thomas Cook. Another momentous shift was an account-management process to review every travelers check account (primarily banks) that had become unprofitable as a result in the drop in interest rates. For the first time, Thomas Cook focused on making each of these accounts profitable, breaking a century-old tradition of serving all customers regardless of their needs or costs of delivering service.

In this shifting environment, McDonald realized that the company in North America was just as "mired in the old ways of doing business" as the UK. He quickly articulated his end game: he decided that within three years the company would generate $25 million in profits. He built his own Creative Execution formula, SPF25, which became the driving force behind all the activities his team engaged in. The formula stands for Strategy, People & Process, and Finance. By managing the disciplined execution of all four of these components, McDonald believed that Thomas Cook could reach its goal of making $25 million in profits in the Americas. And that's exactly what happened, with a twist.

When Thomas Cook saw that its American sibling was restored to health, it decided to sell its Financial Services division to Travelex, a foreign-exchange company with more than 700 kiosks in airports and cities around the world. The deal netted Thomas Cook a cool £450 million (the then-equivalent of $650 million). When the deal came into force, McDonald was well on his way to achieving annual profits of $26 million. He had already hit the $21-million mark after two years at the helm.

McDonald's turnaround of Thomas Cook Americas struck me as a perfect example of Creative Execution in action. It seemed that he got the company firing on all cylinders, not just repeating the SPF25 slogan but actually living it and owning it. If you're the CEO of an organization seeking that kind of transformation, or a manager trying to implement a new IT system in your company, you know how invaluable it is to get people to take ownership of change. Just how did McDonald manage to obtain the total buy-in of his team? He filled in each dimension of the Creative Execution formula, starting with his SPF25 strategy, which would take the company to a new level of performance. "I wanted to establish myself and create an agenda around SPF25 which would emphasize how we would execute each aspect of the formula as a team," he explains.

I spent several months working with McDonald and talking to his team about the gigantic leap forward they executed at Thomas Cook. When I was done recording their story, I looked for the patterns of leadership lessons that flowed from the successful execution of the SPF25 vision, and began to discern the various elements of the Creative Execution formula. In the end, it was clear to me that his turnaround of Thomas Cook Americas could be easily understood against the backdrop of the five dimensions of Creative Execution.

Unique Strategy

Having worked with BCG's strategy consultants in the UK, McDonald understood how important it was for Thomas Cook to shift to more profitable clients and businesses lines and stop relying on interest rates to make money. He started working on a strategic plan for the Americas business, but soon realized the sheer complexity of the plan would daunt anyone who read it. He remembers looking at a 40-page strategy document and thinking, "I can't show anyone in the organization any of these documents. It will scare the hell out of them." Instead he landed on the more simple SPF25 formula, which he buttressed with five priorities and five values. The SPF25 formula was easy to remember and included key indicators for each of the five priorities, which made it actionable as well. "I only had ten fingers," Gary recalls, "so I'd use one hand to describe the five priorities during my presentations, and the other to list our values." That kind of simplicity made the strategy and priorities easy to remember and easy to discuss with people.

Candid Dialogue

Creating open and frequent dialogue about what needs to change is often the most underestimated critical success factor inside organizations. The greatest champion of this principle is Admiral Nelson, who invited his captains to dinner almost every day aboard his flagship the *Victory*, and constantly drew and mentally rehearsed the upcoming battle with the French and Spanish Combined Fleet. McDonald used the same technique, inviting his executives to his house for dinner, or flying them down to Florida for two-day retreats. "I needed to know more about each of my team members than even their spouses did," he explains. "Without their total trust and mutual respect, we'd become dysfunctional."

McDonald hosted "bureaucracy busting breakfasts" with employees around the country, where he invited a small group of employees and asked what got in their way of doing a better job. He designed a live employee feedback system, which asked employees, on a daily basis, to respond to a simple question: "Is today a better day than yesterday?" The nature of the comments would influence a "mood meter" built into the tool. "If it was blue that was rather cold and red was hot and sizzling," Gary recalls. "It was amazing how it changed based on something I or my team had said or done." This may seem benign in the days of Twitter, but it created an invaluable communication pipeline between the leadership team and the employees scattered between his Toronto head office, the United States, and Mexico.

Clear Roles and Accountabilities

One of the first things McDonald did was to change his leadership team. On his first day, he met with his vice-president of human resources and asked him, candidly, to tell him how many of the people on the leadership team were really good. "Only one," he remembers Mike telling him. "And I'm sorry to say, but that's me." McDonald and his HR head spent their first month together reshuffling the team. They landed on six executive roles, down from fifteen. The next task was telling them that each would have to own one aspect of the SPF25 formula, a priority, value, or financial indicator, which wasn't related to their functional role. "That was hugely disruptive," McDonald says. But turning the executive team into owners of a priority ensured that that each would have skin in the game and could be held accountable—by McDonald and their peers on the leadership team—for making the strategy work.

He used the same approach to pick the most talented people inside the business and ask them to spearhead a particular initiative. "We had someone in charge of managing the trade room operations," he explains. "That person was absolutely superb for something we had to do, yet we couldn't afford to lose him in the role he was in." They put him in charge of the change effort, and he executed it better than McDonald had anticipated. "We suffered a bit in the marketplace because we pulled him off his job, but it was worth it." He had learned this lesson in the UK, when he was in charge of developing the global marketing strategy for the company, breaking up the implementation into small project chunks and handing out responsibility to different team members. "There were people who I put in charge of the marketing transformation who were actually much more senior than I was," he recalls. "But the bottom line is we needed skilled players who would feel empowered enough to lead change."

The way McDonald empowered his direct reports was simple. He told them upfront: you're the CEO of your priority or change initiative. And that made it clear to people that they would be accountable for the success or failure of their piece of the pie. As Sharon Groom, who McDonald appointed as general counsel for the Americas, puts it: "We were all encouraged to take responsibility for things. If you didn't like it, you had to fix it. Everyone felt like they had a clear purpose and could make a difference."

Bold Action

To get the message across that he expected everyone to play their part in making SPF25 come to life, McDonald made a number of bold decisions. First, he brought down the walls around his office, so that everyone could walk in and see what he was working on. "People would see me behind a glass door and wonder 'what the heck is he doing in there?'" he recalls. Opening up his office took away the physical and emotional barriers that often isolate CEOs from the real world. "Having people walking by and just saying hi was hugely beneficial," he explains. Once he got his office reorganized, McDonald moved on to the trading floor, which housed more than 40 traders whose main job was to provide exchange-rate quotes and online services for customers. McDonald worked with the traders to redesign the entire floor using a golf-course theme, complete with replica carpets, clocks from famous golf courses, and a nineteenth-hole café. The Eagle's Nest, as the floor soon became known, "created the most energized environment I've ever seen in any organization," he says. "Their business was taking off and they worked together, celebrated, and partied together."

More significant was his decision to drop unprofitable customers, and shift away from some of the big bank relationships that Thomas Cook had been tethered to for years. In the United States, the company had a longtime relationship with Bank of America, which sold millions of travelers checks from their branch operations, but cost Thomas Cook between $3 and $4 million per year. McDonald decided to drop the large banks that wouldn't agree to change the relationship to a win-win model. "We had to all put our hands in the middle to agree with that part of the strategy," he stresses. "That was tough to do, because we were losing market share to American Express, and at one time we were willing to take on any bank at any cost. But at the end of the day if we couldn't turn the relationship into a win-win, we decided we had to resign the account." These Bold Actions made it clear to everyone in the UK and in the Americas that Thomas Cook was serious about getting back to profitability.

Visible Leadership

To get everyone on board with SPF25, from the traders in the Eagle's Nest to the foreign-exchange specialists operating in the Americas cities and airports, McDonald held monthly town hall meetings with employees where he relentlessly explained the five priorities and values. The essence of the SPF25 direction was captured in an article he wrote called "Moving Forward," and forwarded to every employee. He asked every one of his direct reports to complete a 360 review and work with a coach to maximize their personal leadership. "As the lead communicator for making SPF25 happen, I had to rethink how I used my time," he says. "I just couldn't send delegates to meetings with employees or customers. I had to find the time to be there. I had to learn to better delegate and get my hands off things." To ensure that the whole team focused on their own leadership development, he took his leadership team to INSEAD, the business school outside Paris, for a week of leadership-skills development.

While McDonald focused on building up individuals' strengths, he also invested heavily in creating a first-rate team and rewarding his employees' performance. He celebrated every client win by sitting down with employees at the Eagle's Nest café. His philosophy was that, as CEO, one of his biggest roles was to recognize the achievements of his team and encourage high performance through loud rewards. "We even put up a wall of fame to showcase the frontline people who were

215

the key to success," he adds. For employees, McDonald found a simple way to recognize progress. He had soft-drink machines installed in the Eagle's Nest, and every time the company posted a positive monthly result, the price of each can would go down by a quarter or more. There were so many positive months that the price eventually went down to zero, and Gary feared that he would turn Thomas Cook into a soft-drink factory.

Almost 10 years later, he still has regular dinners with his team members, who all remember the ride at Thomas Cook, and McDonald's leadership, with genuine fondness and nostalgia. Sharon Groom recalls how McDonald personified the culture change efforts: "When I first joined the team I could see there was a lack of trust, since we'd had several presidents who came from the UK and didn't fit in well. But McDonald didn't just talk about change. He did things himself to promote the new culture, and he removed the suspicions and distrust by allowing us to truly get to know each other and make sure we all understood how we supported one another. Gary assembled a true team of experts, and he became the heart of it." Perhaps that's a better definition of Creative Execution than any I could provide.

THE FINAL QUESTION

Through the experiences of Barack Obama and Gary McDonald, we can see how Creative Execution flourishes under different circumstances. It doesn't take a mighty conflict like Alexander's march into Persia or Yamamoto's planning of World War II in the Pacific to unleash the power of Creative Execution. And despite its unstoppable march toward the East, Creative Execution isn't extinct in the West. Leaders such as Obama and McDonald remind us that we can still harness the power of developing a Unique Strategy and deploy it through Creative Execution, whether your purpose is to run for higher office or turn around a regional business. The question is: do you have what it takes to become a Creative Execution leader? That's the question we'll try to answer in the final chapter.

Becoming a Creative Execution Leader

The only true voyage of discovery . . . would be not to visit
strange lands but to possess other eyes.

—Marcel Proust

What I've offered in this book is a framework for thinking about the various elements of outstanding execution—from the perspective of a new CEO like Gary McDonald, and through the eyes of remarkably successful leaders such as Admiral Nelson or Issy Sharp. And now we come to you. Do you see yourself as a Creative Execution leader, or are you just striving to achieve mediocre results and keep your head above water, day in and day out?

You may think that Creative Execution worked for Nelson and for Google, but that it may not work for you because you're not running for office, admiral of a fleet, or the CEO of a start-up Internet company. But as you found out reading about these history-defying leaders, Creative Execution isn't just a means to an end. It's a way of thinking and developing your leadership that will help you unlock your potential to achieve breakthrough results against the odds, in any organization.

The true art of leadership is to skillfully navigate your way around the Creative Execution formula, constantly watching out for weaknesses and faults, in order to keep yourself and your organization away from the stumbling blocks that finally tripped Alexander the Great and General Motors. Overcoming the derailment that may follow success could be the single largest challenge for any leader or company. Creative Execution gives you the keys to achieving outstanding results against the odds. But as a custodian of Creative Execution, you must learn to become, in the words of my friend and mentor Bob Rosen, a "just enough anxiety" leader: someone who can lead with confidence, yet be humble enough to perceive your own shortcomings and vulnerabilities. Only that honest insight into yourself will keep you on the road to higher forms of Creative Execution, and put additional distance between you and the global hawks bent on your reversal.

THE PATH TO CREATIVE EXECUTION

Becoming a Creative Execution leader, like any other serious transformation, begins by taking an honest look at yourself: your leadership capabilities, your values, and what keeps you from allowing your bold and creative side to flourish. Most of us bottle up our passions and beliefs, worried that if we let those loose, we will stick out and get shot—in a figurative sense. But think back to Nelson, who took his ship smack into the middle of an enemy formation when his commanding officer had hoisted the flag for retreat. The whole fleet followed Nelson's example, and victory was won.

Sometimes (not every day, nor on a simple whim), you need to take the one risk that will tip the scales in your favor. Just like the Google founders who diverted their plane to London in order to convince AOL to rescind its deal with Yahoo!. Think back on the moments when you held back against your core beliefs or intuition. What were the consequences for you and for the organization? Would you be better off now having listened to that core belief, or are you pleased with how things worked out? Either outcome is possible, but make sure you learn a lesson from it. One day, this core belief that gnaws at you—whether, like in Nelson's case, it is the belief that a radical new strategy will work better than the conventionally accepted one, or, in the case of Sergey Brin and Larry Page, that there is ultimately more money to be made in Internet search than inside a "garden wall" of pay-per-use content—is what will drive you toward Creative Execution.

To get you started on this journey, spend some time assessing your organization's performance from the perspective of Vision, Strategy, Culture, and your own Leadership. Do these four elements blend into a powerful Creative Execution formula that will help you launch the next Google, Four Seasons, or Toyota, and beat the odds in the hyper-competitive century in which we now live? Will they help you create one of the world's most respected NGOs or turn around a fragile health care facility?

Here's a framework to help you come up with your own answers:

1. Are You Asking Enough Questions?

The British commentators who cover the English Premier League, where glorious soccer teams such as Manchester United, Arsenal, and Liverpool battle it out every week, have an interesting way of describing a team that's playing a more aggressive game than the other. They often say, for example, "Arsenal seems to be the team that's asking the questions today"—which is a very English way of saying that they're kicking the other team's butt. In the NFL, we often hear the commentators talk about how one team is so much better at execution—they don't ask questions, they simply kill, destroy, or humiliate the other guys. Whatever sport you prefer, I find the concept of asking more questions intriguing. Didn't Toyota ask more questions than GM over the past 20 years? You bet! They asked how they could adapt the Toyota Production System to the North American market, and how they could achieve *both* quality improvements and cost reductions. They even asked to borrow one of GM's plants to figure out how their production system could be transplanted to North America. Toyota was asking itself a number of important questions: could they be faster to anticipate customer needs in North America? And they kept working at it until they became a little arrogant, apologized to the U.S. Congress and to its customers worldwide, and went back to their culture of deep listening.

By asking enough questions, and challenging traditional thinking, you end up framing the problem differently and coming up with creative solutions that set you apart from competitors and other leaders. Look at what Generals Keane, Petraeus, and Odierno did in Iraq during the 2007 to 2008 surge. They literally took on the most powerful individuals at the Pentagon and in their chain of command, including the then-sitting secretary of defense, chief of the Joint Chiefs of Staff, and commander of CENTCOM—people who not only dominated the way the war in Iraq was being fought, but who were also their superiors in the military hierarchy. Keane, Petraeus, and Odierno started the surge movement by asking themselves what they could do differently to defeat the insurgency. They rewrote the U.S. counterinsurgency manual, peppering it with lessons from Vietnam and Algeria, and emphasized the need to protect the population. They stood by their request for five additional brigades, even when asked if three or four would do. They asked themselves fundamental questions about the desired outcome from the war in Iraq. Was the American goal really to promote democracy in the Middle East? Or was it to stabilize Iraq as the country began to rebuild itself? By asking the questions that the chief of staff and the secretary of defense refused to deal with head-on, the three generals forced a rethinking of the entire U.S. military strategy in Iraq—which became invaluable in Afghanistan when President Obama launched his own surge of U.S. forces in 2009.

In your quest to create your own Creative Execution formula, ask yourself:

- Is your current strategy truly bold, exciting, and differentiated? Does it keep you awake at night, just like Nelson's captains, thinking about the bright possibilities it might unleash?
- Are you letting the voices of outsiders be heard over the cacophony of other voices telling you to keep things the way they are?

- Are you playing defense more frequently than you are playing offense against competitors or regulators? If so, you're not asking enough questions, and you need to have a Candid Dialogue with your team about what your true goals are.

2. Is Your Culture Thriving?

GM didn't feel the need to learn from Toyota until it was too late. Despite their joint venture in California, where Toyota gave GM access to its famed Toyota Production System (TPS), GM continued to operate the same way throughout the 1980s and the 1990s. Instead of incorporating the TPS features into its existing facilities, GM invented a new, separate company, Saturn, to compete directly against the Japanese. Starting in 1984, Saturn began to produce simple, high-quality cars. But Saturn could not, by itself, keep up the Creative Execution feat that was required of GM as a whole in order to beat the likes of Toyota, Honda, and up-and-comer manufacturers like Hyundai. By 2008, Saturn's sales had dropped 22 percent, compared to an 18-percent average drop for the entire automobile market in the United States. And when GM announced its restructuring plans in 2009, Saturn was prominently sitting on the chopping block, along with GM's other ailing brands such as Hummer and Saab. By keeping Saturn as a separate brand, GM went through a feel-good exercise that disguised its ultimate failure. The company's executives could say that they had an answer to Toyota, but by keeping that answer away from its main brands, its lessons never made it into GM's core production system. Saturn is a keen reminder that GM could in fact have turned itself around—if it had applied its lessons learned from Toyota and its own people to the entire company. It took the recession of 2008 to 2009 to force GM to relearn those lessons after it went into bankruptcy.

One of the hardest lessons history teaches us, as we learned with Alexander and Yamamoto, is that success often breeds failure, unless it's accompanied by constant vigilance for lessons learned. In its report on the first space shuttle disaster—*Columbia*'s heartbreaking explosion during liftoff in January 1986—the Presidential Commission appointed by President Reagan reported that one of the fundamental problems had been NASA's reluctance to learn from its successful string of shuttle launches, despite the evidence that the O-rings in its solid rocket boosters were faulty. It wrote that the solid rocket booster (SRB) manufacturer, Morton-Thiokol, and NASA "did not make a timely attempt to develop and verify a new seal after the initial design was shown to be deficient. Neither organization developed a solution to the unexpected occurrences of O-ring erosion and blow-by even though this problem was experienced frequently during the Shuttle flight history."[1]

When the second space shuttle disaster occurred in 2003 with the disintegration of *Columbia* during reentry, NASA had once again committed the sin of not learning from its successes. When it observed that a piece of foam hit the left wing of the orbiter during takeoff, it chose to not investigate the event further until the shuttle's return to Earth, and let *Columbia* get on with its normal mission. This incident had first taken place on *Columbia*'s first flight in 1981, when several pieces of insulating tiles had gone flying off the shuttle during takeoff. At the time, NASA reacted by requesting that ground satellites observe the damage and assess its potential impact. By 2003, NASA had grown so confident that it didn't bother asking for close-in photography to observe the damage to *Columbia*'s left wing. The result was the tragic loss of the orbiter and its seven astronauts, including the first Israeli to fly into space.

Like Alexander and Yamamoto, GM and NASA found it hard to believe that any fatal flaw could undermine their soaring adventures. GM had built the largest company in the world, and had become the de facto American model of a successful enterprise. NASA had built the space shuttle on the heels of the unblemished Apollo missions, where the only near-disaster was Apollo 13. Neither organization expected a sudden reversal, because their culture was fed by years of successful achievements and determination to move forward, despite the accumulating evidence that danger was just around the corner. Ted Rogers, the former president and CEO of Rogers Communications, Canada's largest cable, wireless, and media company, said before he passed away in 2008 that "the seeds of destruction are within us." He knew that rapid growth and financial success can foster a culture of superiority that blinds leaders to the sudden turns on the road ahead, and prevents them from learning what others are doing.

Let's go back to the costly arrogance shown by Admiral Nagumo, who led the Pearl Harbor strike force and came to Midway in 1942 expecting a swift victory over the U.S. Navy. Because of the Imperial Japanese Navy's huge successes following the attack on Pearl Harbor, Nagumo and his pilots believed that they could defeat any U.S. focus they encountered, and easily seize Midway. But in the bloody, desperate battles of early 1942, the Americans had learned what made the Japanese superior, and quickly changed their tactics. For instance, the U.S. Navy's main fighter, the Grumman Wildcat, was slow and cumbersome to maneuver compared to the nimble Zero fighters, but the plane had self-sealing fuel tanks, whereas the Zero did not. This meant that the Zeros would explode almost instantly—killing their pilots—after just a few hits from the Wildcat's machine guns. So the Wildcat pilots adopted a new, deadly effective tactic. A single Wildcat essentially acted as bait, and wildcat pilots would then swoop down over the unsuspecting Zeros to shoot them down from behind and above.

Aboard their aircraft carriers, the Americans also got smarter more quickly than the Japanese by flooding their fuel tanks with carbon dioxide when they came under attack, which prevented the fuel from combusting when the ships were hit by torpedoes or armor-piercing bombs. These important lessons proved essential at Midway, and cost the Imperial Japanese Navy four of its six fast-attack carriers, 4,800 sailors, and 275 planes in one afternoon. Brutally woken up by Japan's attack on Pearl Harbor and its easy conquest of the Philippines, Malaya, and the Dutch East Indies, the U.S. Navy went into fast-learning mode and found ways to turn the tables on the Japanese.

As you strive to learn from others, and avoid the costly road that leads to reversal, ask yourself:

- Are you effectively learning from your competitors, customers, and peers in other organizations?
- Do you believe so strongly in your eventual success that you dismiss warning signals and find yourself blindsided by other companies?
- Are you making it safe for people in your organization to acknowledge when they make a mistake, instead of feeling like they have to conceal doubts or failures for the sake of staying "on plan"?

3. Are You Leading from the Front?

Like Nelson, Alexander, and many other military leaders have shown throughout history, leading from the front is the best way for leaders to stay tightly connected to the forces that drive execution. Even in the age of Twitter and GPS, there's no substitute for a leader, whether a CEO or manager, who spends time in the trenches with the people who deal directly with customers and can feel first-hand the impact of competitors. All the way up to the early twentieth century, leading from the front was the hallmark of every commander, admiral, or general. It was only in World War I, the "war to end all wars" as it was naively thought of at the time, that senior commanders began to lead from remote headquarters, typically in a French chateau miles from the front. This distance between senior leader and those responsible for execution had disastrous consequences. Unaware of the true situation on the ground, French and British commanders designed lofty attack plans that led to the deaths of millions of their soldiers. The same formula was used by the Germans, who were determined to bleed the French Army in places such as Verdun and remained delusional about their ability to win the war even in the face of mounting evidence that their position was quickly deteriorating.

Leading from the front, in warfare or business, is the fairy dust that keeps people focused on their tasks. That's why Katie Taylor, CEO of the Four Seasons, visits an average of 30 hotels every year, and makes sure that she's seen every hotel in the Four Seasons portfolio at least once every three years. She knows that living the Four Seasons values and standards can't be conveyed just through memos and corporate policies.

Here's another striking example: as the commander of the British 7th Armoured Brigade—better known as the Desert Rats—during the 1991 Gulf War, Major General Patrick Cordingley needed to find a way to keep up with his 12,000 men as they charged into Kuwait alongside the U.S. Marines. When the British and U.S. Army practiced maneuver warfare in Europe, they would set up stationary command posts to communicate with troops blocking an anticipated attack by Warsaw Pact forces. But as his brigade broke through enemy minefields and drove a deep wedge into Iraq, Cordingley had to find a new way to stay close to his 300 tanks, armored personnel carriers, and artillery pieces.

After much deliberation with his battle staff, Cordingley decided that he would lead his Desert Rats into battle the old-fashioned way: riding at the head of the formation inside a Challenger tank. As the order to begin the assault came down on February 25, 1991, he jumped into his designated tank and led his troops into eastern Iraq to clear the way for the massive "left hook" that smashed through the Iraqi defenses. The Desert Rats proved their mettle by destroying 300 tanks and armored personnel carriers as they pushed forward. "It became clear," Cordingley wrote after the battle, "that a brigade commander really could work from a tank."

Cordingley's decision to lead from the front reflected his broader commitment to truly understanding the mindset of his soldiers as they prepared for battle. One of his preferred methods was to visit his division's forward posts and invite people to play a game of chess with him. "The minute you'd start playing, people would start asking questions," he explains. "And the questions that came out where the ones they were really concerned about: "When are we going to go home, sir? How long before we attack? Do you think it's going to be alright?" Then someone would get really brave and ask how many chemical weapons the Iraqis had. Would we be able to put on our chemical and biological suits? Would the injection we got against the bubonic plague actually work? Because I was sitting down and they were above me watching, they felt relaxed and the questions would roll."[2]

Just like Taylor and Cordingley, your job as a Creative Execution leader is to be visible, particularly in tough times, in order to lend meaning to your strategy and direction. We all remember that President Bush flew to a remote U.S. Air Force base on 9/11 instead of flying back to Washington, DC, or New York—his first serious mistake as president. Conversely, you might remember pictures of Barack Obama being cheered on by 200,000 Berliners during his 2008 election campaign, or giving a speech in Cairo in June 2009 to start mending the rift between the United States and the Muslim world. Lead from the front, because that's where you'll discover the potential risks that will derail or accelerate your well-laid plans.

LET CREATIVE EXECUTION SURGE

Building your own Creative Execution formula may be the most important investment you make to ensure that you develop the capabilities that you need to win in an ever-more-schizophrenic global marketplace. Just when you thought the world had recovered from the financial crisis of 2008, the European debt crisis happened. Somehow, while we were busy salvaging what we could from the credit meltdown that followed the failure of Lehman Brothers and the near-failure of AIG and other not-so-bright points of light from the U.S. subprime market implosion, the Greeks were presented with their bill for letting tax collections go, well, uncollected, and those of us who hadn't read a Greek tragedy since high school suddenly saw one served up on CNN and the front pages of the financial press on a daily basis. As one eurozone denizen decried in a tweet to BBC World: "Greece up in revolt, Italy near collapse—welcome to 400 BC!"

The point isn't so much that the Greeks almost universally falsify the value of their homes so that they don't pay the commensurate real estate tax, or that Lehman, AIG, and other investment banks securitized subprime loans and forked them over to unsuspecting investors. These two facts only prove what we already know: that <u>when left to their own devices, people will act greedily or unscrupulously.</u> What's more interesting about these twenty-first-century crises is how quickly and ruthlessly they spread to other parts of the world, like a financial H1N1 virus. A housing problem that should have been contained in the United States led to the near-collapse of global credit, while the Greek government's inability to finance its sovereign debt derailed an entire continent's financial system.

Here's an utterly improbable example of how the world is now interconnected: on Monday October 3, 2011, the Greek government announced that it would fall short of its deficit reduction target by roughly 1 percent. Sounds bad, but really it wasn't. The 1 percent gap amounted to about $2 billion—peanuts in the overall European economy, which churns out $20 trillion worth of goods and services annually. To put it differently, a company like Wal-Mart, which made $419 billion in 2011, could have paid off that $2 billion using less than two days' worth of revenues. Yet this small slip by the Greek government triggered a massive slide in European and global markets. The FTSEurofirst 300 Index fell 900 points within two hours of opening, the Dow Jones fell 258 points, and a Belgian-French bank, Dexia, lost 10 percent of its value and had to be taken over by the Belgium government two weeks later.

We have all heard about the butterfly effect, whereby a butterfly flapping its wings in, say, India, triggers a hurricane in Japan. This is an elegant way to describe chaos theory, which was first proposed in 1890 by Frenchman Henri Poincaré. We now live in a world where the butterfly effect is an economic reality. A small event that happened in Greece generated an instantaneous financial firestorm from Asia to America.

The challenges we face in a constant-crisis world may seem insurmountable, but they are not. What is needed—in order to fix economic imbalances, unemployment, climate change, and the financial stagnation that threatens our democratic societies—is a surge of Creative Execution. More importantly, we need new kinds of leaders who won't be afraid to think boldly, collaborate, and embrace the global matrix we find ourselves woven into. We must stop looking back and, like Katie Taylor when she took over from Issy Sharp at the Four Seasons, look forward. Only by upping our game can we hope to change the rules of play.

While no single universal formula can solve the massive challenges we face as a global society, there is a clear pattern among leaders such as Nelson, Alexander, and Google's founders, who have placed big bets and pulled off what most contemporary observers thought were impossible victories. These victories, and the lessons these leaders teach us, contain the essence of what we need to do in order to defeat the negative energy that the global financial crisis unleashed in our bloodstream.

We all remember the stodgy Five-Year Plans that the Soviet state designed with great fanfare during the 80 years of Communist rule in Russia. These Five-Year Plans were supposed to provide a strategic framework for the entire Soviet economy, prescribing everything from who would produce coal to the number of fridges and tanks the country's factories would roll out. These Five-Year Plans became a straightjacket that stunted creativity and innovation, leading to the semi-paralysis of the Soviet economy, which eventually collapsed under its own weight. And so whether your organization is still reeling from the shock of the global financial crisis, or you are starting a new venture or leading a government agency, hospital, or not-for-profit organization, you are in the same position that the hundreds of leaders from Alexander the Great to Toyota's founders have found themselves in throughout history.

Your job is to avoid creating a grand strategy or Five-Year Plan that limits creative thinking and innovation, and focus instead on mobilizing the forces of Creative Execution that exist all around you. You can embrace change and turn the multitude of crises that dot the global playing field into phenomenal opportunities, or bury your head in the sand and hope they will go away.

The choice is yours.

ENDNOTES

INTRODUCTION

1 John F. Kennedy, "We choose to go to the moon" speech, Houston, 1962.
2 Marty Bahamonde testimony before the Senate Committee on Homeland Security & Governmental Affairs, October 20, 2005, as reported in MSNBC. com: "Official: FEMA didn't heed storm warnings", Oct. 20, 2005, p1.
3 Douglas Brinkley, *The Great Deluge: Hurricane Katrina, New Orleans, and the Mississippi Gulf Coast* (New York: HarperCollins, 2006), 37.
4 Ibid., 323
5 Principles of Coast Guard Operations from Coast Guard Publication 1 - U.S. Coast Guard: America's Maritime Guardian, p. 82.
6 Alan Deutschman, "Change or Die," Fast Company, May 2005, p.55.
7 Haridimos Tsoukas and Christian Knudsen, eds., *The Oxford Handbook of Organization Theory: Meta-Theoretical Perspectives* (Oxford: Oxford University Press, 2003), 264.
8 Jack Welch, *Winning*, New York: HarperCollins, 2005, p. 25
9 Christopher Andrew and Vasili Mitrokhin, *The Mitrokhin Archive II: The KGB and the World* (London: Allen Lane/Penguin Books, 2005), 475.
10 Steve Forbes and John Prevas, *Power Ambition Glory: The Stunning Parallels between Great Leaders of the Ancient World and Today* (New York: Three Rivers Press, 2009), 288.

CHAPTER 1

1 Victor Davis Hanson, *Carnage and Culture: Landmark Battles in the Rise of Western Power* (New York: Random House, 2001), 3.
2 Tania Gergel, ed., *Alexander the Great: The Brief Life and Towering Exploits of History's Greatest Conqueror* (New York: Penguin Books, 2004), 8.
3 Gergel, Alexander the Great, 47–48.
4 Hanson, *Carnage and Culture*, 83.
5 Hanson, *Carnage and Culture*, 79.
6 Partha Bose, *Alexander the Great's Art of Strategy* (New York: Penguin Books, 2003), 37.
7 Geoffrey Parker, ed., *Cambridge Illustrated History of Warfare* (New York: Cambridge University Press, 1995), 29.
8 Hanson, *Carnage and Culture*, 77.
9 Bose, *Alexander the Great's Art of Strategy*, 148–49.
10 Gergel, *Alexander the Great*, 30.
11 Steve Forbes and John Prevas, *Power Ambition Glory: The Stunning Parallels between Great Leaders of the Ancient World and Today* (New York: Three Rivers Press, 2009), 101–02.

12 John Keegan, *A History of Warfare* (New York: Alfred A. Knopf, 1993), 260.
13 Gergel, *Alexander the Great*, 71.
14 Bose, *Alexander the Great's Art of Strategy*, 147.
15 Gergel, *Alexander the Great*, 124-25.
16 James Romm, *Ghost on the Throne: The Death of Alexander the Great and the War for Crown and Empire* (New York: Alfred A. Knopf, 2011), 27.

CHAPTER 2

1 Lisle Rose, *Power at Sea: The Breaking Storm 1919–1945* (Columbia, MO: University of Missouri Press, 2007), 217.
2 Colin White, ed., *Nelson: The New Letters* (Woodbridge, UK: The Boydell Press, 2005), 206.
3 Noel Mostert, *The Line Upon a Wind: The Great War at Sea, 1793–1815* (New York: W.W. Norton & Company, 2007), 36–37.
4 John Keegan, *The Price of Admiralty: The Evolution of Naval Warfare* (New York: Penguin Books, 1988), 66.
5 Mostert, *The Line Upon a Wind*, 195.
6 Ibid., 199.
7 Mostert, *The Line Upon a Wind*, 169.
8 Roger Knight, *The Pursuit of Victory: The Life and Achievement of Horatio Nelson* (New York: Basic Books, 2005), 295.
9 Arthur Herman, *To Rule the Waves: How the British Navy Shaped the Modern World* (New York: HarperCollins, 2004), 386.
10 Walter Sichel, *Emma, Lady Hamilton: From New and Original Sources and Documents* (London: Archibald Constable and Company, 1905), 426.
11 John Frederick Smith, William Howitt, and John Cassell, *John Cassell's Illustrated History of England, vol. 2* (London: Cassell, Peter, and Galpin, 1862), 267.
12 Mostert, *The Line Upon a Wind*, 263.
13 Ibid., 505.
14 Knight, *The Pursuit of Victory*, 556.
15 Keegan, *The Price of Admiralty*, 53.
16 Knight, *The Pursuit of Victory*, 556.
17 Alfred Thayer Mahan, *The Life of Nelson, vol. 2* (London: Sampson Low, Martson & Company, 1897), 339–340.
18 Mostert, *The Line Upon a Wind*, 275.
19 Ibid.
20 Adam Nicolson, *Seize the Fire: Heroism, Duty and the Battle of Trafalgar* (London: HarperCollins, 2005), 45.
21 Brian Lavery, *Nelson's Fleet at Trafalgar* (Annapolis: Naval Institute Press, 2004), 149.

22 Mostert, *The Line Upon a Wind*, 504.
23 Herman, *To Rule the Waves*, 384.
24 Lavery, *Nelson's Fleet at Trafalgar*, 135.
25 Herman, *To Rule the Waves*, 398.
26 Ibid., 386.
27 *The Economist*, "Conjuror of victory: how Lord Nelson, a methodical and conservative man, became a romantic hero", June 23, 2005.
28 Knight, *The Pursuit of Victory*, 533.
29 Ibid., 539.
30 Mostert, *The Line Upon a Wind*, 26.
31 Ibid., 27.
32 Ibid., 519.
33 Vincent P. O'Hara, *Struggle for the Middle Sea: The Great Navies at War in the Mediterranean Theater, 1940–1945* (Annapolis: Naval Institute Press, 2009), 261.

CHAPTER 3

1 Ian W. Toll, *Pacific Crucible, War at Sea in the Pacific, 1941-1942* (New York: W. W. Norton & Company, 2012), 49.
2 Constantine Pleshakov, *The Tsar's Last Armada* (New York: Basic Books), 274.
3 Dan van der Vat, *The Pacific Campaign: The U.S.-Japanese Naval War 1941–1945* (New York: Simon & Schuster, 1991), 70.
4 Paul S. Dull, *A Battle History of the Imperial Japanese Navy (1941–1945)* (Annapolis: Naval Institute Press, 1978), 7.
5 Ian Toll, *Pacific Crucible: War at Sea in the Pacific, 1941–1942* (New York: W.W. Norton & Company, 2011) 118.
6 Toll, *Pacific Crucible*, 11.
7 Nathan Miller, *War at Sea: A Naval History of World War II* (Oxford: Oxford University Press, 1995), 207.
8 Dull, *A Battle History*, 5.
9 Miller, *War at Sea*, 195.
10 Dull, *A Battle History*, 10.
11 Miller, *War at Sea*, 371.
12 Van der Vat, *The Pacific Campaign*, 32–33.
13 Thomas E. Griess, ed., *The Second World War: Asia and the Pacific* (New York: Square One Publishers, 2002), 16.
14 Miller, *War at Sea*, 245.
15 Victor Davis Hanson, *Carnage and Culture: Landmark Battles in the Rise of Western Power* (New York: Random House, 2001), 375.
16 Dallas Woodbury Isom, *Midway Inquest: Why the Japanese Lost the Battle of Midway* (Bloomington, IN: Indiana University Press, 2007), 100.

17 Miller, *War at Sea*, 253.
18 Miller, *The War at Sea*, 255–257.
19 Ibid., 256.
20 John Keegan, *The Price of Admiralty: The Evolution of Naval Warfare* (New York: Penguin Books, 1988), 221.
21 Dull, *A Battle History*, 331.

CHAPTER 4

1 Barry Lando, *Web of Deceit: The History of Western Complicity in Iraq* (Toronto: Anchor Canada, 2007), 10.
2 T. E. Lawrence, letter to the editor, *London Sunday Times*, August 22, 1920.
3 Shahram Chubin, "Reflections on the Gulf War," *Survival*, July–August 1986, 308.
4 Dilip Hiro, *Neighbors, not Friends: Iraq and Iran after the Gulf Wars* (New York: Routledge, 2001), 18.
5 William Polk, *Understanding Iraq* (New York: Harper Perennial, 2006), 144.
6 Norman Schwarzkopf, *It Doesn't Take a Hero: The Autobiography of General H. Norman Schwarzkopf* (New York: Bantam Books, 1992), 287.
7 Don Chipman, "Desert Storm and the triumph of joint warfare planning," *Air Power History*, Spring 2005.
8 Ibid.
9 Lt Gen. David Deptula and Major Gen. Charles Link, "Modern Warfare: Desert Storm, Operation Iraqi Freedom and Operation Enduring Freedom," *Air Power History*, Winter 2007.
10 Schwarzkopf, *It Doesn't Take a Hero*, 320.
11 Ibid., 381.
12 Ibid., 413.
13 Ibid., [415].
14 James Dunnigan and Austin Bay, *From Shield to Storm: High-Tech Weapons, Military Strategy and Coalition Warfare in the Persian Gulf* (San Jose: Authors Choice Press, 2001), 282–283.
15 David Lamb, "The Gulf War: Schwarzkopf says Iraq's Military Close to Collapse," *Guardian*, February 21, 1991.
16 Norman Schwarzkopf, "True Leadership: They love their people and do their duty," *Leadership Excellence* 22, no. 11 (November 2005) 3–4, http://www.demariagroup.com/downloads/LE1105_DMG.pdf.
17 Barry McCaffrey, "Lessons of Desert Storm," *Joint Force Quarterly* (Winter 2000–01): 12–13.
18 Schwarzkopf, *It Doesn't Take a Hero*, 356.
19 PBS Frontline, *The Gulf War: An in-depth examination of the 1990–1991 Persian Gulf crisis, Oral History: Norman Schwarzkopf*, http://www.pbs.org/wgbh/pages/frontline/gulf/oral/schwarzkopf/1.html.

20 Schwarzkopf, *It Doesn't Take a Hero*, 359.
21 Ibid.
22 Ibid., 383.
23 Michael R. Gordon and General Bernard E. Trainor, *The Generals' War* (Boston: Little, Brown, 1995), 397.
24 Schwarzkopf, *It Doesn't Take a Hero*, 384.
25 Ibid., 411–12.
26 George Gendron, "Schwarzkopf On Leadership: General Norman Schwarzkopf discusses some of the principles that helped him win the Gulf War," *Inc.*, January 1, 1992, http://www.inc.com/magazine/19920101/3858.html.
27 Schwarzkopf, "True Leadership," 3.
28 Robert M. Citino, *Blitzkrieg to Desert Storm: The Evolution of Operational Warfare* (Lawrence, KS: University Press of Kansas, 2004), 290.
29 Citino, *Blitzkrieg to Desert Storm*, 297.
30 David Cooper, *Broken America* (Lincoln, NE:iuniverse), 32.
31 Thomas Ricks, *The Gamble: General David Petraeus and the American Military Adventure in Iraq, 2006–2008* (New York: The Penguin Press, 2009), 9.
32 Ibid., [129].
33 Ibid., 14.
34 John McCain, "McCain Opening Statement before Armed Services Committee Hearing With General Petraeus and Ambassador Crocker," Washington, DC: September 11, 2007, http://mccain.senate.gov/public/index.cfm?FuseAction=PressOffice.PressReleases.
35 [President's Address to the Nation, 10 January 2007].
36 Ricks, *The Gamble*, 116.
37 Ibid., [128].
38 Ibid., [157].
39 Ibid., 215.
40 Ibid., 107.
41 Donna Miles, American Forces Press Service, U.S. Department of Defense, "Petraeus Notes Difference Between Iraq, Afghanistan Strategies," Washington, DC: April 22, 2009, http://www.defense.gov/news/newsarticle.aspx?id=54036.
42 Rod Norland, "A False Spring," *New York Times*, April 26, 2009, New York edition.

CHAPTER 5

1 Julia Loffe, "A Green City Blooms in the Desert," *Fortune*, December 8, 2008.
2 Dambisa Moyo, *How the West was Lost: Fifty Years of Economic Folly—and the Stark Choices Ahead* (New York: Farrar, Straus and Giroux, 2011), 173.

3 Michael Lewis, *Boomerang: Travels in the New Third World* (New York: W.W. Norton & Company, 2011), 177.

4 Deepak Ramachandran and Paul Artiuch, "Harnessing the Global N-Gen Talent Pool," New Paradigm Learning Corporation, July 2007.

5 Juha Alho et al., "New Forecast: Population Decline Postponed in Europe," *Statistical Journal of the United Nations* ECE 23 (2006): 1–10.

6 Population Division of the Department of Economic and Social Affairs of the United Nations Secretariat, World Population Prospects: The 2008 Revision. Author's Note: For an enlightening visual representation of these population shifts, go to http://populationpyramid.net/.

7 Donald Kagan, *Pericles of Athens and the Birth of Democracy* (New York: The Free Press, 1991), 2.

8 *Tracking GhostNet: Investigating a Cyber Espionage Network*, TheSecDev Group and Munk Centre for International Studies at University of Toronto, March 29, 2009.

9 See: http://topics.nytimes.com/top/reference/timestopics/subjects/c/computer_malware/stuxnet/index.html

CHAPTER 6

1 *Time*, January 2, 1956.

2 Micheline Maynard and Nick Bunkley, "Foreign Automakers Pass Detroit in Monthly Sales," *New York Times*, August 2, 2007.

3 Alex Taylor III, "GM and Me," *Fortune*, December 8, 2008.

4 Thomas Friedman, *The World is Flat: A Brief History of the Twenty-First Century* (Vancouver/Toronto: Douglas & McIntyre, 2007) 165.

5 William J. Duiker and Jackson J. Spielvogel, *World History 5th Edition* (Belmont, CA: Thomson Wadsworth, 2007) 615.

6 Jeffrey Liker, *The Toyota Way: 14 Management Principles from the World's Greatest Manufacturer* (New York: McGraw-Hill, 2004), 16.

7 David Magee, *How Toyota Became #1: Leadership Lessons from the World's Greatest Car Company* (New York: Penguin Group, 2007), 15.

8 Liker, *The Toyota Way*, 21.

9 Magee, *How Toyota Became #1*, 29.

10 Ibid., 19.

11 Ibid., 20.

12 Hirotaka Takeuchi, Emi Osono, and Norihiko Shimizu, "The Contradictions that Drive Toyota's Success," Harvard Business Review, June 2008.

13 Magee, *How Toyota Became #1*, 60.

14 Ibid., 76.

15 Ibid., 39.

16 Liker, *The Toyota Way*, 23.
17 Magee, *How Toyota Became #1*, 38.
18 Healthy Companies International, "Best Practices: Listening Below the Surface at Toyota," Arlington VA, 2006.
19 Magee, *How Toyota Became #1*, 45.
20 Jim Lentz, address to AIADA Annual Meeting, February 12, 2008.
21 Liker, *The Toyota Way*, 25.
22 Jeffrey Liker and Michael Hoseus, *Toyota Culture: The Heart and Soul of the Toyota Way* (New York: McGraw-Hill, 2008), 11.
23 Magee, *How Toyota Became #1*, 107.
24 Toyota Global Vision 2020, http://www.toyota-global.com/company/vision_philosophy/toyota_global_vision_2020.html
25 Takeuchi, Osono, and Shimizu, "The Contradictions," June 2008.
26 Ibid.
27 Ibid.
28 Alex Taylor III, GM and Me, *Fortune Magazine*, December 8, 2008, p 97.
29 Magee, *How Toyota Became #1*, 53.
30 Ibid., 78.
31 Alex Taylor III, "How Toyota Lost Its Way," *Fortune*, July 26, 2010.
32 Magee, How Toyota Became #1, 174–75.
33 Ibid., 176.
34 Ibid., 178.
35 Healthy Companies International, "Listening Below the Surface at Toyota," 2006.
36 Liker, *The Toyota Way*, 186.
37 Magee, *How Toyota Became #1*, 98.
38 Motor Trend Names Redesigned Toyota Camry 2007 Car of the Year, *Motor Trend*, January 2007.
39 Alex Taylor III, "Toyota: The Birth of the Prius," *Fortune*, February 21, 2006.
40 Ibid.
41 Ibid.
42 Liker, *The Toyota Way*, 51.
43 Micheline Maynard, "New Leader Expected at Toyota Next Year," *New York Times*, December 24, 2008.
44 Magee, *How Toyota Became #1*, 48.
45 Bill Vlasic and Martin Fackler, "Car Slump Jolts Toyota, Halting 70 Years of Gain," *New York Times*, December 23, 2008.
46 Jim Lentz, AIADA Annual Meeting and Luncheon, San Francisco, CA, February 11 2008.
47 Nick Bunkley, "In Detroit, Toyota Vows to Earn Trust," *New York Times*, January 10, 2011.
48 Ibid.

CHAPTER 7

1 Isadore Sharp, "The Unseen but Decisive Factor in Entrepreneurial Success," address to the Canadian Club of Toronto, May 25, 2004, http://www.cana-dianclub.org/Libraries/Event_Transcripts/2905_pdf.sflb.ashx.
2 Ibid.
3 Isadore Sharp, "The Ultimate Host," *Time*, September 21, 2007, http://www.time.com/time/specials/2007/article/0,28804, 1663316_1684619_1694700,00.html.
4 Ibid.
5 Author interview.
6 Sharp, "The Unseen but Decisive Factor."
7 Ibid.
8 Olive, *No Guts, No Glory*, 93.
9 David Olive, *No Guts, No Glory: How Canada's Greatest CEOs Built Their Empires* (Toronto: McGraw-Hill Ryerson: 2000), 84.
10 Sharp, "The Ultimate Host."
11 Ibid.
12 Leonard Brody and David Raffa, *Everything I Needed to Know about Business . . . I Learned from a Canadian, 2nd edition* (Mississauga, ON: John Wiley & Sons Canada, 2005) 141.
13 Roger Martin, "Isadore Sharp: Creating the Four Seasons Difference," *Globe and Mail*, November 20, 2007.
14 Olive, *No Guts, No Glory*, 97.
15 Erik Stern and Mike Hutchinson, *The Value Mindset: Returning to the First Principles of Capitalist Enterprise* (Hoboken, NJ: John Wiley & Sons, 2004), 13.
16 Healthy Companies International, "Turn Your Values into Action: An Interview with Isadore Sharp," *What CEOs Do*, March 2005.
17 Author interview.
18 Isadore Sharp, interview in *Hotels*, August 1, 2006.
19 Healthy Companies International, "Turn Your Values into Action."
20 Author interview.
21 Author interview.
22 Sharp, "The Unseen but Decisive Factor."
23 Sharp, "The Unseen but Decisive Factor."
24 Healthy Companies International, "Turn Your Values into Action."
25 Issy Sharp, The Ultimate Host. Time.com, 14 December 2007
26 Olive, No Guts, No Glory, 81.
27 Isadore Sharp, *Four Seasons, The Story of a Business Philosophy* (Toronto, Canada: Penguin Group, 2009), 89:
28 Olive, *No Guts, No Glory*, 111.
29 Sharp, *The Unseen but Decisive Factor*.
30 Healthy Companies International, "Turn Your Values into Action."
31 Martin, "Isadore Sharp."

32 Olive, *No Guts, No Glory*, 109.
33 Author interview.
34 Healthy Companies International, "Turn Your Values into Action."
35 Joseph Weber and John Rossant, "The Whirlwind at the Four Seasons: Luxury Hotel Chain Founder Issy Sharp Is on a Global Tear," *Businessweek*, October 13, 1997, http://www.businessweek.com/archives/1997/b3548138.arc.htm.
36 Olive, *No Guts, No Glory*, 90.
37 Author interview.
38 Qian Yanfeng, Hot Hotels, in the *China Business Weekly*, 24 November 2008.
39 Joseph Michelli, *The New Gold Standard: 5 Leadership Principles for Creating a Legendary Customer Experience Courtesy of The Ritz-Carlton Hotel Company* (New York: McGraw-Hill, 2008), 60.
40 Ibid., 21.
41 Author interview.
42 Isadore Sharp, interview in *Hotels*.

CHAPTER 8

1 Jeff Jarvis, *What Would Google Do?* (New York: HarperCollins Publishers, 2009), 40.
2 Vise, *The Google Story*, 271.
3 Randall Stross, *Planet Google: One Company's Audacious Plan to Organize Everything We Know* (New York: Simon & Schuster, 2009).
4 Stross, *Planet Google*, 67.
5 http://www.google.com/corporate/tenthings.html
6 David Vise, *The Google Story* (New York: Bantam Dell, 2005), 38.
7 Ibid., 60.
8 Stross, *Planet Google*, 50.
9 Ibid., 56.
10 Vise, *The Google Story*, 63.
11 Ibid., 68.
12 Stross, *Planet Google*, 64.
13 http://www.google.com/corporate/tenthings.html
14 Michael Specter, "Postcard from Silicon Valley: Search and Deploy", *The New Yorker*, May 29, 2000.
15 Danny Sullivan, "Yahoo Partners with Google", *The Search Engine Report*, July 5, 2000.
16 Vise, *The Google Story*, 119.
17 Google Books Library Project overview, 2011, http://www.google.com/googlebooks/library.html.
18 Stross, *Planet Google*, 92.
19 "Google Buys YouTube for $1.65 Billion", MSNBC.com, *The Associated Press*, October 10, 2006.(URL: http://www.msnbc.com/id/15196982/)

20 Vise, *The Google Story*, 170.

21 Google Investor Relations, 2004 Founders' IPO Letter: "An Owner's Manual" for Google's Shareholders, http://investor.google.com/corporate/2004/ipo-founders-letter.html.

22 Adam Lashinsky, "Chaos by Design: The Inside Story of Disorder, Disarray, and Uncertainty at Google. And Why It's All Part of the Plan," *Fortune*, October 2, 2006.

23 Stross, *Planet Google*, 8.

24 Ibid., 9.

25 Vise, *The Google Story*, 118.

26 Ibid., 2.

27 John Battelle, "The Birth of Google," *Wired*, August 2005.

28 Vise, *The Google Story*, 21.

29 http://www.google.com/corporate/tenthings.html

30 Google Investor Relations, 2004 Founders' IPO Letter.

31 Stross, *Planet Google*, 11.

32 Stross, *Planet Google*, 179.

33 Vise, *The Google Story*, 207.

34 Laura Holson, "Putting a Bolder Face on Google," *New York Times*, March 1, 2009, B1.

35 Lee Spears and Brian Womack, "Facebook May be More Expensive than Google", Bloomberg.com, 2 February 2012.

36 Miguel Helft and Jessi Hempel, "Facebook vs. Google: The Battle for the Future of the Web," *Fortune*, November 21, 2011.

37 Paul Tassi, "A Eulogy for Google Plus," *Forbes*, August 15, 2011.

38 Claire Cain Miller, "In a Quest for Focus, Google Purges Small Projects", *The New York Times*, http://bits.blogs.nytimes.com/2011/11/10, 10 November 2011.

39 Lashinsky, "Chaos by Design."

CHAPTER 9

1 Joe Klein, "Study McCain and Do the Opposite: And Other Lessons for Candidate Whitman from a Renowned Campaign Watcher," *Fortune*, March 30, 2009, 68.

2 Ryan Lizza, "Battle Plans: How Obama Won," *New Yorker*, November 17, 2008.

3 Barack Obama, National Democratic Convention Keynote Address, Fleet Center, Boston, MA, 27 July 2004.

4 Klein, "Study McCain and Do the Opposite."

5 Barry Libert and Rick Faulk, *Barack Inc.: Winning Business Lessons of the Obama Campaign* (Upper Saddle River, NJ: FT Press, 2009), 22.

6 Libert and Faulk, *Barack, Inc.*, 80.
7 Libert and Faulk, *Barack Inc.*, 46.
8 Lisa Taddeo, "The Man Who Made Obama," *Esquire*, March 2009.
9 Obama's Aide Plouffe Plots Victory From Background (Update1)By Julianna Goldman - June 16, 2008 , Bloomberg.
10 Obama Speech to Campaign Staff, June 27, 2008.
11 Tim Dickinson, "Obama's Brain Trust," *Rolling Stone*, July 10, 2008.
12 Libert and Faulk, *Barack, Inc.*, 35.
13 James O'Toole, "Obama vs. Clinton: Leadership Style", in *Business Week*, February 8, 2008
14 Libert and Faulk, *Obama, Inc.*, 134.
15 Jabari Asim, *What Obama Means . . . For Our Culture, Our Politics, Our Future* (New York: William Morrow, 2009), 219.
16 Libert and Faulk, *Obama, Inc.*, 111.
17 Tim Butcher, Barack Obama uses Israel visit to reassure Jewish voters, *The Telegraph*, July 23, 2008.
18 David Leonhardt, "After the Great Recession," *New York Times* Magazine, May 3, 2009, 76.

CHAPTER 10

1 Report of the Presidential Commission on the Space Shuttle Challenger Accident, June 1986.
2 Major General Patrick Cordingley, Leading in Times of Crisis, Healthy Companies International, *What CEOs Do*, Arlington, VA, 2009.

INDEX

Abbas, Mahmoud, 208
Aboukir Bay, 5, 43
Abraham Lincoln (carrier), 99
Abu Dhabi (Dubai), 112, 113–14
Abu Ghraib, 199
Achaemenid dynasty, 27
Achilles, 32
Adsense program (Google), 193
advertising. *See* online advertising
Afghanistan, 34, 35, 83, 101, 108, 122, 204, 205, 208, 220
Africa, 14, 116, 118, 125, 134, 206 (*See also* North Africa, South Africa)
aging population, 120
Ahmadinejad, Mahmoud, 206
AIG, 226, 227
Airbus, 114
aircraft carriers, 62–63, 79, 223
AirLand joint operations, 87, 99
Akagi (carrier), 58, 64, 67, 69, 72, 73
AKPD (media firm), 202
al-Allawi, Iyad, 100
Albermale (ship), 54
Aleutian Islands, 70, 74
Alexander the Great, 9, 12, 15, 36, 52–54, 216, 217, 221, 224, 228
Alexander the Great, battles. *See* Chaeronea, battle of; Issus, battle of; Guagamela, battle of; Granicus, battle of
Alexander the Great—Creative Execution, 26–27
    bold action, 31–33
    candid dialogue, 29–30
    clear roles/accountabilities, 30–31
    unique strategy, 27–29
    visible leadership, 33–35
Alexandria (Egypt), 36, 160
Algeria, 104, 220
Allen, Thad, 4
al-Qaeda, 103, 104, 108, 110
al-Sadr, Muqtada, 107
AltaVista, 176, 179
al-Waleed bin Talal, Prince, 150, 160, 161, 167, 168
America Online. *See* AOL
American Express, 215
American International Group. *See* AIG
American War of Independence, 55
Amman (Jordan), 160

Amtrak, 114
Anatolia, 22
Ando, Tadao, 113
andon cord, 134–35, 137
Android mobile devices, 174
anti-Americanism, 83, 207
AOL Europe, 191
AOL, 177, 182, 186–87, 192, 218
AOL–Google partnership, 191
Apollo 13, 82, 222
Apollo missions, 82, 222
Apple Store, 8
Arab Spring, 122
Arctic, oil/gas reserves, 125
Aristotle, 18, 29
Arizona (ship), 68, 69, 78
Artiuch, Paul, 119
Asia, 9, 13, 14, 15, 17, 20, 24, 27, 28, 32, 34, 68, 78, 97, 118, 122, 130, 159, 169, 170, 171–72, 174, 227
Asim, Jabari, 206
Ask Jeeves, 182
Ask Network, 192
assembly line production, 132, 137
Athens, 19, 20, 21, 121–22
atomic bomb, 78
Australia, 134
automobile industry, 127–48
Axelrod, David, 202–3, 204, 207
axis of evil, 98, 206
Ayers, Charlie, 175, 188

Baby boomers, 119-20
Babylon, 18, 26, 35
Baghdad, 84, 88, 89, 99, 102, 107, 108, 110
Bahamonde, Marty, 2
Baku (Azerbaijan), 171
Bali, 159
Ballmer, Steve, 175
Bangladesh, 134
Bank of America, 214–15
Barack, Inc. (Libert/Faulk), 200, 201
Bartello, John, 188
Battle of Britain, 57
Battle of the Atlantic, 57–59
Battle of Trafalgar, xvi, 12, 14, 15, 40–42, 44–49, 50, 51–52, 55, 59, 60, 82, 92, 96, 166 (*See also* Nelson, Horatio—Creative Execution)
Battle of Waterloo, 12, 14

Battleship Row (Pearl Harbor), 64, 78
Bechtolsheim, Andy, 179
Beijing, 111, 114, 115, 169, 170
Belgium, 227
Bellerophon (ship), 49
Berlin Airlift, 81
Berlin Crisis, 81
Berlin Wall, 83, 208
Berlin, Obama speech, 226
Berlusconi, Silvio, 121
Biden, Joe, 202
Bismarck (ship), 57
Bligh, Captain, 48
blind belief in strategy (BSS), 7
blunt, top-down execution, 11–12
Boeing, 114
book digitization program (Google), 182–84, 190
Boomerang (Lewis), 117
Borneo, 61
Borodino (ship), 60
Bose, Partha, 29, 31
Boston Consulting Group (BCG), 5–6, 210, 211
Boulogne (France), 40
Bounty (ship), 48
boutique hotels, 170
Brazil, 116, 118, 174
Brin, Sergey, 11, 176–80, 185–95, 218, 219, 228
Brinkley, Douglas, 3
British 7th Armoured Brigade. *See* Desert Rats
British Admiralty, 46, 47, 50, 51, 54
British Army, 224
British Grand Fleet, 40, 123
British Royal Navy, 68
Brown, Michael, 1, 2, 3, 4
Bucentaure (ship), 45
Bucephalus (Alexander's horse), 20
Buffett, Warren, 188
Burma, 162
Bush, George H.W., 92, 93, 122
Bush, George W., 1, 2, 4, 98, 99, 121, 199, 205, 226
butterfly effect, 227

Cadiz (Spain), 40, 41, 44, 50
Cairo, 160, 169
California (ship), 68
Camry, 129, 133, 144
Canada, 119
Canary Islands, 12, 51
Cape St. Vincent, battle of, 42–43
Carnage and Culture (Hanson), 18
carrier-based raids, obstacles to, 62–63
Carson, Jon, 203
Casey, George, 105
cavalry warfare, 19, 22, 24, 28, 30, 31, 32, 33, 37, 38 (*See also* Companion Cavalry)

CENTCOM, 91, 97, 99, 103, 109, 220
Centers for Disease Control and Prevention, 1
centres of gravity approach (military), 28, 54
CEOs, salaries, 116, 146
Chaeronea, battle of, 19, 20, 21, 32
Chalabi, Ahmed, 100, 101
chaos theory, 227
Charidemus (adviser), 22–23, 30
chemical warfare, 85, 225
Cheney, Dick, 86, 93
Chernobyl, 5
Chertoff, Michael, 1, 3
Chevrolet, 132
China, 114–15, 116, 117, 118, 119, 120, 124, 125, 134, 168–70, 171
Chrome (web browser), 175
Chrysler, 127, 128, 129, 132, 137, 144
Churchill, Winston, 51, 78
Citino, Robert, 97
Cleitus, 35–36
Clift Hotel (San Francisco), 155
climate change, 115, 124–25, 128
Clinton, Hillary, 197, 198, 199, 203, 205, 207, 208
Clinton/Obama debate, 206–7
close-quarters combat, 41, 46, 54
CNN, 184, 226
CO_2 emissions, 112–13, 124
Cold War, 2, 84, 137
Collier, Robert, 153
Collingwood, Cuthbert, 47
Columbia explosions, 222
command-and-control model, 6–7
Communism, 228
Companion Cavalry, 20–21, 22, 23, 25, 26, 28, 30, 31–32, 33, 53–54
computer attacks, 123–24
comScore, 174, 192
Condé Nast, 155, 162
Consumer Confidence Index, 116
continuous improvement, 138
Convis, Gary, 133, 142, 145–46
Cooper, Simon, 169
Copenhagen, battle of, 43, 48, 191
copyright infringement, 182–83
Coral Sea, battle of the, 70, 74
Cordingley, Patrick, 224–25
core beliefs, 218–19
Corolla, 134, 144
corporate credos
    don't be evil (Google), 180, 185, 188, 195
    Gold Standard (Ritz-Carlton), 169–70
    Golden Rule (Four Seasons), 156–59, 161, 164, 166, 167, 170, 172
    Toyota Way, 138
Corsica, 39

Courtyard (hotels), 170
creative disobedience, 47, 50, 54–55, 91, 143, 195, 218
creative execution
    components, 9–12
    defined, 4, 9
    (See also under names of people, companies)
Creative Execution—building your own
    asking enough questions, 219–21
    culture, 221–24
    in constant-crisis world, 226–29
    leading from the front, 224–26
creativity, 6, 8, 110, 126, 131, 138, 172, 186, 190, 228, 229
credit meltdown, 226, 227
Credit Suisse First Boston, 185
Credit Suisse, 113
Cuba, 199, 206
Cuban Missile Crisis, 81
culture of contradictions, 141
culture of superiority, 222–23
culture, deep listening. See deep listening culture
Cunard Line, 111
Curtice, Harlow, 127
customer service, 8, 140, 149, 150–51, 152, 154, 156, 161, 163–64, 165, 166, 169–70, 172

Dace (submarine), 76
Daihatsu (Toyota subsidiary), 146
Damascus (Syria), 160
Darius III (king of Persia), 17, 20, 21–26, 28, 30, 31, 33, 34–35, 36, 54
Darter (submarine), 76
De Chucurra, Cosme, 44
Dead Sea Scrolls, digitized, 194
Death of Nelson (painting), 52
debt-ceiling debate (2011), 120–21
deep listening culture, 134, 220
Dell Inc., 150
Dell, Michael, 150
Delphi (car parts supplier), 128
democracies, 120–22
Democratic National Convention (2004), 199, 206
demographic shifts, 115–20
Desert Rats, 94
Desert Shield, 86–87, 91
Desert Storm, xviii, 15, 88–97, 110, 137
detached leadership, 102
Detroit, 128, 129, 130
Dexia (Belgian-French bank), 227
Dickinson, Tim, 203
don't be evil corporate philosophy, 180, 185, 188, 195

Doha (Qatar), 160
Dorchester Hotel, 152
dot-com meltdown (2000), 174, 179
DoubleClick, 175
Dow Jones, 227
Dreadnought (ship), 123
Dreamliner (aircraft), 114
droughts, 125
Dubai, 111–14, 160, 169
Dull, Paul S., 61, 66, 77
Dunnigan, James, 90
Dutch East Indies, 63, 68, 69, 73, 223

Eagle's Nest (Thomas Cook), 214, 215, 216
EarthLink, 182
earthquake (Japan), 5, 129, 147
Eastern Europe, 120
eBay, 174
Echo Boomers, 119–20
Edwards, John, 203
Egypt, 43–44, 85, 87, 103
Eichner, Itamar, 208
Ellen DeGeneres Show, 201
Emanuel, Rahm, 204
Emirates Park Towers (Dubai), 112
Enterprise (carrier), 64, 71, 72, 73
entrepreneurial organizations, 7
Excel, 175
Execution Curve, 8

Facebook, 173, 174, 176, 192–94, 195, 198, 200–1
Fadhil (Baghdad), 108
Fairmont (hotels), 168
Fast Company, 6
Fastabend, David A., 107
Faulk, Rick, 200, 201–2, 203, 205, 207
FEMA (Federal Emergency Management Agency), 1–4, 5
Fiat, 129
financial meltdown (2008-09), 121, 134, 146, 157, 168, 181, 186, 198, 221, 226, 228
    (See also credit meltdown; subprime mortgage crisis)
First Gulf War (See Desert Shield; Desert Storm; Schwarzkopf, Norman—Creative Execution)
Fischer, David, 193
Five-Year Plans, 228, 229
flat organizations, 165, 189–90
Fletcher, Frank J., 72, 74
Ford, 127–28, 132, 133, 134, 135, 137, 139, 141, 142, 144, 146
foreign-exchange business. See Thomas Cook Financial Services

Fortune, 128, 133, 141, 142, 144, 157, 194, 195, 198
Foster & Partners, 113
founder-led organizations, 7
Four Seasons (Macau), 169
Four Seasons (NY), 150, 170
Four Seasons (Rome), 154
Four Seasons Four Seasons Hotels and Resorts, 148
Four Seasons Hotels, 9, 148–172, 224–25 (*See also* Sharp, Isadore [Issy]—Creative Execution)
Four Seasons London, 171
Four Seasons Motor Hotel, 150–52
Four Seasons Residence (condos), 161–62
Four Seasons Residence Club, 161
Four Seasons Resort and Club Dallas at Las Colinas, 149
Four Seasons Tented Camp, 162
France, 27, 39, 41, 43, 57, 85, 87, 97, 100, 101, 115, 119, 122, 130
Franco-Spanish Combined Fleet, 40–41, 42, 44–45, 92
Franks, Tommy, 93, 102
Freedom Tower (NY), 112
French 6th Division, 94
French Army, 224
French Foreign Legion, 94
French Indonesia, 68
French Institute for Radiological Protection and Nuclear Safety, 5
French Revolution, 39
FSB (Federal Security Service, Russia), 10
FTSEurofirst 300 Index, 227
Fuchida, Mitsuo, 67, 69
Fukushima Daichi nuclear disaster, 5
fundraising, political, 204–5

Garner, Jay, 100
Gates, Bill, 150, 161, 167, 168
Gates, Robert, 105, 205
Gaul, 27
Gay, George, 73
Gehry, Frank, 113
Gen X, 6
Genda, Minoru, 62, 69
General Electric, 9–10,123, 175
General Motors. *See* GM
Generation Y, 119–20
George V Paris, 150, 160
George W. Bush (aircraft carrier), 79
Georgetown (KY) plant (Toyota), 134, 135, 145
Germany, 58, 85, 97, 100, 113, 118–19, 120, 129, 208–9
Ghazaliya (Baghdad), 108

GhostNet virus, 124
global financial crisis. *See* financial meltdown (2008–09)
Global Innovation 1000 study, 126
globalization, 15, 119, 227
GM, 11, 127–29, 133, 135, 136, 137, 141, 142, 144, 145, 146, 217, 221, 222–23
Gmail, 184, 186, 190
Gold Standard (Ritz-Carlton credo), 169–70
Golden Rule (Four Seasons credo), 156–59, 161, 164, 166, 167, 170, 172
Goldman Sachs, 115
Google Books, 183, 194
Google Cultural Institute, 194
Google Desktop Search, 175
Google Docs, 175
Google Earth, 184, 191
Google Health, 194
Google Labs, 194
Google Maps, 184, 192
Google Mars, 186
Google News, 184, 192
Google Power Meter, 194
Google Video, 184
Google, 9, 11, 15, 173–95, 217, 218
Google+, 174, 190, 194
Google—Creative Execution
  bold action, 190
  candid dialogue, 188–89
  clear roles/accountabilities, 189–90
  unique strategy, 186–87
  visible leadership, 191–92
Googleplex, 174, 189
Gorbachev, Mikhail, 10, 208
Gordian knot, 32
Grande Armée, 39–40
Granicus River, 32, 33–34, 44
Granicus, battle of the, 21, 22, 23, 24, 26, 32, 34, 36, 37, 52
Gravière, Jurien de la, 49
Great Deluge, The (Brinkley), 3
Greater East Asia Co-Prosperity Sphere, 69
Greece, 7, 117, 121, 226–27
greed, 227
green energy, 124
Greenland, 124
Groom, Sharon, 214, 216
Grosvenor House, 152
Grummar Wildcat, 223
Guadalcanal, 78
Guagamela, battle of, xv, 17, 24–26, 27, 28, 29, 31, 33, 34, 36, 37, 53–54, 92, 96
Guam, 68
Guangzhou (China), 169, 171
Guantanamo Bay (Cuba), 199

Index

Hainan (China), 124, 169
Hakodate (harbor), 130
Halsey, William, 76–77
halting production. *See* andon cord; *jikoda*
Hamas, 208
Hamilton, Lady Emma, 41, 46, 51
Hanson, Victor David, 18, 26, 30
Harding, Warren, 198
Hardy, Captain, 51
Hawaii, 58, 62, 65
Helft, Miguel, 194
Hempel, Jessi, 194
high-speed rail, 114–15
Hilton (hotels), 151, 154, 164
Hiro, Dilip, 85
Hiroaki, Abe, 73
Hiroshima, 78, 207
Hiryu (carrier), 58, 64, 71, 73, 74
Hitler, Adolf, 36, 57, 86
HMS *Hood* (ship), 57
Holbrooke, Richard, 204
Holiday Inn, 152, 153
Hölzle, Urs, 179
Homeland Security, Dept of, 1, 2–3
Honda (company), 129, 221
Hong Kong, 68, 111, 150, 159, 164, 166
Hornet (carrier), 71, 72
hotel industry. *See* luxury hotel industry
How This Ends (Fastabend), 107
Howe, Earl, 48
Hughes, Chris, 198–99, 201, 202
humility, 134, 139, 145, 167–68
Hurley, Chad, 183
Hussein, Saddam, 81, 83, 84–86, 97–98, 100
Hyatt, 149, 154, 169
hybrid vehicles, 140, 143, 144–45, 146
Hyundai (company), 221

ice shelf, melting, 124, 125
Ich bin ein Berliner speech, 208
immigration, 120, 151
Immortals (Darius's guard), 20, 54
Imperial Japanese Army, 60, 66, 68
Imperial Japanese Navy, 14, 58, 62, 67, 68–69,
    74, 75, 223
improvised explosive devices (IEDs), 102
Inchon, 82
India, 26, 34, 35, 101, 114, 116, 119, 120,
    168–69, 170
Indochina, 82
Indonesia, 61
Industrial Revolution, 15, 131
initial public offering (IPO), 185–86,
    188–89, 191
Inn on the Park (London), 153, 163, 168

Inn on the Park (Toronto), 152, 163
innovation spending, 126 (*See also* creativity)
INSEAD (business school), 215
Internet Explorer, 175
Iran, 24, 109, 119, 121, 174, 206, 207
Iran-Iraq war, 84–85, 86, 95, 98
Iraq Petroleum Company, 84
Iraq, 18, 24, 83–110, 184, 205, 208, 220
    (*See also* Desert Shield; Desert Storm;
    surge—Creative Execution; Operation
    Iraqi Freedom; Schwarzkopf, Norman—
    Creative Execution)
Iraqi Air Force, 89
Iraqi Army, 84, 87, 88, 98, 100, 101, 108, 110
Iraqi National Museum, 102
Iraqi police, 107
Isenberg, Alice, 200
Israel, 124, 194, 208
Issus, battle of, 23, 24, 26, 28, 34, 36, 37, 53–54
Istanbul, 157
Italy, 119, 120, 121, 226
ITT Sheraton, 154–55, 163
Iwo Jima, 78

Jakarta, 159 (Indonesia)
Japan, 12–14, 100, 117, 119, 120, 121, 121,
    129, 130–31 (*See also* Pearl Harbor, attack
    on; Toyota)
Jarvis, Jeff, 174
Jervis, John, 42 43
jikoda, 134–35, 136, 138
Joint Chiefs of Staff, 82, 86, 91, 92, 103, 220
Jordan, 103
Juilliard, Colette, 113–14
Julius Caesar, 12, 26–27
just-in-time (JIT) production, 135, 147

Kaga (carrier), 58, 64, 73
Kagan, Donald, 122
Kagoshima Bay, 65
kaizen, 129, 137, 138, 141, 175
Katrina (hurricane), 1–4, 184
Keane, John, 105, 109, 220
Keegan, John 34, 42, 74
Kennedy, John F., 198, 208
Kerry, John, 206
KGB, 10
Kimmel, Husband E., 14
Kingdom (yacht), 167
Klein, Joe, 198, 200
Kleiner Perkins Caulfield & Byers, 179, 180, 181,
    185, 191
Knight, Roger, 44, 47
Knyaz Suvorov (ship), 60
Koga, Mineichi, 66

Kondo, Nobutake, 74
Korean War, 82, 86
Kosygin, Alexei, 152
Kotter, John, 6
Kranz, Gene, 82
Kriegsmarine, 57
Kublai Khan, 12
Kuwait City, 160
Kuwait, 83, 84, 85–87, 224
Kyoto Protocol, 124
Kyushu (Japan), 59

L'Orient (ship), 44
Laos, 162
Lashinsky, Adam, 186, 195
Latin America, 120, 150
Latvia, 117
Lawrence of Arabia, 84
leadership from the front, 224–26
lean manufacturing. See jikoda; just-in-time
    (JIT) production; pull production system)
left hook maneuver, xviii, 88, 91–92, 95, 97,
    98, 224
Lehman Brothers, 226, 227
Lentz, Jim, 138, 146, 147
Leonidas (king of Sparta), 32
Lewis, Michael, 117
Lexington (carrier), 70
Lexus, 144, 146
Leyte Gulf, 75–77
Libert, Barry, 136, 200, 201–2, 203, 205, 207
Libya, 123, 125
Liker, Jeffrey, 132, 145
line-ahead (military) tactic, 43, 46–47, 54–55
live employee feedback system, 212–13
Lizza, Ryan, 199
loyalty, 47–48, 167
Luck, Gary, 93
Lushun (China), 59
Lutz, Bob, 145
luxury hotel industry, 148–72

MacArthur, Douglas, 75, 82
Macau, 169
Macedonia, 19, 20
MacKenzie, Angus, 144
Maeda, Kosei, 69
Magee, David, 132, 134–35, 136–37, 138, 139,
    141, 142, 144
Malaya, 68, 69, 73, 223
Manchukuo (China), 60
Manchuria, 69
Mandarin Oriental, 149, 166
Manhattan Project, 78
Mao Tse-tung, 206

Marathon, battle of, 17
Marrakesh (Morocco), 171
Marriott International, 159, 170
Marriott, J.W., Jr., 170
Mars (ship), 45
Marshall Plan, 81, 102
Marshall, George, 81
Martin, Roger, 154, 165
Maryland (ship), 68
Masdar (Abu Dhabi), 112–13
Masdar Institute of Science and Technology
    (MIST), 113
Massachusetts Institute of Technology
    (MIT), 113
matrix management, 7, 141, 143
Max Sharp & Son, 151
Maya (ship), 76
Mayer, Marissa, 182, 192
McAlpine family, 152–53, 168
McCaffrey, Barry, 91
McCain, John, 105, 198, 199, 203, 205, 207, 208
McDonald, Gary, 10–11, 197–98, 209–14, 217
McDonald, Gary (Thomas Cook)—Creative
    Execution
  bold action, 214–15
  candid dialogue, 212–13
  clear roles/accountabilities, 213–14
  unique strategy, 211–12
  visible leadership, 215–16
McGraw-Hill, 182–83
McNamara, Robert, 102
Medvedev, Dmitry, 122
Meiji era (Japan), 130–31
Mexico, 119, 213
Microsoft Office, 175
Microsoft Outlook, 175
Microsoft Word, 175
Microsoft, 15, 174, 175–76, 183, 184, 187,
    190, 195
Midway, battle of, 14, 69–75, 223
Mikasa (ship), 59–60
military organization, 12–15
Millennial generation, 6
Miller, Nathan, 65, 70
Mitchell, George, 204
Mitsubishi armament factory, 78
moon landing (1969), 81, 82
morale, 8, 29, 46
Morgan Stanley, 185
Morton-Thiokol (company), 222
Moscow, 170
Mostert, Noel, 42, 43, 46, 48, 54, 170
motive vs. strategy, 27
Motor Trend Car of the Year award, 144
Motorola Mobility, 174

Mountain View (CA), 174, 188
Moxie Software, 119
Moyo, Dambisa, 115
MSN, 193
Mulally, Alan, 141, 146
Munk Center for International Studies
    (U of T), 124
Musashi (ship), 75, 76
Mutsuhito, emperor of Japan, 130
Mutton, Nick, 156, 157
My.Obama.com (MyBo website), 201, 205
MySpace, 201

Nagasaki, 78, 207
Nagato (ship), 67
Nagoya (Japan), 134
Nagumo, Chuichi, 64, 66, 67–69, 71–72,
    74, 223
Napoleon, 12, 14, 36, 39–40, 41, 57
NASA, 222–23
natural resources, 125
Nelson Touch, xvi, 41–42, 47–49, 69
Nelson, Horatio, 12, 15, 51–55, 212, 217, 218,
    224, 228
Nelson, Horatio—battles. *See* Cape St. Vincent,
    battle of; Copenhagen, battle of; Nile,
    battle of the; Trafalgar, battle of
Nelson, Horatio—Creative Execution
    bold action, 50
    candid dialogue, 47–48
    clear roles/accountabilities, 48–49
    unique strategy, 45–47
    visible leadership, 50–51
Netscape, 187
New Orleans, 1–4
New Paradigm Learning Corporation, 119
New York Stock Exchange, 191
N-Gen, 119
Nicolson, Adam, 49
Nile, battle of the, 12, 15, 43–44, 48, 50, 52, 82
Nimitz class (aircraft carriers), 79
Nimitz, Chester W., 70, 71, 76
    9/11, 1, 2, 98, 101, 159, 166–67, 226
Nissan, 129
No Guts, No Glory (Olive), 153
North Africa, 40, 44, 122
North Korea, 82, 206, 207
Northrup Grumman Newport News, 123
Norway, 120
Norwegian Institute for Air Research, 5
NUMMI (New United Motor Manufacturing, Inc.)
    partnership, 133–34, 136, 138, 142, 143

O'Hara, Vincent, 55
Obama 08 (iPhone app), 20

"Obama for President" users group, 201
Obama, Barack, 11, 109, 110, 121, 123, 197–99,
    216, 226
Obama, Barack—Creative Execution
    bold action, 204–5
    candid dialogue, 200–2
    clear roles/accountabilities, 202–4
    unique strategy, 199–200
    visible leadership, 206–9
Obama, Michelle, 207
Oberoi (hotels), 168
obeya (large open spaces), 141–42
Occupy Wall Street protests, 116
Odgers Berndtson, x
Odierno, Raymond T., 105, 109, 220
Ohio, McCain visit, 209
oil, 84, 85–86, 125, 129
Oil-For-Food program, 98
Oklahoma (ship), 68
Okuda, Hiroshi, 138, 143
Olive, David, 153, 155, 163
Olmert, Edhud, 207
Olympic Hotel (Seattle), 155
one-child policy (China), 117
online advertising, 173, 180–81, 186, 187,
    188, 190
online political donations, 205
OPEC, 85
Operation Iraqi Freedom, 3, 99–102, 103
Operation SHO, 66, 75–77
Order of Canada, 149
Organization Man archetypes, 8
organizational inertia, 7
Orkut (social networking), 174
Osono, Eml, 134, 140
Ottoman Empire, 83, 84
overconfidence, 40, 71
Ozawa, Ichiro, 75

Pace, Peter, 103, 105
Page, Larry, 11, 176–80, 185–95, 218, 219, 228
PageRank algorithm, 176–77, 178, 179, 180,
    181–82, 185, 186–87, 195
Pakistan, 109, 204
Palestinian National Authority, 207
Palo Alto (CA), 173, 178, 179, 190
Parmenion (general), 21, 24–25, 26, 29–30, 31,
    32, 33, 34, 35
Pearl Harbor Naval Shipyard, 70–71
Pearl Harbor, attack on, xvi, xvii, 14, 15, 58–59,
    61–69, 78–79, 223
Pei, I.M., 113
Penguin (publisher), 182–83
Peninsula Hotels, 166
Pennsylvania (ship), 68

"People in the Marketplace" program, 166
Perry, Matthew, 130, 131
Pétain, Maréchal, 100
Petraeus, David, 104, 105–6, 109, 110, 220
phalanx formation, 21, 22, 25, 28–29, 30, 38, 54
Philip II (king of Macedon), 19, 20, 21, 22, 36
Philippines, 63, 68, 69, 73, 75, 223
Pierre Hotel (NY), 155
pincer battle maneuver, 44
Pinelli, Ron, 128
Platt Brothers, 131
Playboy magazine, 186
Plouffe, David, 198, 202, 204
Plutarch, 24
Poland, 86
population growth, global, 117–19
Port Arthur (China), 59, 60
Powell, Colin, 93, 102
Power Ambition Glory (Forbes/Prevas), 12
    PowerPoint, 175
presidential approval ratings, 121
Press, Jim, 133–34, 145
Prevas, John, 33
Prince of Wales (ship), 68
Prius, 128, 144–45
Procter & Gamble, 175
Pryor, Mark, 2
pull production system, 136–37
purpose, sense of, 31, 139, 214
Putin, Vladimir, 122, 125

Qatar Museum of Islamic Arts, 113
Qatar, 160
Queen Elizabeth (liner), 111

Radisson (hotels), 169
Ramachandran, Deepak, 119
Ramses (pharaoh), 12
Rape of Nanking, 61
Reagan, Ronald, 83, 208
Red Army, 36
Redoutable (ship), 52
Reed, John S., 6
Regent (hotels), 169
Regent International Hotels (Hong Kong),
    159–60, 166
Renaissance Hotels, 170
Republican Guard, 85, 88, 90, 97–98
Repulse (ship), 68
research & development spending, 126
respect, 29, 143, 168, 212
RevPar metric, 161, 154, 166, 168, 170
Rhoesaces (commander), 21
Ricks, Thomas, 103–4, 108
ringi system, 143

Ritz-Carlton, 149, 151, 153, 155, 156, 159, 161,
    164, 166, 168–70
Riyadh (Saudi Arabia), 89, 96, 160, 168
Rodney, Sir George, 42, 55
Rogers Communications, 223
Rogers Ted, 223
Rolling Stone, 203
Romm, James, 35
Roosevelt, Franklin D., 59, 65
Rosen, Bob, 218
Rotman School of Management (U of T), 154
Rowley, Philip, 191
Royal Military Academy (Paris), 39
Royal Navy, 43, 48, 55
Royal Sovereign (ship), 49
Rumsfeld, Donald, 101, 102, 105, 205
Russia, 83, 84, 103, 114, 115, 118, 119 120,
    122, 125
Russian Baltic Fleet, 14, 131
Russian Pacific Fleet, 59–60
Russo-Japanese War, 59–60, 67

Saadiyaat Island (Abu Dhabi), 113
Saint Helena, 40
Saints, battle of the, 55
Sakhalin Island, 60
Salamis, battle of, 17
San Bernardino Strait, 75, 76
Sandberg, Sheryl, 193
Santa Ana (ship), 49
Santísima Trinidad (ship), 40
Sanya (China), 169
Saturn (company), 221
Saturn V (rocket engine), 82
Saudi Arabia, 85–87, 101
Savoy (hotel), 152, 163
Schmidt, Eric, 178, 189, 192, 193, 194
Schwarzenegger, Arnold, 121
Schwarzkopf, Norman, 15, 79, 99, 102, 110
Schwarzkopf, Norman—Creative Execution,
    90–91
    bold action, 95–96
    candid dialogue, 92–93
    clear roles/accountabilities, 94–95
    unique strategy, 91–92
    visible leadership, 96–97
Second Gulf War. *See* Operation Iraqi Freedom
Securities and Exchange Commission, 185, 191
Sequoia Capital, 179, 180, 181, 183, 185, 191
Shanghai, 111, 114, 115, 169
Sharp, Isadore (Issy)–Creative Execution,
    162–63
    bold action, 166–67
    candid dialogue, 164–65
    clear roles/accountabilities, 165–66

unique strategy, 163–64
visible leadership, 167–68
Sharp, Max, 150, 167
Sharp, Rosalie, 152
Shenzhen (China), 169
Sheraton (hotels), 151, 153, 164 (*See also* ITT Sheraton)
Shia, 83
Shimizu, Norihiko, 134, 140
Shimoda (harbor), 130
shock-and-awe, 98–99
Shoho (carrier), 70
Shokaku (carrier), 58, 64, 70, 71
Siemens, 124
Singapore, 63, 68, 69, 170
solid rocket booster (SRB), 222
Sons of Iraq, 105, 108
Soryu (carrier), 58, 64, 71, 73
South Korea, 82
South Manchurian Railway, 60
Soviet Union, 10, 81, 83, 122, 137, 228
Space Shuttle disasters, 22
Spain, 16–17, 119
Sparta, 17–18, 19
SPF25 (Strategy, People & Process, and Finance), 11, 210, 211, 212, 213, 214, 215
Sponsored Links, 180–81
Spruance, Raymond A., 72, 74
St. Vincent, battle of, 50
Stalin, Joseph, 78, 206
Stanford University, 15, 176, 177, 178, 188
Starwood Hotels, 154
Station Hypo, 70, 71
Stern, Erik, 156
Street View (Google), 184
Stross, Randall, 176, 178, 180, 183, 189, 190
Stuxnet worm, 124
submarines, 64–65,123
subprime mortgage crisis, 226, 227
Sun Microsystems, 179
Sunnis, 83
Superdome (New Orleans), 4
surge (2007–8)—Creative Execution
bold action, 107–8
candid dialogue, 105–6
clear roles/accountabilities, 106–7
unique strategy, 104–5
visible leadership, 108–9
Surigao Strait, 75
sustainability, 125
SUVs, 128, 144
Sweden, 116, 120
Switzerland, 120
Syria, 87, 101, 206

Takao (ship), 76
Takeo, Kurita, 75–77
Takeuchi, Hirotaka, 134, 140
talent pool, 119–20
Taliban, 98, 109
Taranto, raid on, 62, 66
Tarmiyah (Iraq), 109
Task Force 38 (U.S. naval group), 75–76
Taylor, Alex, 128, 141
Taylor, Katie, 153, 159, 166, 168, 169, 170, 171–72, 224–25, 226, 228
Tea Party Movement, 121
technology-based warfare, 83, 90–91, 98–99
Temple of Amon (Egypt), 25
Ten Thousand (Greek army), 18, 27
Tennessee (ship), 68
Tented Camp. *See* Four Seasons T ented Camp
TEPCO (Tokyo Electric Power Co.), 5
terrorism, 1, 2–3, 122–24
TF34 (U.S. carrier force), 76
Thailand, 129, 134, 162, 170
Thebes, 19, 21
Thermopylae, battle of, 17–18, 32
TheSecDev Group, 124
Thessalian cavalry, 30
Thomas Cook, 197
Thomas Cook Americas, 209–15
Thomas Cook Financial Services, 10–11, 16, 27, 211
Togo, Heihachiro, 15, 59–60, 67, 69
Tokyo, 78, 130, 159, 170
Toll, Ian, 62, 65
Toronto Sheraton, 155
torture, 199, 208
Toulon (France), 41
town hall meetings, 202, 215
Toyoda Automatic Loom Works, 131–32
Toyoda, Akio, 145, 146, 147
Toyoda, Eiji, 143
Toyoda, Kiichiro, 131–32, 139, 148
Toyoda, Sakichi, 131, 132, 134, 139, 151, 162
Toyota City, 130, 146
Toyota Motor North America, 133, 142
Toyota Production System. *See* TPS
Toyota Way (corporate credo), 137, 138
Toyota, 15, 219–20, 221 (*See also* deep listening culture; TPS)
Toyota—Creative Execution formula, 134–35; unique strategy, 139–40; candid dialogue, 140–41; bold action, 143–45; visible leadership, 145–46; clear roles/account-abilities, 11–43
TPS (Toyota Production System), 132, 134–37, 175, 219, 221

travel and foreign exchange. *See* Thomas
  Cook; Travelex
Travelex, 11, 211
Treaty of Paris (1919), 83
trench warfare, 82
Truman, Harry, 78, 121
trust, 46, 47–48, 121, 148, 190, 208, 216,
  212, 216
Tsushima (Japan), 13, 59–60
Tsushima, battle of, 69, 131
Turkey, 18, 21, 22, 85

U.S. 7th Marine Expeditionary Brigade, 96
U.S. Air Force, 89, 90
U.S. Armed Forces, 83, 97, 101, 105
U.S. Army, 90, 104, 224
U.S. Central Command. *See* CENTCOM
U.S. Coast Guard, 5, 27
U.S. Joint Staff Officer's Guide, 28
U.S. Marines, 88, 89, 91, 94, 224
U.S. National Weather Service, 3
U.S. Navy, 2, 58, 63, 67, 70, 71, 74, 90, 223
U.S. Pacific Fleet, 14, 58, 61, 65, 68
U.S. Special Forces, 89
U.S. State Department, 101
U.S. VII Corps, 93, 94, 95, 98
U.S. XVIII Corps, 94, 95, 98
U.S.Coast Guard, 2, 3–4
U-boats, 57 (*See also* submarines)
underway replenishment, 63
unemployment, 116–17 (*See also* talent pool;
  young labor)
United Arab Emirates, 113
United Nations Framework Convention on
  Climate Change, 124
United Russia party, 122
University of Michigan, 182, 183, 190
uranium, 124

Value Mindset, The (Stern), 156
Venezuela, 206
Venza crossover, 144, 145
Verdun, battle of, 224
Victory (ship), 12, 40, 49, 50, 52, 96, 212
Vietnam War, 82–83, 96, 87, 88, 91, 92, 93, 95,
  97, 102, 104, 110, 123, 220
Villeneuve, Pierre-Charles, 40–41, 49, 50
Virginia (submarine), 123
Vise, David, 177, 178, 179, 182, 185, 187, 191
vision, 9, 139–40, 168 (*See also* corporate
  credos)
Visteon (car parts supplier), 128
vitality curve, 9–10
Volt (hybrid car), 129

volunteerism, political, 203–4
Vuono, Carl, 92, 93

Wagoner, Rick, 128
Wake Island, 64
Waldron, John, 72–73
war games, 62, 65, 86, 224
War on Terror, 98, 110, 122, 199, 200
Warden, John, 88
Warsaw Pact, 137, 224
Watanabe, Katsuaki, 146
Water Tower complex (Chicago), 155
weapons of mass destruction, 98, 100, 101
Web Properties rankings, 192
Wehrmacht, 97
Welch, Jack, 9–10
West Bank, 208
West Indies, 40
West, Benjamin, 52
William the Conqueror, 12
Wilson, Arnold, 84
Wilson, Woodrow, 122
windfarms, 113
Winning (Welch), 9
World War I, 55, 82, 83, 84, 123, 224
World War II, 55–79, 81, 83, 97, 102, 119, 127,
  132, 138, 151, 216
Wright, Rev. Jeremiah, Jr., 207

Xerxes (king of Persia), 32

Yahoo!, 174, 176, 181, 182, 191, 192, 194, 218
Yamamoto, Isoroku, 14, 15, 58–61
Yamamoto—Creative Execution, 61–64
  bold action, 67–68;
  candid dialogue, 65–66
  clear roles/accountabilities, 67
  unique strategy, 64–65
  visible leadership, 68–69
Yamato (ship), 71, 75, 76
Yorktown (carrier), 70, 71, 72, 73–74
young labor, 119–20
youth population, 118
youth unemployment, 116–17
YouTube, 183–84, 201, 205, 206
Yugoslavia, 83

Zero fighters, 58, 65, 67, 72, 73, 223
zero-carbon emission city. *See* Masdar
  (Abu Dhabi)
Zinni, Anthony, 99–100, 101
Zuckerberg, Mark, 193, 194
Zuiho (carrier), 76
Zuikaku (carrier), 58, 64, 70, 75, 76

ABOUT THE AUTHOR

Eric Beaudan is the Global Practice Leader for Leadership Assessment at Odgers Berndtson, one of the world's top executive search firms. He developed the LeaderFit™ method which is used to assess executives in the private and public sectors.

Teddy Melvin, Photographer

Eric started his consulting career with Watson Wyatt (now Towers Watson) in Toronto and Ottawa, and was a Principal with Healthy Companies International in Washington DC. He also headed the Organization Development function for Rogers Communications Inc. and Bank of Montréal, both in Toronto.

He has written numerous articles for *The Globe & Mail*, the *Christian Science Monitor* and the *Ivey Business Journal*. He also writes Fortune 500 CEO interviews which are published by Healthy Companies International and Odgers Berndtson.

Eric holds a Master of International Affairs from Columbia University. He grew up in Paris and now resides in Oakville, Ontario. He has two children.